REVOLT in the NETHERLANDS

REVOLT IN THE NETHERLANDS
The Eighty Years War, 1568–1648

ANTON VAN DER LEM

Translation by Andy Brown

REAKTION BOOKS

Published by Reaktion Books Ltd
Unit 32, Waterside
44–48 Wharf Road
London N1 7UX, UK
www.reaktionbooks.co.uk

First published in English 2018
English-language translation © Reaktion Books 2018
Translation by Andy Brown

This book was first published in 2014 by Uitgeverij Vantilt, Nijmegen, under the title *De Opstand in de Nederlanden 1568–1648: De Tachtigjarige Oorlog in woord en beeld* by Anton van der Lem
© Anton van der Lem and Uitgeverij Vantilt, Nijmegen, 2014

This publication has been made possible with financial support from the Dutch Foundation for Literature

Nederlands letterenfonds
dutch foundation for literature

All rights reserved

No part of this publication may be reproduced, stored in a retrieval system, or transmitted, in any form or by any means, electronic, mechanical, photocopying, recording or otherwise, without the prior permission of the publishers

Printed and bound in China

A catalogue record for this book is available from the British Library

ISBN 978 1 78914 086 6

Contents

Foreword to the English-language Edition 8

Introduction 11

1 The 'Lands Over Here' 17
The Netherlands under Burgundian and Habsburg Rule until 1555

2 The Troubles 35
Loyal Opposition against Philip II: 1555–1567

3 Loyalty Tested 69
Under Alba's Repression: 1567–1573

4 The Netherlands, or *Belgium Nostrum* 95
From War to Pacification: 1573–1576

5 The Netherlands Divided 117
The Short-lived Success of the Moderate Centre: 1576–1584

6 An Offensive War 135
The North against the South: 1584–1609

7 The Twelve Years Truce 161
Division in the North, Recovery in the South: 1609–1621

8 **The Long Road from Truce to Peace**   177
The North Victorious, the South between Hammer and Anvil: 1621–1648

Epilogue: By Way of Conclusion   203

CHRONOLOGY OF MAIN EVENTS   209

MAPS   214

REFERENCES   219

BIBLIOGRAPHY   237

LIST OF ILLUSTRATIONS   255

ACKNOWLEDGEMENTS   259

INDEX   261

OPPOSITE: 1 Daniel van den Queecborn (attrib.), *William, Prince of Orange*, donated to Leiden University in 1598 by his son Maurice.

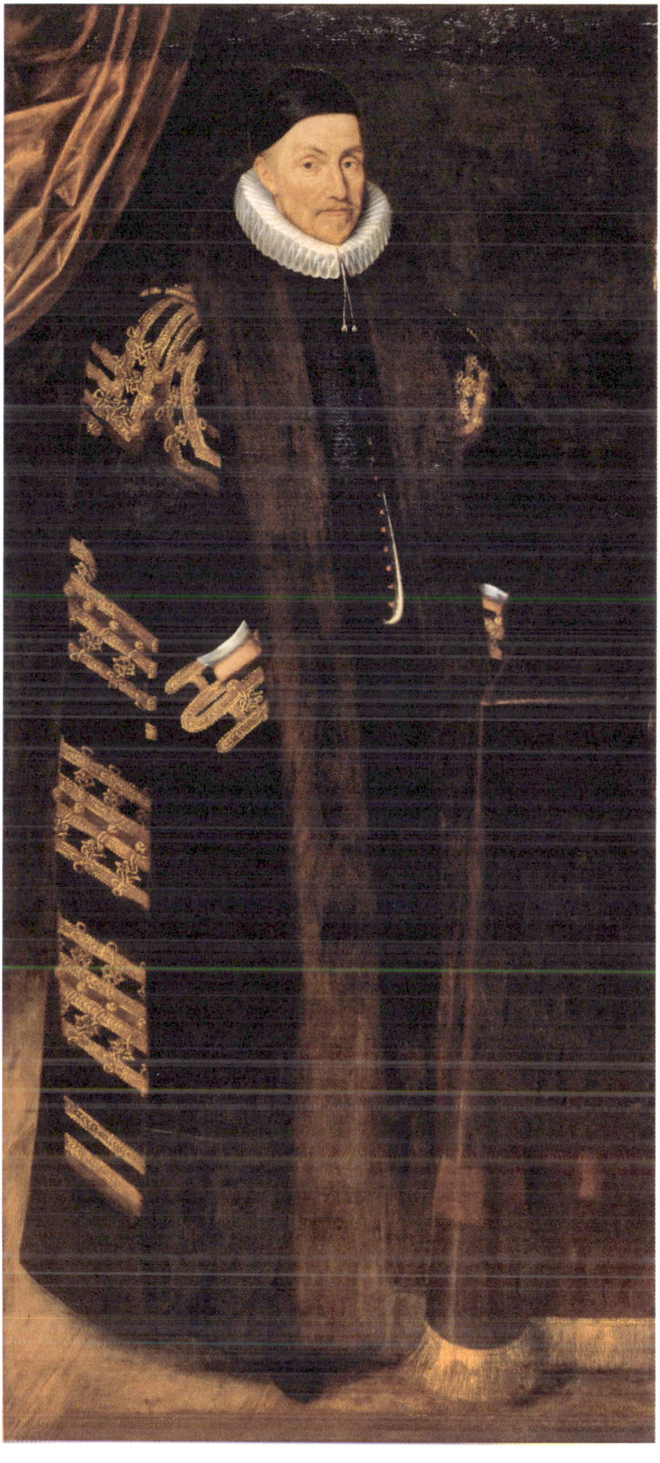

Foreword to the English-language Edition

THE REVOLT IN THE NETHERLANDS has always aroused great interest in the English-speaking world. In his *The Rise of the Dutch Republic* (1856), the American John Lothrop Motley gave a comprehensive and evocative description of the Revolt. He identified completely with the inhabitants of the Low Countries and fervently described the role of William, Prince of Orange as that of a Dutch George Washington. His romantic portrayal of the Revolt was translated into Dutch by Reinier C. Bakhuizen van den Brink, then director of the national archives. Bakhuizen van den Brink was ruthless in his criticism, however, adding countless notes to the text in which he modified or contradicted Motley's insights and assessments. In the second half of the twentieth century, and indeed up to the present day, it was British historians like Geoffrey Parker, Jonathan Israel and Alastair Duke who had the greatest impact on the debate. Their international influence has been decisive, including on historians from the Netherlands, Belgium and Spain.

The complex power game of revolt and war in the Low Countries continues to endlessly fascinate historians, resulting in an enormous number of books and articles, both academic and popular. They examine a wide range of aspects of the conflict, political and military, religious and social, economic and cultural. They can be national or international in scope, sometimes even global. Others study the Revolt in a specific region or in one town. Unfortunately, most historians who work on the Revolt are reluctant to offer a summary for a wider, non-professional readership because they are so aware of its complexity. And yet, someone must dare to take the step. This book is aimed at those readers.

In the anniversary year 2018 – 450 years after the Battle of Heiligerlee – this introduction to the Eighty Years War (1568–1648) presents an overview based on the current state of historical research. It offers the latest insights in text and image. Many of the illustrations are lesser known and come from the Special Collections of the University Libraries in Leiden. The university's website on the Revolt (http://leiden.dutchrevolt.edu) provides a platform to access or present further information.

The title of this English-language book is not *The Dutch Revolt*. That is first out of respect for the standard work by Geoffrey Parker with the same title. Second, as Parker also makes clear, the Dutch did not revolt, but were an outcome of the Revolt. Moreover, as not only Parker but also Dutch historians like Johan Huizinga and Ernst Kossmann before him have emphasized, the inhabitants of the Low Countries did not want to rise up in revolt at all. They did not consider themselves rebels and wanted only to defend the traditional system of government in which the sovereign of the land ruled in consultation with their representatives and in accordance with the rights and privileges he had sworn to respect at his inauguration. Opposition emerged only when the sovereign started to behave more and more like an absolute ruler, answerable only to God. At first, it took the form of open criticism, and then hardened into political and, later, military resistance. Many, however, remained unconditionally loyal to the king as their legitimate sovereign. Contemporaries, too, saw that the Revolt was actually a civil war, one that split towns and regions, indeed families. While in the beginning, religious persecution by the Spanish rulers drove those in favour of religious reform abroad, after the success of the revolt in the Republic, many Catholics chose exile because they wanted to practise their faith in freedom. For that reason, this book is called 'The Revolt *in* the Netherlands' and not 'The Revolt *of* the Netherlands'.

It is too simple and actually incorrect to see the Revolt in the Netherlands as the Dutch war of independence. Under the lords of the Burgundian and later the Habsburg dynasties, the seventeen provinces of the Low Countries formed an autonomous, independent and personal union. For the sake of convenience, the ruler is referred to in the history books as the Lord of the Netherlands. Yet, it would be equally correct to refer to the same ruler as the sovereign of the Spanish kingdoms. Like the Netherlands, these realms were not a unified state but a personal union, consisting of Castile, León, Aragon, Valencia, Navarre and so on. Again for the sake of convenience, the ruler is known as the King of Spain. Problems arose only when Philip II, who was king of the Spanish kingdoms, also began to conduct himself as the king of the Netherlands. At the same time, the Spaniards began to see the Netherlands as a Spanish possession. Consequently, in the Netherlands, the Eighty Years War came to be – and continues to be – seen as a struggle for freedom and independence. In Belgium, through the creation of the independent Belgian state in 1830, the myth has arisen of centuries of foreign domination, the 'Spanish' era being followed by an 'Austrian' and a 'Dutch' period. This myth was debunked in the early years of the twentieth century but stubbornly refuses to disappear even in the present day.

In this book, 'the Low Countries' or 'the Netherlands' refers mainly to the provinces that now make up the area of the Benelux (Belgium, the Netherlands and Luxembourg) plus the current French departments of Nord-Pas-de-Calais. In actual fact, before using the word 'Dutch', historians should take their lead from art historians and use the terms 'Netherlandish' and 'Netherlanders' when dealing with almost the entire sixteenth century. In this book, the word 'Dutch' is not used until quite late on, that is, for events after 1588. The name 'Holland', so often used for the whole of the present-day Netherlands, is a *pars pro toto*, whereby the name of a part is used to describe the whole: the Netherlands referred to by the name of its most important county, later province. Here, I use Holland only to refer to the county/province and not the current Kingdom of the Netherlands. The same applies to 'Flanders'. In Spanish, the war in the Low Countries as a whole has been referred to since the sixteenth century as *la guerra de Flandes*. Here, I use Flanders only for the illustrious old county, not the Flemish region in the current federal state structure of Belgium.

It was Louis-Prosper Gachard, then director of the Belgian national archives, who set a good example around 1840 by making a start on exploring and presenting the data on the Netherlands in the Spanish national archives, the Archivo General de Simancas. Many Belgians have since followed in his footsteps, while Dutch historians joined the search only in recent decades. John Lothrop Motley learned many languages, including French, Spanish, Italian and Dutch. He passionately chose the side of the rebels in the revolt against Spain. Historians from the whole world now read sources in all these languages to understand the conflicts of those years and to do justice to everyone's standpoint and convictions.

Introduction

What It was About and Why We Need to Know

The history of the Revolt in the Netherlands, or the Eighty Years War, is a complicated story. What was the war about? Why do we need to know? And why did it last so long? To gain a clear understanding of that complex reality, it is important to identify in advance the three most important reasons for the differences of opinion that led to protest, unrest and, ultimately, war and civil war. All of the complications and points of dispute, all alliances and treaties, can be traced back to one or more of these main reasons. They were grounded in three fundamental rights that apply at all times and in all countries but which, unfortunately, are still often not always guaranteed in modern times: the freedom of religion and conscience, the right to self-determination and the right of participation.

Freedom of Religion and Conscience

The Eighty Years War became a conflict *about* religion, while William, Prince of Orange fought for *freedom* of religion. Repeatedly, negotiations on a ceasefire or peace agreement ran aground because the warring parties could not agree on the mutual and equal recognition of two or more religions. On 31 December 1564 the prince stated in the Council of State in Brussels that, though he was a good Catholic, he could not approve of princes wishing to rule over the consciences of their subjects. That was a principled stand, but also one driven by practical considerations: if Catholics, Mennonites, Lutherans and Calvinists lived alongside each other, it was ridiculous for them to be at each other's throats. When the prince was recruiting men for the army that would win its first victory at the Battle of Heiligerlee (23 May 1568), he did so in the name of 'liberty of religion and conscience'. That goal was achieved in January

2 The Netherlands as they were in 1555, when Charles V abdicated in favour of his son Philip II. Wall map for history lessons, Groningen, 1955.

1579, with the inclusion in the Union of Utrecht of a provision stating that no one could be investigated, let alone prosecuted, because of their religion. That meant de facto freedom of conscience and was a major step towards achieving freedom of religion. The prince succeeded in getting religious freedom adopted, to the extent that anywhere where more than 100 heads of household asked to be allowed to practise their religion freely, they would be permitted to do so. Between 1578 and 1580 this was tried out in practice in 27 towns in the Low Countries. That is very few in modern terms but it was a lot in the context of the hard battle being fought at that time. Moreover, within a short time, the experiments failed everywhere. Tolerance had to be learned at a cost of much injustice, blood and sorrow.

The Right to Self-determination

Every community wishes to govern itself according to its own laws and freedoms, and not be subordinated to the interests of a greater whole if that means it is being discriminated against. Examples abound in today's world. In the sixteenth-century Netherlands, many people believed that their interests were being given lower priority than those of other parts of Philip II's large empire. They felt that they were increasingly being subordinated to the politics of the royal dynasty and were not being governed in a way that served their own interests.

The Right of Participation

Today, in democratic countries, people can make their voices heard by voting in elections and choosing their representatives. Governments are accountable to the representatives of the people. This was in principle no different in the Netherlands at that time, though that representation was organized differently. The Council of State, which advised the monarch, comprised members of the clergy, nobles and the 'third estate' (burghers and peasants). The representatives of these three estates formed the 'States' for their province, and the representatives of the States met in the 'States General'. Together with them, the sovereign lord represented the general interests of the country. There were of course differences of opinion, but the Council and the States functioned as consultation bodies. The States had agreed with the sovereign, for example, that he would not declare war or impose taxes without their approval. The king, however, increasingly departed from this traditional consensus model. He believed that his power derived exclusively from God and that this allowed him to rule as an absolute monarch. In his eyes, it was the duty of the Council and the States to obey only him.

Why It Lasted So Long

Religion

The Roman Catholic Church proclaimed – and still does – that there is no salvation outside the Church. There is only one True Faith. Protestants were heretics and Muslims were unbelievers. In turn, followers of the Reformed church considered their religion to be the only True Faith and referred to Catholics as papists. And because no two Truths can exist alongside each other and the Catholic King of Spain would tolerate no other religion in his kingdom, the war lasted for eighty years.

Self-determination

The Netherlands formed an independent state consisting of seventeen provinces. Their sovereign lord was also head of state of the Spanish kingdoms: first Charles v and then Philip II. That gave rise to the misconception that the Netherlands belonged to Spain – a misunderstanding that lives on in Spain to this day. The Spanish king was the ruler of an empire and the most powerful figure in the international political arena. He made the Netherlands subordinate to his international political interests. The Netherlands, however, wished to be ruled in accordance with their own interests, in control of their own affairs, politically, militarily, economically and in matters of faith. If Spain had been willing to acknowledge the Netherlands' right to self-determination, the king's other domains – in the first place in Italy, but also in Spain itself – would have demanded the same status. That would have meant loss of face, of *reputación*, for the Spanish crown. The king could not afford to let this happen, which was another reason why the war lasted for eighty years.

Participation

Decisions were imposed on the people of the Netherlands without consultation, first by the king and then by his representative, the Duke of

Alba. The king and his representatives ignored the Council of State, and the States General were no longer convened. The policies they imposed included Alba's *Tiende Penning* (Tenth Penny), a tax that the Netherlands refused to pay. The followers of the Prince of Orange actually paid much more than the *Tiende Penning*, but Orange's tax was imposed with their consent and in their own interest. Alba himself observed this with amazement. He and his successors never understood this principle – and that, too, was a reason why the war lasted for eighty years.

3 The arms of the Seventeen Netherlands, with Brabant as the most prominent, in the centre. Centuries later, the arms of Brabant would become those of Belgium. From *Lofsang van Brabant* (1580), written in French and Dutch by the poet Jan van der Noot.

I

The 'Lands Over Here'
The Netherlands under Burgundian and Habsburg Rule until 1555

The House of Burgundy

Anyone interested in how the Revolt led to the Netherlands dividing in two will first need to know how those lands came together in the first place. The driving force that brought together what we can now call the Low Countries was the House of Burgundy, originally a branch of the French royal House of Valois. The Duchy of Burgundy, with Dijon as its capital, was a fief of the French crown. Jean II, King of France, ceded the duchy to his son Philip (known as 'the Bold') in 1363 as a source of revenue. Philip married the wealthy heiress of the Count of Flanders and Artois, thus acquiring these rich counties in the north. The marriage also meant that he acquired the Free County of Burgundy, the Franche-Comté, to the east of the Duchy of Burgundy, strengthening his position in the south. Their grandson, Philip the Good, who came to power in 1419, succeeded in increasing his domains mainly to the north, acquiring first Namur, then Brabant and Limburg-Overmaas, followed by Holland and Zeeland, and finally Luxembourg. And in the bishoprics, where it was impossible to acquire a domain through succession, he had his illegitimate sons elected as bishops. These various domains did not yet have a collective name. Philip was known as the Duke of Burgundy and Brabant, and the Count of Flanders, Artois, Hainaut, Holland, Zeeland, Namur and so on. The name 'the Low Countries by the sea' was only geographically correct, but even then did not apply to his land of origin, Burgundy. Philip's domains were thus described from the perspective of the duke himself, who usually resided in Flanders or Brabant, as *les pays de par deçà*, the 'lands over here'. Burgundy itself was referred to as *les pays de par delà*, the 'lands over there'. The word *pays* (land) could refer to a duchy (Brabant, Gelre), county (Flanders, Holland) or a lordship like Mechelen or Friesland. This remarkable combination of widely varying domains clearly shared no common language. Those in the south spoke French, while those in the north spoke Flemish or Dutch. 'The lands over here' was not a name that could easily be used as a battle cry. Soldiers on the battlefield need a short, concise cry, like 'Bourgogne, Bourgogne!', 'Ghent, Ghent!' or 'Holland, Holland!' 'The lands over here' was simply too much of a mouthful. Philip the Good's prosperous patrimonial domains lacked nothing, except a collective name for the whole.[1]

All of these different domains had only the modest beginnings of a joint state structure. The main factor that united them was that they shared the same sovereign lord. There were also certain similarities in their social structure. Nearly all of them comprised the three estates: clergy, nobility and the 'third estate' (burghers and peasants). The duke chose his advisers and the commanders of his armies from the nobility. He endowed them with low-ranking positions, such as bailiff, governor of a citadel, or as his deputy or stadtholder,[2] in domains where he could not regularly be present in person. For nobles from the oldest and most prominent families, the sovereign had a special honour: the Order of the Golden Fleece. This was a very exclusive club to which the highest-ranking nobles were very keen to belong and through which the duke was able to assure himself of their loyalty.

The rich burghers in the cities, who had accumulated their wealth by trade and industry, could lend the duke money to finance his wars and the luxurious life at court. If he needed money he would submit a request, known as an 'aid', to the States, in which the three estates of his subjects were represented. The States in each domain would meet at the duke's invitation. In exceptional circumstances, the duke could call the States together at the same time in the States General. The States General met for the first time in Bruges in 1464. The richest provinces were Flanders, Brabant, Holland and Zeeland, which had often been in conflict with each other in the past.[3] Under the House of Burgundy they were now ruled by the same sovereign lord, averting much of the friction between them. The representatives of these four wealthy provinces met regularly to discuss trade disputes, traffic over land and water, and problems with tolls and currency. The merchants had much to gain from a stable and powerful government that kept the currency strong. Even more important was the protection they enjoyed against foreign

4 Sandstone gable relief showing Emperor Charles v. Utrecht, *c.* 1550–60.

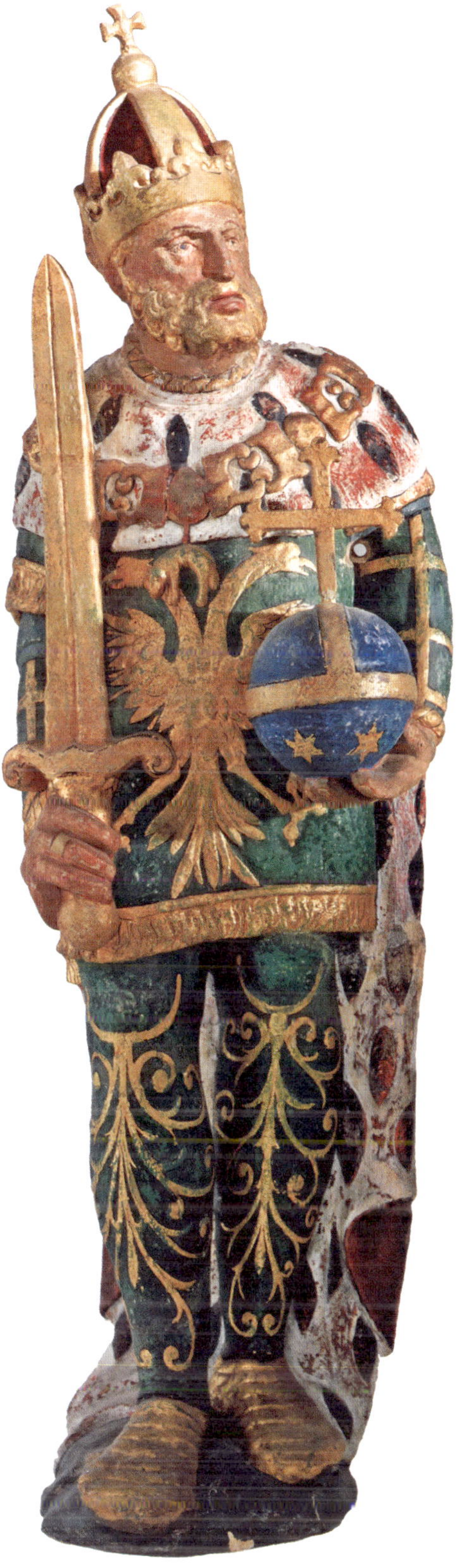

competitors. The duke supported them, for example, in disputes with the Danish king or the Hanseatic League in the Baltic region. Map 1 (see p. 215) shows the core area of the Low Countries. These provinces together were the economic heart of the Burgundian state and accounted for 80 per cent of the taxes collected within it. Those in the north, east and south were less important, economically and politically.

Under the rule of Philip the Good, through cooperation with the duke and with each other, a sense of solidarity – still far too vague and intangible to be called national awareness – gradually evolved in the Low Countries. It first developed around the ducal dynasty and was especially prevalent among the upper layers of the bureaucracy and the Church, which had regular contact with the duke's court. Philip fostered good relations with the individual provinces by respecting their privileges as much as possible. He pursued political unification only very slowly, by, for example, introducing general rules separately in each province. He assured himself of the loyalty of the nobility and burghers by making cautious changes in influential positions. In his turn, the duke had to solemnly swear at his investiture to respect the rights of his subjects. The document that imposed the most restrictions on his own rights was known as the *Blijde Inkomst*, or Joyous Entry. It was on this document that he swore his oath at his investiture in Brabant. (This tradition has survived to the present day, with the monarchs of Belgium and the Netherlands being invested rather than crowned. They now swear their oaths on the Constitution, in the same way that the Dukes of Brabant did on the Joyous Entry.[4]) The document stipulated, for example, that the lord was not permitted to wage war or impose taxes without the States' permission. By agreeing to this, he recognized the right of his subjects no longer to obey him if he knowingly did anything to harm their interests. This article could, however, be interpreted very differently by the lord and by his subjects. Many provinces could not fall back on such a charter giving the inhabitants freedom to escape their obligations to the ruler. More than a century later, however, the terms of the Joyous Entry were invoked to justify ceasing to recognize the authority of King Philip II.

The son of Philip the Good, Duke Charles the Bold, who was in power from 1467 to 1477, waged war almost continually to expand his territories. He also had the ambition of incorporating all these lands into a single kingdom, of which he would be the king. Only the pope or the Holy Roman Emperor had the power to 'elevate' domains to the status of kingdom. The Holy Roman Empire is sometimes referred to as the German Empire, and its head of state as the German emperor, but this is actually incorrect. Besides the German territories, the empire also included Austria, parts of northern Italy and, until 1648, the Low Countries, too. We will therefore speak here consistently of the Holy Roman Empire. The emperor came from the House of Habsburg, also known as the House of Austria. Charles the Bold had only one child, Mary of Burgundy. Charles proposed to the emperor, Frederick III, a marriage between Mary and Frederick's son Maximilian, in exchange for elevation of the Burgundian domains to a kingdom. The negotiations had reached an advanced stage and the marriage agreed when the emperor suddenly took off, leaving the duke behind without a kingdom.

Charles the Bold died on the battlefield in 1477. His daughter was only seventeen years old and had little political experience. It was therefore good, in terms of preserving the state structure of the Netherlands, that the States had several decades' experience of sharing responsibility for government. That experience led the States to take two important decisions. First, they resolved to keep all the lands together. That was necessary because the French king was reuniting the Duchy of Burgundy with the French crown. He also invaded the Netherlands, to take advantage of the absence of a male ruler. Second, the States General increased their own influence on government. They compelled the young duchess not only to consent to a Joyous Entry, but also to approve what were known as *Groot-Privileges* (Great Privileges), which would limit her authority even more compared to her father and grandfather. The States could, for example, now convene on their own initiative, that is, without having to wait for a summons from the ruler. Under Mary's more powerful successors, the Great Privileges fell again into disuse. Of lasting importance was that the Burgundian complex of duchies and counties survived the shock of 1477, largely due to the response of the States, so that the ties between the 'lands over here' remained intact. But the Duchy of Burgundy would from then on belong to France.

How the Netherlands and the Spanish Kingdoms Came to be Governed by the Same Ruler

Today it is almost impossible to imagine just how closely, in medieval and early modern society, the fate of a county, duchy or kingdom was linked to that of their ruling dynasty. A marriage, a birth or a death could determine whether they merged or separated. Of course, in their charters and the Joyous Entry, their people protected themselves against alliances that would not be in their interests, for example, by explicitly insisting that princely marriages require their consent. For a long time, in the prominent noble families of Europe, it had not been unusual to seek a bride or groom from another country, sometimes even from a far-off land. Philip the Good had married a Portuguese princess, and Charles the Bold an English one.

As mentioned above, the engagement of Mary and Maximilian had already been agreed by their fathers. After Charles the Bold's premature death, it seemed sensible to proceed with the marriage without delay. Maximilian's power could offer an effective counterbalance to the ambitions of the French king. It proved impossible, however, for Maximilian to pursue a purely 'national' policy, and certainly after he had been elected King of the Romans – that is, heir apparent to the Holy Roman Emperor – in 1486. Although Louis XI had seized the Duchy of Burgundy for the French crown, Franche-Comté remained a territory of the House of Burgundy, which, after the marriage of Mary and Maximilian, could also be called the House of Habsburg. Franche-Comté would now be governed from Brussels. From this time, we see the States developing their own 'Netherlands policy'. Maximilian had his own agenda, which often clashed with the interests of his subjects in the Low Countries. Under his government, the States learned how to cooperate with a lord who also had interests elsewhere. After Mary's unexpected death in 1482, the States thus succeeded in keeping Maximilian's regency for his young son Philip the Fair (1482–1506) to a minimum. In 1494, they declared Philip of age and capable of taking over government of the Netherlands as a 'natural prince'. Of course, the young ruler was closely supervised by a number of indigenous advisers.

Maximilian would settle for nothing less than the daughter of a king as a bride for Philip. Consequently, in 1496, Philip the Fair married Joanna, a daughter of Ferdinand, King of Aragon and Isabella, Queen of Castile, the two most important Spanish kingdoms. The chances that the marriage would lead to a merger of the domains of the bride and groom were extremely slim, as Joanna was preceded by a brother and an older sister in the line of succession. But, with a degree of improbability only to be found in real history, both siblings died prematurely. From the moment that Philip and Joanna – who would later suffer from mental illness – had the prospect of acceding to the thrones of Castile and Aragon, Philip's 'Netherlands policy' was as good as finished. Only his

The 'Lands Over Here'

early death in 1506 may have prevented an inevitable clash between the ruler and his subjects in the Netherlands – and possibly with his Spanish kingdoms, whose wrath he had incurred by favouring nobles from the Low Countries.

Once again, the 'natural prince' was still too young to govern: Philip's first son, Charles, had been born in Ghent on 24 February 1500. As had happened with his father, the States decided to declare Charles of age while he was still very young, and in 1515 he accepted the role of ruler of the Netherlands. After the death of his grandfather Ferdinand of Aragon in 1516, he inherited the Spanish crowns of Aragon and Castile. Habsburg gold – borrowed from the German banking family Fugger – ensured his election in 1519 as Holy Roman Emperor, after which he became known as Charles v. Half of Europe fell under his rule or within his sphere of influence: the Spanish kingdoms, including half of Italy,

5 The arms of Charles v, bearing the most important of his many domains. The upper half shows the Spanish kingdoms; at bottom left are Austria and Burgundy. The golden lion against a black background is Brabant, and the black lion on a gold background is Flanders. Tapestry, *c.* 1540–55.

23

the rich Low Countries, Austria and the bordering territories. Columbus's voyages of discovery had led to South and Central America being seized for the Spanish crown (that is, Castile), giving it access to the gold and silver from the mines of Peru and Mexico. Such a state, made up of a number of totally different component parts, is known as a composite monarchy.[5] Charles v's coat of arms could only reflect the most important of these territories: of his domains in the Netherlands, it featured only the lions of Brabant and Flanders. In order to be represented in all of his domains, he was replaced in the Spanish kingdoms by regents, in Naples by a viceroy and in the Netherlands by a governor-general. Charles delegated his authority in the Netherlands first to his aunt, Margaret of Austria (who was governor-general from 1507 to 1530), and later to his sister, Mary of Hungary (who took over from 1531 to 1555). Their family pride was even greater than that of the emperor himself, if that was possible, and while they had no political ambitions whatsoever, they were very dedicated to preserving Habsburg interests. However, both also defended the interests of the Netherlands, which they governed with a resolute hand.[6]

Lutherans and Anabaptists

The rule of Charles v became a succession of wars. The old rivalry with France continued unabated. The emperor and the French king disputed the principalities in northern Italy, and for Charles, reconquering the Duchy of Burgundy – no matter how unrealistic an ambition – was a matter of honour. These wars cost enormous amounts of money, all of which had to be collected from Charles's subjects in the Netherlands and elsewhere in his realm. No less formidable was the other traditional enemy, the Ottoman Empire, who had to be fought from time to time. The Christians considered the Muslim Ottomans to be unbelievers, and the Muslims felt the same way about the Christians. For the Catholic Charles, the fight against the Ottomans was essentially a crusade.

After 1520, however, an unexpected enemy reared its head, more dangerous than any worldly prince: the Reformation, which emerged in Germany. For many centuries, the Roman Catholic Church had been the only Christian church in western Europe. It professed – and still professes – to be the only universal church, outside which there is no salvation. Throughout almost its entire history, the Church had been under fire from critics who disagreed with the lifestyle of the clergy or with

6 Poor Jesus and the rich Catholic Church. An appeal to practise what you preach, as we would say nowadays. Images like this were very popular in the sixteenth century.

certain articles or practices of the faith. They were especially censorious of the Church's excessive material wealth. But, time and again, the Church had succeeded in absorbing reform movements, or getting the secular government to punish the reformers. In the first half of the sixteenth century, Erasmus of Rotterdam and, in Germany, Martin Luther were sharp critics of the Church. While Erasmus remained loyal to the Church and worked to achieve change from the inside, Luther pushed for more radical reform, which eventually led to a break with Rome. In the eyes of the Church and of Emperor Charles v, Luther was a heretic. And why should the apostate Augustine monk from Wittenberg not be treated in the same way as other heretics who had gone before him? But, against expectations, things turned out different: Luther enjoyed the support of a number of German Prince-Electors – there were seven of these in total, so called because it was their task to elect a new emperor. Those who backed Luther did so not only because they agreed with his reforms, but also because they had cast their greedy eyes on the Church's wealthy and expansive possessions.

25

Charles V saw it as his Christian duty to fight against Luther and the Protestant princes. In his campaign in Germany, he naturally made use of army commanders from his other domains. Consequently, the Spanish Duke of Alba fought alongside Maximilian of Egmont, the Count of Buren, whose daughter Anna would later marry William, Prince of Orange. In the end, Charles V was unsuccessful in his attempts to defeat the German Protestants, and in 1555 the Peace of Augsburg was concluded, establishing the principle that the people of a principality would have the same religion as its ruler. This principle, expressed in the Latin *cuius regio, eius religio* (whose realm, his religion) would later become widely applicable.

The people of the Netherlands thus saw how a different Christian faith was permitted in a number of principalities within the Holy Roman Empire. That was completely unprecedented. The very existence of a deviant, 'heretic' religion, also based on the Bible and the Fathers of the Church, undermined the worldwide authority of the Church of Rome. The Peace of Augsburg also gave Charles a free hand in the Netherlands. Since the German Lutheran princes never used their influence to advocate the spread of Protestantism in the Low Countries, the Lutherans were never of great significance there. Charles had no other choice than to allow German Lutheran merchants to do business in the trading centre of Antwerp, but, as far as politics were concerned, they behaved impeccably, mainly so as not to cause offence.

Much more of a threat were the Anabaptists, who had a radically different interpretation of the Christian faith. They did not agree with baptizing children immediately after birth; baptism had to be a conscious choice made at a later age, and for that reason they had themselves re-baptized. Although this in itself was sufficient to make them candidates for the stake, their social convictions – the ideal of joint ownership of goods and banning private property – ensured that the secular government, too, prosecuted them as agitators.

The Anabaptists believed that, in advance of the Kingdom of God, they could achieve a kingdom of heaven on Earth. In 1534, led by two men from the Netherlands, they took over the city of Münster in Westphalia. They wanted to make Münster – 1,500 years after the crucifixion and resurrection of Christ – the heavenly Jerusalem. Several thousand devotees from the Low Countries headed for Münster in the hope of building a better life there. But the established order could not tolerate such a radical renunciation of everything they considered as God-given reality,

Haer nieuwe Gheeft die heeft gheblaeckt, alft openbaer heeft ghebleken,
By der ftraet loopende moeder naeckt, en hebben t'huys aen brant ghefteken,

Anabaptists walk through the streets of Amsterdam naked, warning of the end of times.

and in 1535 the Anabaptists of Münster were besieged, defeated and executed as agitators and rebels. Similar scenes were narrowly avoided in Amsterdam, where Anabaptists almost succeeded in taking over the city. A small group of naked men and women ran through the city centre, calling out hell and damnation. The authorities responded with a hard hand and the Anabaptists ended up on the gallows as insurgents. Despite these severe repercussions, Anabaptists remained more numerous in the Netherlands than Lutherans. They themselves also realized that the situation in Münster had gone too far, and from then on they preached absolute non-violence. Following the example of their leader Menno Simons, they continued to believe in adult baptism and rejected the notion of swearing an oath: they believed that every word they uttered was spoken before God and that a simple promise should therefore suffice. As pacifists, they have since been known for their peace-loving mission, but within their own ranks, Menno tolerated no dissent. That led to a number of schisms, with each group claiming to be the 'true congregation'.[7]

Charles v issued decrees (known as placards) against 'heretics' time and time again, ordering the strictest measures to be taken. The placards were mainly directed at the Mennonites and were responsible for the majority of deaths of those whose lives ended at the stake. But the emperor already had a record of harsh religious persecution: the first Lutherans – Hendrik Voes and Jan van Essen, two monks from the Augustinian monastery in Antwerp – were executed on 1 July 1523 in Brussels, as martyrs to the Protestant faith. In practice, many lower-level authorities ignored the emperor's orders. In the provinces and the cities there was growing reluctance to execute people because of their religious beliefs. So they simply looked the other way and feigned innocence. When the emperor passed the government of the Netherlands on to his son Philip, he boasted that the problem of heresy was almost completely under control in the 'lands over here'.

During the religious persecution conducted under Philip II, people often looked back nostalgically to 'the times of Emperor Charles'. In reality, however, the emperor had repeatedly stepped up the persecution of heretics. This reached its high point in the 'blood placards' of 1550.

The Low Countries United

Besides policies on foreign and religious affairs, Charles v also had a domestic policy for the Low Countries. In the tradition of the Burgundian dukes, he tried to expand his territories in the region. His power and status as King of Spain and Holy Roman Emperor enabled him to take over the secular power of the bishopric of Utrecht in 1528 with little difficulty. In doing so, he added the lands of Utrecht, Overijssel and Drenthe to his empire. In 1530, the pope even granted him permission to choose the bishops himself, after which the Holy See would grant its

8 The Leo Belgicus, the Netherlands depicted as a lion, 1617.

official approval. Charles did not succeed in adding Gelre to his domains in the Netherlands until 1543. The Dukes of Gelre had been troublesome neighbours for more than a century. As allies of the French kings, they contested the lands of the Burgundian dukes and spread death and destruction with raids that penetrated as far as The Hague. When Charles v finally brought the Duke of Gelre to his knees in 1543, there was great relief and joy in the surrounding provinces of Holland, Zeeland, Brabant, Utrecht and Overijssel. One citizen of Utrecht was clearly so pleased with Charles that he had a statue of the emperor mounted into the facade of his house (see illus. 4). The Zuiderzee now changed from a maritime war zone to a peaceful inland sea, which was good for trade and shipping. It is tempting to say that Charles v's sphere of influence in the Low Countries now formed a geographical whole, but this was only true inasmuch as their eastern border corresponded to the present-day borders of the Netherlands, Belgium and Luxembourg. However, Charles v also acquired the county of Lingen (see Map 2, p. 216), which now lies completely outside present-day Netherlands and Belgium, but which Charles counted as part of his domains in the Low Countries. He also wanted to add the county of East Friesland and the bishopric of Münster, but these ambitions were never realized. It is, however, important to remember these intentions, so that we do not consider the later state borders as somehow 'natural', 'self-evident' or 'complete': this is simply what we have become accustomed to.

Because of the wars with France, Charles v required the close cooperation of the Netherlands' provinces and therefore did nothing to curtail their rights. As far as possible, he also appointed only 'indigenous' officials to the administration. A number of high-ranking officials did come from Franche-Comté, but this traditional Burgundian land had provided a whole generation of excellent jurists and administrators, which successive rulers had been delighted to make use of. As the role of the government became more expansive and complex, the specific expertise of the jurists from Burgundy and the other provinces meant that they gradually acquired increasing influence. They were known as *conseillers de robe longue*, councillors in long togas, a reference to their official attire. The most deserving among them were elevated to the low nobility. Alongside the old nobility, the *noblesse d'épée*, or nobles of the sword, who had proved their worth on the battlefield, a new nobility of administrators emerged, the *noblesse de robe*. These new nobles acquired such influence that the governor-general, Mary of Hungary, wrote to Charles that the other aristocrats had complained, feeling discriminated against. The Burgundians were referred to as 'foreigners'. Yet – to use a modern word – professionalization of the administration was unavoidable, and in 1531 Charles reorganized his advisory councils. Under his predecessors, too, there had been separate councils for justice and for financial affairs. Charles's desire to make his government more equal to the demands of the modern age was therefore nothing new. He set up three councils, which would later be known as Collateral Councils. First, there was the Council of State, which advised on policy and comprised the most prominent nobles, and once again the inevitable jurists. Second, there was the Privy Council, which was concerned with general legislation and jurisprudence. Only well-educated jurists – those who had attended university – were eligible for the work of this council. Third, there was the Council of Finance, which could also only comprise professional civil servants with the required experience. Philip II later took over this whole system of Collateral Councils from his father.

In the same year, Charles V consented to his brother Ferdinand being elected King of the Romans, meaning that he would be expected to succeed Charles as Holy Roman Emperor. The two brothers, both heads of two branches of the House of Habsburg or Austria, generally worked closely together. That was also necessary to present a united front in the joint fight against Lutheranism and the Ottoman threat. That does not mean to say, however, that there was no rivalry between them. After the Duke of Alba crushed the German Protestant princes in 1547 at the battle of Mühlberg, Charles V held supreme power in the Holy Roman Empire. That also gave him the opportunity to acquire a piece of the cake for himself at the Diet of Augsburg.

Because of their remote location, the Netherlands' ties with the Empire had become somewhat looser over the centuries; this applied to many other peripheral imperial territories, such as northern Italy, Switzerland and Hungary. Charles had inherited a number of these domains from his father – roughly, the Low Countries south of the major rivers (Rhine and Maas), plus the county of Holland. These were known as the patrimonial domains. Charles himself had acquired the other lands to the north of the rivers: Utrecht and Overijssel, Friesland, Groningen and Gelderland. All the Low Countries were still strictly speaking part of the Empire, with the exception of Flanders, to the west of the River Scheldt, and Artois, which was a fief of France. So, in 1548, Charles transferred Flanders and Artois to the Empire and unified all of the Low Countries in what was known as the Burgundian Circle. Since 1500, the Empire had been divided into administrative 'circles', aimed at strengthening cooperation between the regions to counter the progressive erosion of the state structure. At the same time – and this was to be the source of many problems – Charles gave the circles much greater independence from the Empire.

The Empire granted the Netherlands their old freedoms and privileges and would no longer intervene in the internal affairs of the Burgundian Circle. Furthermore, imperial law would no longer apply, while representatives from the Netherlands would be permitted to attend the Imperial Diets. As a token of their friendly intentions, the Netherlands would still make an annual voluntary financial contribution, equal to twice what a Prince-Elector had to pay. This increasing independence was seen as enormously weakening the Empire: Charles essentially created for himself a new state, where his son Philip would succeed him as ruler. Only the crown was lacking. It was also typical of Charles that he called it the *Burgundian* Circle, while the Prince-Electors would have preferred the 'Netherlandish Circle'. With this choice of name, Charles was emphasizing his place, as he saw it, in the Burgundian tradition. The addition of Flanders and Artois was a meaningless gesture. The Netherlands did not pay the contributions to the Empire, and the custom of paying tribute to the emperor as their sovereign quickly fell into disuse. All the Empire was still permitted to do was provide assistance in the event of war – in other words, if France were to invade the Low Countries. When the Netherlands found themselves caught up in internal conflict during the Revolt, the electors of the Empire – in their turn – refused to take action.[8]

After this diplomatic victory in the Empire, Charles focused on the next step. In 1549, he had all the provinces of the Low Countries consent to what was known as the Pragmatic Sanction, an edict in which they pledged to accept his son Philip as their ruler after Charles's death. That offered the perfect opportunity to bring Philip from Spain and introduce him to the domains he was set to inherit. When he came to the Netherlands he was 22 years old, but by no means an inexperienced youth. He had been born in Valladolid in 1527 and was the only son of Charles V and Isabella of Portugal, who also had two daughters, Maria and Juana. Partly because of the prolonged absence of his father, he had been very close to his mother, who acted as Charles's regent in the Spanish kingdoms. When Philip lost his mother at the age of eleven, it was a great shock. And, although still only about sixteen, it fell to him to deputize for his father in governing the Spanish kingdoms while Charles was away. Although his father, of course, wrote to him to give him guidance, he performed his role as regent well. He was resolute in his consultations with the Spanish 'States', the *Cortes*, and in keeping the aristocratic families – which had a tendency to form clans – on a tight rein. In 1543 he married Maria of Portugal. However, Maria died in 1545 after giving birth to their son, Don Carlos, and Philip was overcome with guilt and sorrow. He had therefore already acquired considerable political and life experience before coming to the Netherlands. In addition, he always remained calm and self-controlled, as was expected of a prince, and in Spain especially.[9] After Philip's experiences in Spain, it was therefore perfectly logical for Charles to introduce him to his domains in the Netherlands. He arrived there in 1549, by way of his father's domains in Italy, Austria and Germany.

With the exception of those in the far north (Friesland and Groningen), Philip visited all the provinces of the Low Countries, to allow them to pay homage to him as their future sovereign lord.[10] The cities that the prince honoured with a visit made sure he saw them at their best: they arranged receptions, processions, theatre performances, gifts, effusive speeches and, of course, expansive banquets washed down with plenty of drink. The report of Philip's visit to Antwerp was published in Latin, French and Dutch. The sober prince, who had simple tastes, must have found the Low Countries a veritable 'Land of Cockayne'. Nevertheless, while he refrained from eating and drinking to excess, he did retain a love of the Netherlands' gardening culture, music and painting.

9 Margaret of Parma, governor-general of the Netherlands, 1559–67.

2

The Troubles
Loyal Opposition against Philip II: 1555–1567

The Succession

On 25 October 1555, Charles v transferred the government of the Netherlands to his son Philip II. The main court in the palace on Coudenberg hill in Brussels was not decorated festively for the ceremony. The walls were still hung with black drapes, marking the death of the emperor's mother, the so-called Joanna the Mad, earlier that year. Whether intentionally or because there was no money for more appropriate decoration, the drapes had been left in place and emphasized the sombre nature of the occasion. Although, on paper, Charles was the most powerful monarch in the world, this felt like the day he petitioned for the bankruptcy of his policies. The many wars he had waged had emptied his coffers. At the age of 55, he was worn out – by the pressures of government, his many overseas campaigns and the constant strains of war. And, in his latter years, he also suffered from gout.

Voluntary abdication was highly unusual.[1] Monarchs derived their authority from God, and, relying on God's almighty power, they generally reigned until their deaths. Emperor Charles, however, announced that, as a pious Catholic, he wished to spend his final years preparing for death in luxurious quarters adjacent to a monastery in Spain. In reality, he was completely disillusioned mentally and a physical wreck. He had been unable to hold back the Reformation within the Holy Roman Empire. He had suffered a painful defeat in the war with France in the battle for the bishopric and city of Metz. Returning from that campaign, he no longer wished to live in Coudenberg Palace and took up residence in a small house on the edge of the park in Brussels.[2] There may have been another political reason for his abdication. In the latter years of his rule, he received reports that there was considerable doubt, even resistance, in government circles in the Netherlands regarding his possible succession by the unknown prince Philip.[3] That may have led him to arrange the transfer of power himself, to ensure that he was succeeded by his son.

Philip's life had changed radically when he married the Catholic Queen Mary I of England on 25 July 1554. Mary was the eldest daughter of the Protestant King Henry VIII, who had torn the English Church away from Rome. Mary and Philip succeeded in restoring Catholicism in England, without the possessions that Henry had seized having to be returned to the Catholic Church. That was no mean feat. When Charles summoned his son to Brussels at the end of 1554, Philip refused, feeling that his presence in England was vital to the good government of the country. Furthermore, Mary was pregnant and he wanted to stay until she had given birth. Only after this proved – distressingly – to be a phantom pregnancy did Philip see the possibility of leaving England, temporarily. He responded to his father's summons, and on 8 September 1555 they were reunited in Brussels.[4]

During the ceremonial transfer of power, it became clear just how bad Charles's health was. He supported himself with a stick in his right hand and with his left hand on the shoulder of the young Prince William of Orange. William, only 22, was not yet a stadtholder or a member of the Council of State. He was an army commander in the war with France and the emperor had called him to Brussels especially for the ceremony. Historians from the Low Countries emphasize that the emperor was especially fond of the prince. It is, however, more likely that William had the honour of supporting the emperor since, as the Prince of Orange, he was the highest in rank. And emperors simply do not lean on a count or a duke if there is a prince present.[5] One Spanish historian would accuse the prince of later showing a lack of gratitude for this gesture by inciting the States against Philip.[6]

Every description of the abdication of Charles V emphasizes that Philip II stumbled over his words and apologized for not having a sufficient command of French to address the gathering. He left it up to his adviser Granvelle. Antoine Perrenot, Lord Granvelle and Bishop of Arras (1517–1586), came from Franche-Comté. His father had been one of Emperor Charles's leading advisers and had educated his son to follow in his footsteps. The young Granvelle was extremely intelligent, spoke many languages fluently and had a talent for high politics. He advised the young Philip so well and, especially, so tactfully that the latter always felt that he had come up with his ideas himself.[7] At the abdication, Granvelle

10 The earliest portrayal in a Dutch historical work of Charles V leaning on the shoulder
of the Prince of Orange. In Gerard van Loon, *Beschryving der Nederlandsche historipenningen*
(Description of Dutch Commemorative Medals; vol. 1, 1723).

had also spoken on behalf of the emperor, but Charles had added a short personal speech in which he even asked those present to forgive him if he had done anyone an injustice. This established a clear contrast between the father, human and clearly concerned about the Netherlands, and the son, distant and unable even to speak the language.

We thus see here three figures who will feature prominently in the drama described in this book: Philip, Prince William of Orange (referred to below simply as 'Orange' or 'the prince') and Granvelle. The illustration above is the first to depict the emperor leaning on Orange's shoulder. A completely different portrayal of the scene can be seen in the former Granvelle Palace in Besançon, Granvelle's birthplace. It shows Philip II kneeling at Charles V's feet and kissing his hand, under the approving gaze of Granvelle himself, who is standing at the same height as the emperor. A nineteenth-century tile picture in the meeting room of the States of Friesland depicts a version of Philip's investiture much loved by the Frisians: the king looks alarmed on his throne, because the Frisian representatives refuse to kneel to take the oath of allegiance. In reality, however, there was no need for them to kneel, as both parties swore the oath to each other while standing. This shows how the later writing of

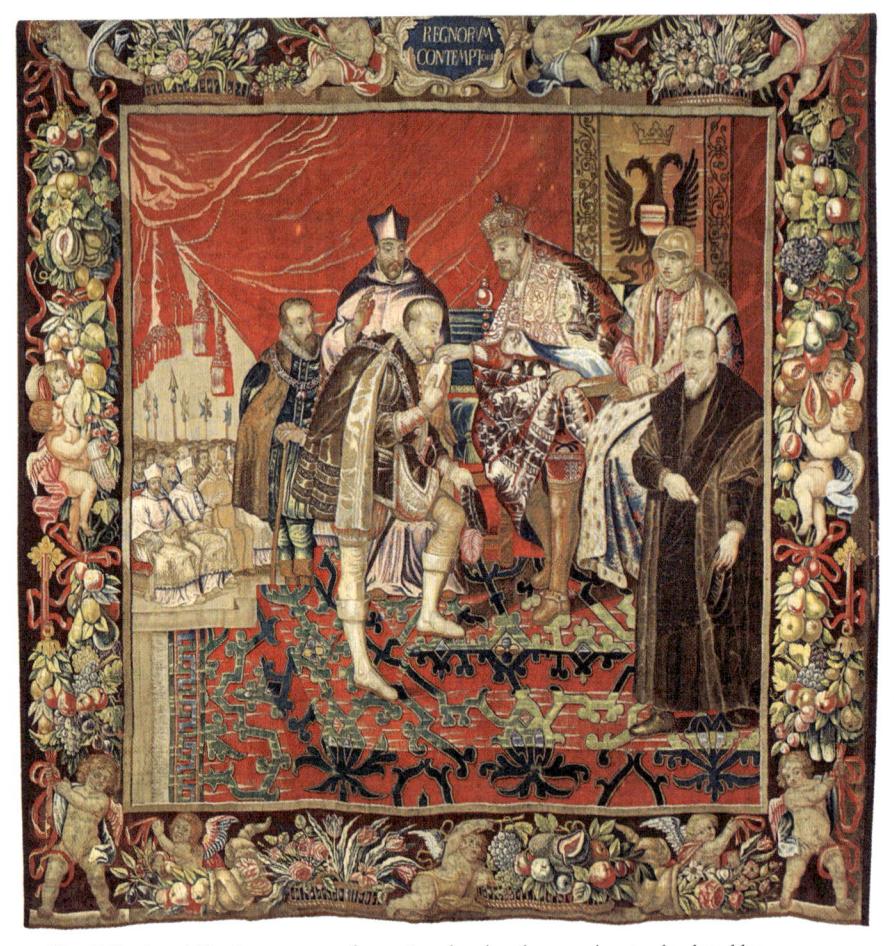

11 *The Abdication of Charles v*, tapestry from 1630 showing the prominent role played by Granvelle in the succession. Note Philip II kissing his father's hand.

history and the visual arts can influence our interpretation of an event. We therefore have to be careful in interpreting written accounts and using illustrations as historical sources.

The abdication and swearing of the oath took place over several days. The representatives from Brabant and Flanders took the oath on 26 October, and the other provinces followed the next day. On 16 January 1556, also in Brussels, Charles V abdicated as king of the Spanish kingdoms and their overseas territories.[8] He continued to interfere with government affairs, however, not only while he was in the Low Countries, but also after he had left for Spain in September 1556. This severely irritated Philip II, whom many people still considered incapable of governing efficiently.[9]

The Troubles

Certainly in the early years of his rule, but also throughout his reign, Philip pursued the policy line set out by his father as closely as possible. Yet it was his father who had passed on his greatest problem: a hopeless financial situation. This was a great obstacle to both his domestic and his foreign policies. In fact, in the final years of Charles v's rule, the state should have been declared bankrupt. But the emperor's honour prevented him from doing so. Immediately after his investiture, Philip ordered a commission to draw up a report on the financial situation across his whole empire – the Netherlands, the Spanish kingdoms and all the domains belonging to them – and how it could best be reorganized. That led to the appointment of a factor, whose task was to draw up an inventory of all debts, revenues and expenditures and then take control over them. It was also decided that the factor should be located in the Low Countries. Philip wasted no time, appointing banker Gaspar

12 The Friesland delegation led by Gemme van Burmania refuses to kneel when swearing the oath to Philip II, as portrayed in a 19th-century mural in the Provincial Hall in Leeuwarden. This proud moment in Frisian history is, however, a fable, as the delegates did not have to kneel.

Schetz to this important post on 31 October. But, as Philip had not yet been appointed king of the Spanish kingdoms, the Spanish saw their opportunity to put a spanner in the works. They argued for the appointment of a permanent second factor, also to be located in the Low Countries but who should be a Spaniard. His duties were described in such a way that he would essentially hold the reins. Philip agreed with the proposals, to the severe irritation of his advisers from the Netherlands. Because of this divided mandate, and even more so because of the widely varying interests of the different parts of the kingdom and the unmanageability of day-to-day practice, this plan – which sounded so good on paper – died an early death. But at least those at the head of the kingdom were aware of the essential nature of the problem.[10]

In 1557, in an attempt to get a grip on these dire financial problems, Philip reduced the interest on the national debt unilaterally to 5 per cent. In reality, this amounted to a declaration of bankruptcy.[11] (Philip would do this again three times during his reign, in 1560, 1574 and 1596.) That in particular made it even more important to consult with the States General on how to assure the nation's finances. The States of Holland already managed the majority of the province's financial transactions. The rich merchants who financed the provincial debt by buying *renten* (bonds) had, as provincial administrators, oversight and control of that debt. Their right hands knew perfectly well what their left hands were doing. Antwerp bankers who wanted to borrow money in Holland for the central government asked the States of Holland to stand surety for the interest payments.[12] The credit and trust enjoyed by the States thus compared favourably with Philip's state of bankruptcy.

As a result of this control by the States of Holland, the province's balance of payments improved year by year.[13] The representatives met on their own authority and had an aversion to tax on trade, but not to imposing a *tiende penning* (tenth penny) if they considered it necessary for their own finances. That did not mean that they were prepared to impose extra taxes to help the government out of trouble.[14] Holland's guarantee on loans to the central government were the most important because, during the Revolt too, the province would bear most of the costs. The lessons learned about financial management under Charles v and Philip II were probably important preconditions for the Revolt taking place at all, and perhaps also for its ultimate success. The States of Holland knew that princes were insatiable spendthrifts with no idea of how and where the money had to be raised. Philip II had once written to an adviser:

> You know of my ignorance in financial matters. I cannot distinguish a good memorandum from a bad one in this respect. And I am not going to addle my brains trying to understand something that I do not understand and have not understood for my whole life.[15]

Unfortunately, the situation in the two most important provinces in the country, Brabant and Flanders, was in no way comparable to that in Holland. They may have been richer, but there were also more voices to impede the decision-making process. That applied to both the guilds in the cities and the clergy, which was taxed separately. Furthermore, the big cities had their sights set on the surrounding countryside and rivalry between them was fierce. And because so many institutions and individuals enjoyed tax exemptions, the burden was even heavier for those who did have to pay tax.[16]

In 1558, a year after the state had been declared bankrupt, the States General convened again, now in Arras. Philip was still sensible enough to allow the States' representatives to consult with each other.[17] He wanted them to agree to a turnover tax, like the one he had seen imposed in Spain. That would make his income independent of the States' approval of the *beden* (aids) that he had to submit to them every year. The States of course realized that themselves and rejected the proposal. They were prepared to provide Philip with money only under strict conditions. Were they taking a leaf out of Holland's book? The States General demanded control and joint management of how the money was spent. In place of the turnover tax that Philip requested, they offered to provide him with a fixed sum for nine years. That was not exactly in line with how Philip wished to rule, but the same method was applied in Spain. The king made an urgent personal appeal to the States, but they ignored it. Philip could no longer get his way simply by invoking respect for the monarchy.[18] What is remarkable is that Granvelle, so often praised for his intelligence and who managed his own finances so well, did not persuade the king of the advantages of joint management of his finances. This Burgundian royal servant was only interested in currying favour with Philip and agreed completely that the States General should no longer come together. Shared responsibility for the financial affairs of the Low Countries would have been better for the position of both country and monarch. But there were simply no separate budgets and financial responsibilities in Philip II's different domains. This non-transparent financial situation fuelled allegations that the interests of the Netherlands' provinces were being sacrificed to those of Spain. At the same time, however, the Spanish kingdoms complained bitterly that they continually had to throw money into the bottomless pit of the Netherlands.

During the years that Philip was in the Netherlands, Brussels functioned as the capital of his empire. That meant that he had an international entourage around him, with international advisers. Consequently, he had little or no time to fulfil his obligations in the governing institutions of the Netherlands. Although he was therefore himself present, immediately after his investiture he appointed a governor-general to deputize for him: Emmanuel Philibert, Duke of Savoy, whose duchy was occupied by France.[19] This enabled Philip to concentrate on international politics. In 1555 an Italian cardinal was chosen as the new pope. Paul IV was not favourably inclined towards Spain and the Spanish, and in 1556 he declared war on Philip in Italy. Philip II charged the Duke of Alba with defending the Spanish crown's possessions in Italy. His orders were not to spare Paul IV personally, but to treat the pope, as head of the Roman Catholic Church and the Holy See, with all due respect. Alba fulfilled this delicate mission with great success.[20] His pacification of Italy was sufficient to spare the country from war for half a century.

13 Portrait of Philip II, dressed in simple clothing, made when he was staying in the Netherlands and as the high nobles and burghers would have seen him. It is an engraving, only 15.3 by 10.7 cm, by Jan Vermeyen of Beverwijk, c. 1600. Around Philip's neck is the medallion of the Order of the Golden Fleece. The Latin inscription reads 'Philip, King of the English, Prince of the Spanish'. The image therefore dates from before his acceptance of rule of the Netherlands.

Philip's major headache in foreign policy was the war with France. He felt that France could best be fought from the Low Countries.[21] In July 1556 the war escalated again and Philip thought it high time to visit his wife, Mary, in England. He stayed in the country for the second – and last – time from the end of March to July 1557, where he successfully persuaded the English that their interests were also under threat. On 1 June 1557, Mary signed a declaration of war with France.[22] Philip wanted to fight the French with English troops that same year and ordered

Emmanuel Philibert, who was the commander of his armies in the Low Countries, to wait with the deciding battle until he arrived with his English reinforcements. He intended to lead his troops into battle himself for the first time and prove himself as their supreme commander. But the moment was too favourable for the Duke of Savoy to miss, and on 10 August he won a decisive victory over the French at Saint-Quentin. This victory was, to a large extent, thanks to the Count of Egmont, who led the cavalry and for whom the road to Paris now lay open. Philip arrived just in time to inspect the victorious troops.[23] He dared not risk the road to Paris, leading instead the siege and capture of Saint-Quentin. This is the only time in Philip's life that we see him so close to the field of battle. According to all reports, he was in his element.[24] From then on, he would lead all wars and sieges from the study rooms in his palaces. A year later, in 1558, Egmont defeated the French decisively for a second time, this time at Gravelines, just to the south of Dunkirk.[25] The victory was partly due to the English fleet, which pounded the French troops with cannon shot from offshore. That was no coincidence: the fleet was passing that stretch of the coast at Philip's urgent request.

Although we seem now to have strayed far from the topic of this book, that is not the case. What this shows us is that, for a ruler like Philip II, domestic and foreign policy were interwoven. A monarch who has successfully restored the Catholic Church in a country like England will not move an inch on religion in his own lands. A lord who is also the king of other kingdoms will surround himself with an international group of advisers. In the Low Countries, the indigenous Council of State continued to function, but Philip's real advisers were the members of his personal or Spanish councils, and that was a cause of irritation to the officials of the Low Countries. They therefore had their ruler in their midst, but they did not have his ear. In his major work *The Mediterranean*, French historian Fernand Braudel asked for some understanding of Philip II's position as the ruler of a large, complex empire: distances were great and communication sometimes took weeks, making it by definition impossible for Philip to respond quickly and adequately if a crisis occurred somewhere in his lands.[26] Although this observation is correct, it is also clear from the period when Philip governed from Brussels, when he was right on the spot to react to developments in the Netherlands, that he was an inaccessible and indecisive administrator.

Friction

In 1559, Spain and France concluded the Peace of Cateau-Cambrésis (a small town to the east of Cambrai). It was an advantageous agreement for Spain, confirming its hegemony. To ensure compliance with the peace, Henri II of France was permitted to choose three hostages. He chose – in hierarchical order – the Prince of Orange, the Duke of Alba and the Count of Egmont. All three stayed at the French court and there is no evidence of animosity between the nobles from the Netherlands and the Spanish grandee, who were all prominent servants of the same lord. In later years, Orange circulated a fable about his time at the French court. He claimed that Henri II had secretly agreed with Philip II to pursue the fight against heresy together, and without mercy. Assuming that Orange knew about these plans, the French king had discussed them with him in detail. After that, the prince knew what he could expect of Philip.[27] In reality, however, the prince's thoughts were far from religion: the year before, his wife Anna van Buren had died and he was preoccupied with looking for a suitable, rich second wife – Catholic or Protestant, it made no difference to him. The conversation with King Henri II is added to his *Apology*, a piece of propaganda published in 1580, in which the prince justified his actions after the fact.

Philip had no choice but to go to Spain, given the political necessity of having himself invested as king after the death of his father. There, too, because of the dire financial situation, the people were on the point of rebellion.[28] When his ship left Flushing (modern-day Vlissingen) on 25 August 1559, there was no reason to assume that he would ever again return to the Netherlands. He was expected, just as his father had done, to strengthen his royal authority in his various domains through his regular personal presence and, when circumstances or necessity demanded it, to return to the lands he had inherited in the Netherlands. Philip had seen himself how his absence in England for a year and a half had cost him most of his political influence.[29] Would he have learned from that experience not to stay away from the Netherlands for too long?

Like his father in earlier times, he appointed a female governor-general to represent him in the Low Countries, his half-sister Margaret of Parma. There was, however, one small problem which went back to her birth: she was the illegitimate daughter of Emperor Charles V. Whether this weighed more heavily than her lineage as a daughter of the emperor depended on how favourably inclined people were towards her.[30]

Philip made no changes to the basic structure of the government: the three councils advising the governor – the Council of State, the Privy Council and the Council of Finance – had now been operational for a quarter of a century. The governor-general herself chaired the Council of State. The Privy Council had a very capable chairman, in the person of Wigle Aytta van Zwichem, known as Viglius. Viglius was an outstanding jurist with a solid understanding of state affairs, and a proponent of a stronger central government. As a Frisian, he could provide objective judgment on conflicts between representatives from Flanders, Brabant and Holland. He even received widespread appreciation in the final year of his life when he made a complete U-turn and supported a policy of moderation to settle the differences between rebels and a seemingly uncompromising crown. The Council of Finance was chaired by Charles de Berlaymont, a high-ranking noble who held the position owing entirely to royal favour and who proved extremely useful in the job, largely as a result of his many children. There is no mention of him possessing any special qualities, but Orange sought his support on two occasions.

Older histories of the Eighty Years War generally claim that Philip formally appointed Granvelle, Viglius and Berlaymont as a kind of secret Privy Council – *Consulta* or, in Dutch, *Achterraad* – to advise Margaret. That is, however, difficult to prove. Allegations of backroom politics are to be found everywhere and at all times. Philip did instruct the governor to consult only these three high-ranking officials when making important decisions or appointments, consciously bypassing the high nobility. The extent to which the three advisers were able to influence policy was a consequence of the daily practice of government. High-ranking nobles did sit on the Council of State, but, if they were also stadtholders, they would have spent more time in their provinces than in Brussels. The jurists, on the other hand, were never absent in the capital, and given the permanent presence of the three high-ranking advisers in the city and Granvelle's unlimited access to the governor, it did appear as though Philip had appointed them as a separate council.[31] Viglius and Berlaymont were also by no means anti-national in their ideas. Viglius would become a constant source of irritation for Alba since, as a jurist, he dared to challenge the duke's decisions time and again as illegal and unfair. Berlaymont, for his part, warned the king that the Netherlands could not be governed in the same way as his domains in Italy.[32] The only Spaniard to remain in the Netherlands after Philip's departure was Thomas de Armenteros, a confidant of Margaret of Parma. Yet the king always retained the last word, as was his right as sovereign lord of the land. That led to France and England recalling their representatives from Brussels because everything was decided in Spain.[33]

While all this was played out virtually behind the scenes as an affair between high-ranking nobles, people in the street were more irritated by two specific matters. First, because of the war with France, some 3,000 of Philip's troops were still stationed in the border provinces. People therefore felt that they were paying for troops who were 'occupying' their country. That was not Philip's original intention: he had promised to remove the troops from the country after the peace, but, as long as he did not need them anywhere else, he left them where they were. The second source of popular annoyance was that the king persisted unabated with his policy of religious prosecutions. Was it really still necessary to prosecute people for their religious beliefs? To cause them pain, force them to recant and then – even after they did recant and admitted to their 'aberration' – make them suffer a violent death?

The number of prosecutions and executions was, incidentally, much lower than has traditionally been assumed. The most recent calculations are those of Alastair Duke, who arrived at the following figures for the period before 1566, on the basis of trial reports and other official sources: Arras about 9, Brabant 228, Flanders 265, French Flanders about 60, Friesland 102, Gelre 16, Groningen 1, Hainaut 44, Holland 403, Limburg-Overmaas 6, Luxembourg 0, Mechelen 11, Namur 12, Overijssel 35, Tournai and the Tournaisis 53, Utrecht 31, Zeeland 23 and Maastricht (governed together with the Bishop of Liège) 21. In the independent bishoprics of Liège and Cambrai, there were 26 and 6 victims, respectively. In total, there were records of some 1,300 victims.[34] Compared to the number of victims of religious persecution elsewhere in Europe, that was an enormous figure.[35] Even the Spanish Inquisition, in the first few centuries of its existence, had only pronounced around 200 sentences. It was, however, very different to the thousands, even tens of thousands, cited in the propaganda war surrounding religious persecution. In his Justification of 1568, for example, Orange referred to 50,000 victims, while, in his perspective on the Revolt, jurist Hugo Grotius even spoke of 100,000 victims.[36]

The steadfastness of their faith and the piety with which those who were persecuted suffered their fate invoked respect and sympathy among many people. Although the number of persecuted Protestants remained a small minority in the Low Countries, their suffering roused compassion among the rest of the population, including the Catholics, who continued to account for the majority. It is in any case very difficult to distinguish between Catholics and Protestants in the sixteenth century, especially the first half. In his *Friesland in Hervormingstijd* (Friesland during the Reformation), Leiden historian J. J. Woltjer did make a useful distinction within the Catholic Church at the time of the Reformation between traditional believers, who accepted what the Church told them, and 'Protestant-minded Catholics', in other words, Catholics who were sympathetic to the reforms proposed by the Protestants. There were therefore no clear dividing lines but a sliding scale, from traditional Catholic, via Protestant-minded Catholic, to Protestant.[37] After the Roman Catholic Church decided at the Council of Trent (Trento, Italy) to reform the Church themselves from the top down (the Counter-Reformation), it became difficult for Catholic believers to uphold Protestant ideas within the Church. Tighter rules prescribed exactly what Catholics should believe and what religious practices were and were not permitted. These 'new' Counter-Reformist Catholics would be extremely aware of the differences between Roman Catholic and Protestant.

In the sixteenth century, unlike today, religion was not something that people practised only in their homes or at church. In the Catholic Church, it was customary (and still is in many parts of the world) on religious festival days to hold a procession through the town. Shops had to be closed and people were expected to decorate their houses. The high point of the procession was the passage of the Blessed Sacrament – the bread consecrated during the Holy Mass and carried by the priest in a gilded monstrance. For Catholics, through the process of transubstantiation, consecrating the bread made it literally the body of Christ. As the procession passed them in the streets, bearing this Real Presence, the faithful would kneel, remove their hats and make the sign of the cross. Most Protestants, on the other hand, deny transubstantiation: for them,

14 *Bartel Jacobsz. Bart, 's morgens preekt hij in het wit, 's avonds in het zwart'* (He preached in white in the mornings and in black in the evenings). Bartel had been a priest in Oostzaan in North Holland since 1561. In 1565, however, he converted to the Reformed church, taking most of his parishioners with him. A year later, when the religious conflict had intensified, he fled to England.

the bread remains bread and only symbolizes the body of Christ. Nor are kneeling or making the sign of the cross part of the Protestant liturgy. Consequently, whenever a procession was held, these expressions of religious differences were thrown into sharp relief. Some people would refuse to kneel, remove their hats or cross themselves, leading to irritation on both sides, and conflict. Protestants would not kneel to what they called 'the bread God', while Catholics would say, why should I not kneel before my Lord and Saviour?

The New Bishoprics

As a result of the political alliance of the Burgundian and Habsburg princes, the Netherlands constituted a relatively new state, one whose borders did not coincide with the existing ecclesiastical divisions. The Low Countries traditionally fell partly under the French archbishopric of Rheims and partly under the German archbishopric of Cologne. The lands around Groningen (*Ommelanden*) belonged to the bishopric of Münster. Only four bishops were responsible for the religious welfare of the people of the Low Countries: of Utrecht, Arras, Tournai and Cambrai (all except the last appointed by the king). Plans for a new ecclesiastical organization had already been developed under Emperor Charles but international political developments had prevented them from ever being realized. As a Counter-Reformation Catholic, however, Philip II wanted to make serious work of the reorganization. A committee led by Viglius prepared the plans in the deepest secrecy. Such caution was necessary first to ensure that the French and German bishops did not get up in arms because they would lose a large part of their wealthy domains, and second because many objections could be expected in the Low Countries themselves, as the new structure would unavoidably affect established interests. The person given the difficult task of bringing this to a satisfactory conclusion in Rome was Franciscus Sonnius, later the first Bishop of 's-Hertogenbosch and, after that, of Antwerp. On 12 May 1559 the pope placed his signature beneath the reorganization plan.[38] Philip was in Zeeland, about to leave for Spain, when he received the news of the papal approval.

The Netherlands would from then on form a single autonomous ecclesiastical province, divided into three archbishoprics. The French-speaking provinces and Walloon Brabant would fall under the archbishopric of Cambrai. The important, densely populated provinces of Flanders and Brabant became a single archbishopric, with the archbishop in Mechelen. Third, the old bishopric of Utrecht was promoted to an archbishopric that embraced all provinces above the major rivers, together with Zeeland. In total, the three archbishoprics were divided up into fourteen bishoprics. Furthermore, the bishops now needed to have certain minimum education qualifications: a degree in theology or canon law. The nobility, who liked their younger sons to become bishops, now had to send them to university first. The new bishops were obliged to live permanently in their bishoprics, to set up a seminary to train priests, and to inspect all parishes regularly. In the same bull, the pope – of course, at the king's request – established a new university in the Netherlands, at Douai. This French-speaking Flemish town was chosen because there were as yet no printers there to spread heretical ideas. French-speaking students from the Low Countries would now have to study there, while Dutch-speakers went to Leuven. Studying abroad was allowed only in Rome, or elsewhere with special permission.[39] Philip had appointed Granvelle as Archbishop of Mechelen and therefore 'Primate' of the Netherlands. The pope later promoted him to cardinal. Granvelle himself claimed that he had nothing to do with the plans but Viglius, who partly had Granvelle's protection to thank for his career, had kept him closely informed from beginning to end.[40]

From the point of view of the Church, the reorganization was a very sensible and responsible move. If there was such fierce criticism of wrongdoings in the Church, of unknowing clergy at lower levels or of those of high level abusing their offices, then surely it was to be welcomed that the Church wanted to introduce improvements? And how better to achieve these improvements than to increase supervision of the Church's doctrines and how its followers put them into practice? As a humanist and supporter of Erasmus, Viglius was already convinced of the senselessness of violent prosecution. He felt that the best and only way to defeat heresy was to improve the situation within the Roman Catholic Church itself, thereby removing its causes. But this is not how the plans were interpreted. Nearly everyone believed that Cardinal Granvelle had cooked the whole thing up behind the scenes, in the first place to increase the influence of the crown within the Church, but also for his own personal gain. High clergy had traditionally enjoyed priority over high nobility, and now it was the turn of Granvelle to be given preference. When Orange returned to the Council of State in 1562, he found the top chair occupied by Granvelle and had to settle for second place.

In addition, criticism flared up within the Church itself. To give the bishoprics more financial room for manoeuvre, it was decided that every bishop would also be the abbot of a rich abbey in his bishopric. He would be represented there by a deputy, but the revenue of the abbey would benefit the 'bishop's table', that is, the expenses incurred by the bishop's household. The Bishop of Haarlem would thus also become Abbot of Egmont, the Bishop of Antwerp was allocated St Bernard's Abbey in Hemiksem, the Archbishop of Mechelen acquired Affligem Abbey, and so on. Appointing the bishops as abbots also had intentional political consequences: the abbots often took part in the meetings of the provincial States. The Abbot of Affligem, for example, was one of the most prominent ecclesiastical members of the States of Brabant. The most important secular leader in these States was Orange, as Baron of Breda. And just how important it was to have a seat in the States of Brabant is shown by the fact that the Count of Egmont, stadtholder of Flanders, bought the domain of Gaasbeek in Brabant, largely to be represented in the States. That the places of the abbots would in the future be taken by bishops appointed by the king was widely seen as an attempt on the monarch's part to increase his influence in the States.[41]

15 Granvelle, effective ruler of the Netherlands, after his appointment as cardinal in 1561.

Later, Granvelle and the others involved admitted that the annexation of the abbeys had been a mistake. The blow was somewhat softened on 30 July 1564, when the incorporation was revoked and, instead, the abbots would from then on have to allocate 8,000 guilders a year to the bishopric. The bishops continued to sit in the States but, to Philip's annoyance, they proved not to be simple 'yes-men'. They generally voted in favour of the interests of the province, even if that was not in his interest. Nevertheless, the resistance was so resolute that dissatisfied parties, like the city of Antwerp and the States of Brabant, sent representatives to the king in Spain to express their displeasure and to argue for other solutions. Antwerp, for example, was afraid that the suspected stricter religious control would harm trade and commerce. But their efforts were in vain – king and Church continued to impose their will.

The Inquisition

Every bishop traditionally had two officials under him, known as episcopal inquisitors, who investigated whether there were cases of unbelief or heresy in the bishopric. The secrecy surrounding the reorganization of the Church fuelled rumours that the king also wanted to introduce what was known as the Spanish Inquisition in the Netherlands. There are few institutions in history about which so many fables and fabricated stories have been told as the Spanish Inquisition. This was all connected to the Black Legend, a complex of myths and fables – some based on fact and some completely fabricated – depicting Spanish history in an unfavourable light, which was – and continues to be – popular in certain circles.[42] The working methods of the episcopal inquisitors in Spain were strictly regulated. Large parts of the country's population valued the Inquisition's activities as a kind of spiritual health-care: people could testify to their piety and thereby put a stop to false accusations and rumours. Most of them were not afraid of the Inquisition but welcomed it, the exceptions being Muslims (*moriscos*) and Jews (*conversos*), compelled to convert by force.[43] Gatherings of *luteranos*, heretics, had been discovered in several prominent Spanish cities, causing great consternation and a closing of the ranks in the Church.[44] Cutting and burning was a secular form of punishment, contrasted with which the methods of the Inquisition were much more humane: trial procedures were strictly prescribed and observed. If it was decided to interrogate a suspect by inflicting pain, only one form of torture was permitted: hanging the suspect up by the arms, which were tied together behind their backs. There were very clear rules about how long and how often this method could be applied, and there were exceptions. Pregnant women, for example, could not be interrogated under torture. Confessions obtained through torture had to be repeated voluntarily to be legally valid. Philip II never had the intention to introduce the Spanish Inquisition in the Netherlands and responded to such allegations by saying that the existing inquisition there was adequate and much stricter than its counterpart in Spain. How did that come about?

When numbers of religious dissidents increased in the course of the sixteenth century, papal inquisitors were appointed in addition to the existing episcopal inquisitors. The most notorious of these was Pieter Titelmans, appointed in 1545 as inquisitor for both Dutch and French-speaking Flanders. In the twenty years from 1545 to 1566, he brought more than 1,500 cases of heresy, 127 of which ended with a death sentence. His 'success' was largely due to the support of the central government in Brussels, allowing him to withstand the resistance from local authorities.

There was also a Spanish Augustine monk active in the Low Countries. Lorenzo de Villavicencio was the chaplain for Spanish merchants in Bruges and a man after the king's heart. Villavicencio was fully convinced that the great majority of the people in the Netherlands were loyal Roman Catholics. Nevertheless, he saw heresy and heretical activities everywhere and cherished a deep mistrust of city leaders, especially those in Bruges, and of many high-ranking 'indigenous' officials. He wrote letters and reports to Spain, which determined Philip's view of the religious situation in his domains in the Low Countries. Villavicencio considered Viglius, as a leading figure in the regime, as mainly to blame for the lax prosecution of heretics. Yet his efforts to discredit him with Philip and Margaret had little impact in practice.[45] At the foot of the pyramid of government, he believed that city officials – and pensionaries in particular – shared in the guilt of not prosecuting heretics. In his eyes, they were cut from the same cloth as Viglius. Philip granted Villavicencio a gratuity of 200 ducats and gave the monk permission to write directly to him. The king was actually very well informed about cases of heresy even in the farthest flung corners of his empire. He heard, for example, that on the island of Texel – in the church (a Catholic church, of course) – there had been a public dispute between the priest and a number of Mennonites about religion and child baptism. Everyone could identify the Mennonites, but the sheriff – who wanted to earn back the money his position had cost him(!) – could do nothing about it as the magistrates did not want to pass sentence on their fellow citizens, and the provincial government in The Hague could not support him.[46]

Futile Missions to Spain

If it proved necessary to criticize the ruler or the government of the land, the high nobles considered it their task to do so. At a time before participatory bodies, public surveys, opinion polls or protest demonstrations, the high nobles were the voice of the people. Orange, Egmont, Horn and their supporters felt neglected by the king, the governor-general and her advisers, and that they were being systematically and persistently excluded from government affairs. The Council of State seemed to take important decisions when they were in Holland, Flanders and elsewhere fulfilling their duties as stadtholders. Their anger was grounded in the fact that they formally shared responsibility for measures that they did not support and about which they had not been able to express their opinions. Their opposition was also inspired by fear that their traditional right to participate in decision-making – the possibility for the people of the Netherlands to have some influence on government through the meetings of the States – would come to an end.

Orange and Egmont could no longer accept this state of affairs, and on 23 July 1561 they wrote a letter of protest to the king, complaining that they had hardly any influence, if at all, on government. This was five months after Granvelle had been appointed cardinal (on 26 February).[47] A little less than a year later, nothing had changed in the government's policy, and the high nobles decided to coordinate their criticisms and present a united front in Brussels as a 'loyal opposition'. They joined forces in a league, in the same way as their counterparts in France had done. Baron de Montigny, a brother of the Count of Horn and Governor of Tournai, went to see the king as their spokesman. He returned with little more than fine-sounding words.

On 11 March 1563, Orange, Egmont and Horn wrote a new letter, requesting the king to dismiss Granvelle and refusing to share responsibility for government of the country any more.[48] At the end of the same year, the high nobles came up with an absurd form of protest. They had all their servants dress in the same livery, a sort of uniform of simple grey material. It was officially to save on costs, but they also wanted something to symbolize their displeasure. Fate chose Egmont to devise the symbol. He chose a fool's cap, embroidered on the top of the sleeves of the servants' livery. Everyone understood that this was intended as criticism of the cardinal.[49] As unofficial prime minister in Brussels and cardinal, Granvelle seemed to personify the subordination of the interests of the Netherlands to the Spanish monarchy. All stadtholders and knights of the Golden Fleece endorsed this standpoint, with the exception of Berlaymont and Groningen stadtholder Arenberg. What the high nobility had in mind was a government of king and nobility together, as in the *curia*, the royal court in medieval times.

In the same year, the governor-general also decided that she no longer wished to work with Granvelle, because she felt that he was secretly working against her in his letters to the king. As Duchess of Parma and Piacenza, Margaret was very keen to get her hands on the citadel of Piacenza, which would require the king to remove the Spanish garrison.

The cardinal had advised the king against this, which Margaret found difficult to accept. This illustrates how, in serious conflicts where major interests are at stake, issues that may seem more insignificant can lead to an unexpected rift. Philip gave the cardinal permission to visit his old mother in Franche-Comté. It was a pretext to remove Granvelle without loss of face, but the people of the Low Countries, from nobleman to beggar, saw through the ruse. Granvelle's political friends in Madrid were, in any case, not at all disappointed at his departure from the Netherlands: they had always seen his appointment there as far below his station.[50] After the cardinal had left, the high nobles returned to the Council of State and once again took part in the discussions. They soon noticed that changing a few faces did not automatically improve the situation in the country. The strict prosecution of heretics was one of the king's personal policy priorities, which he could not be persuaded to abandon. Even his loyal followers Viglius and Granvelle had called on the king to be lenient and proposed allowing Protestants in the Netherlands to live like Christians in the Turkish empire: to let them go their own way as long as they behaved properly and made a financial contribution. But the king would hear nothing of it and held on rigidly to his strict principles.

On 31 December 1564, Orange made a speech in the Council of State, in which he outlined the principles of the matter, saying, 'Though I am a good Catholic, I cannot approve of princes attempting to rule over the consciences of their subjects.'[51] Granvelle had been very positive about the prince's Catholic convictions, asserting that he knew nothing about William that appeared suspicious or could cause harm to the faith.[52] Such an outspoken plea for freedom of religion had never been heard before, including in the Holy Roman Empire, whose inhabitants were expected to practise the same faith as their lord. The princes' proposal essentially came down to permitting two or more religions to coexist. That was not naïve idealism, but a practical, supra-religious standpoint based on reality: if Roman Catholics, Mennonites, Lutherans and Calvinists live together in one society (not to mention many other smaller groups), it makes little sense to prosecute them, sometimes to the death.

Since the king and his main council were not in agreement, the best solution seemed to be to send a representative to the king on behalf of the nobles to clarify their standpoints and, if possible, to change his mind. Besides moderation in religious prosecutions and the desire for more participation in policy-making, the nobles also wanted a resumption

16 Anonymous portrait of the Count of Egmont, possibly German. Egmont's execution also generated great indignation in the Holy Roman Empire.

of the war with France. Egmont, a prominent noble who had twice defeated the French, seemed the perfect choice for the mission to Spain. He stayed at the court from early February to the beginning of April. The king was not pleased about the entire visit, but both monarch and court showed their best side. Receptions, banquets and tournaments gave Egmont the impression that the king appreciated his mission. Philip did, however, immediately sweep one thing from the table: he wished to preserve peace with France at all costs. He would rather have lost the Netherlands than resume the war with France.[53] This can justifiably be emphasized, as it is often ignored by historians: they are keen to shine the spotlight on the nobles as representatives of the real interests of the Netherlands and attribute to the king an anti-national standpoint, but it was with the interests of the Netherlands at heart that he wanted to preserve peace with France. Egmont spoke with the king several times, the last time on 4 April in Aranjuez. The king asked him what the nobles had intended by dressing up all their servants in the same livery, adorned with fool's caps. Egmont responded that it had been only a game, to which the king replied, 'Conde, no se haga mas', which roughly translates as 'Count, this has to stop.'[54] In reality, they did not discuss anything substantial; the king assured Egmont of his concern for the welfare of the Netherlands and sent him home with gifts and vague statements. There was considerable agitation in the Council of State when Egmont, on being pressed by William, had to confess that he had been unable to arouse any greater understanding of the situation from the king, let alone a prospective change in policy. In a letter dated 13 May, the king ordered the execution of six Mennonites whose sentence had been suspended in the Netherlands.

Philip preferred to listen to Villavicencio, whom he first granted an audience on 29 July 1565. The conversation lasted for two hours. The king invited the monk to put his findings down on paper and come back within four days. Villavicencio had a fiery and compelling character with great powers of persuasion, and was eventually to become the voice of Philip's conscience. Margaret was still under the spell of the nobles and endorsed their demands: the dominance of the nobility, religious tolerance and convening the States General. It was more than was to be expected when Philip agreed to a religious conference in the Netherlands. Six members of the clergy and three jurists came together, joined – inevitably – by Viglius and Joachim Hopperus of the Council of State. Their recommendations were better education for the young, stricter controls on the clergy and the possibility of sentencing heretics to the galleys rather than to death. Villavicencio was very unhappy about this: he believed that such a meeting was not a task for the government and would rather the Church had held a regional synod. He expressed his radical standpoint and, referring to Church Father St Augustine, emphasized that heretics do not convert out of love but only out of fear of the stake. If civic magistrates did not want to act, they would have to be replaced. All of the problems until then had, after all, been caused by laxity. The possibility had to be explored of executing people in secret and the existing inquisition had to be supported as much as possible. Lastly, he expressed the opinion that Margaret could not be expected to make such a change for the better. When Philip was hesitant in making a decision, Villavicencio pointed out the consequences of his procrastination for the afterlife.[55] Finally, Philip took the plunge, and on 17 and 20 October, from his country house in the woods of Segovia, he wrote the notorious letters ordering the strict placards to be enforced to the letter.[56] The governor-general hardly dared to discuss the letters in the Council of State, but Orange insisted she revealed their contents. The king's immutable policy only added to the dissatisfaction and criticism.

The Compromise of Nobles

In December 1565, Brussels celebrated the wedding of the governor's son, Alexander Farnese, Prince (later Duke) of Parma.[57] Many guests gathered in the city. During the festivities, after many meetings and consultations, twenty lesser nobles set up a league called the Compromise of Nobles. Since Egmont's failed mission to Spain, they felt that they had to do something to promote the interests of the fatherland, by collectively expressing their opposition to the placards and religious persecution. Louis of Nassau, a younger brother of the Prince of Orange, and John Marnix, Lord of Toulouse, a lesser noble of Calvinist persuasion, drew up a petition. Several copies were made and sent around the country to collect signatures. Some 400 nobles, both Catholic and Protestant, most of whom were probably averse to any pronounced religious beliefs, requested that the States General be convened and the placards and prosecutions suspended. Orange advised both the governor-general and the nobles to soften the blow by delivering the petition as an official Request. Margaret hesitantly agreed, and on 5 April 1566, 200 nobles marched, unarmed, to the palace in Brussels. The lower-ranking nobles were at the front, with those higher in rank behind them and, right at the back, Count Henry of Brederode and Louis of Nassau, who were to hand over the Request. The governor-general responded by saying that she could make no concrete promises but promised 'moderation' in enforcing the religious placards.

When he noticed how nervous this incident had made Margaret, Berlaymont said to her, 'N'ayez pas peur, Madame, ce ne sont que des

17 *The Mast of the Inquisition*, anonymous, April–June 1566. To the left, the beggars try to pull the mast over while, to the right, Catholic clerics try to keep it upright. The texts at the top are in Dutch and French, the two languages of the land. Granvelle sent a copy of this print to Philip II in Spain, where it is still kept in the national archives at Simancas. This copy is from the Leiden University library.

gueux' (Do not be afraid, Madame, they are only beggars). The nobles did indeed come begging, but not for themselves: they were asking for leniency for those with other religious beliefs, and for the States General to be convened. That many of them were heavily in debt did not make them beggars in the conventional sense of the word. The new wealth in the Netherlands may have had its basis in trade and commerce, but old money from owning land or serving at court was not yet lost. Historians writing in the Netherlands in the nineteenth century and well into the twentieth tended to portray the nobility as ignorant down-and-outs with little real influence on events. This portrayal was not rectified until the studies of H. A. Enno van Gelder and Henk van Nierop, who reassessed the significance of the nobility at its true value.[58] In the southern Netherlands, it was less common to underestimate the role of the nobility, reflecting the much more important place they held in the economy and government of provinces like Artois, Hainaut and Namur. A few days after they had submitted the Request, the nobles adopted the name *gueux*, beggars, as a badge of honour. They hung begging bowls or 'geuzen medals' around their necks and adopted the slogan *Fidèles au roy, jusqu'à la besace* (Loyal to the king, unto the beggar's pouch). The high nobility sent Montigny on a second mission to Madrid, this time accompanied by the Marquis of Bergen op Zoom. On 30 July 1566, twelve representatives of the lesser nobles – soon dubbed the twelve apostles – submitted a second request to the governor-general. They now even asked for full freedom of religion and for the government to be transferred to the loyal nobles, Orange, Egmont and Horn. Their ambitions were thus twofold: religious and political.

In France, too, the nobles considered themselves the mouthpiece of the nation and felt it their duty to defend the interests of the country, even to the point of rebellion. One high noble, requested to participate in the resistance against the monarch in defence of the fatherland, answered that those who did so always came off worst: kings always proved strongest and those who resisted them ended up on their knees.[59] In the French situation this was undoubtedly good advice, given that it would be another two centuries before the revolution would succeed there. But it is advisable to remember this example, as, in part of the Netherlands, it would be the king himself who would end up on his knees.

Annus Horribilis or *Annus Mirabilis*?

The strictness of the Spanish-Brussels government was based not only on principled religious conviction but also on political policy. France had clearly shown how religious differences could divide and ruin a country. After the Peace of Cateau-Cambrésis in 1559, King Henri II of France had been mortally wounded during a tournament and had died in the prime of his life. He left four underage sons behind, all of whom suffered from weak health and the eldest of whom became King Charles IX, with his mother acting as regent. The Catholic court, supported by the powerful House of Guise, was opposed by prominent Protestant families like Condé and Coligny, referred to in France as Huguenots. The conflict between the two parties fell little short of a civil war. When the Huguenots were defeated in March 1562, many Protestants crossed the northern border of France to Valenciennes, Tournai and Antwerp.[60] One of their leaders was Guido, or Guy, de Brès (1522–1567), who had been a pastor in Tournai since 1559. There, in 1561, he wrote his *Confession de foy* (Confession of Faith), published a year later in Dutch as *Belydenisse des gheloofs*. As the *Confessio Belgica* (Belgic or Netherlandish Confession) it would become popular in the Reformed churches of the Netherlands as a confession of their faith. In the autumn of the same year, De Brès threw a stone over the wall of the castle at Tournai, with a letter attached.

It was addressed to the king and stated that the members of the Reformed church wished to be loyal subjects. Margaret of Parma sent the letter on to Philip II on 19 December 1561. The first Calvinist service took place in the open air in Bailleul (Belle) on 12 July 1562. On 1 May 1565 there were so many Calvinists in Ghent that they asked the magistrate for permission to build their own church. By the summer of 1566, the open-air services were attracting thousands of people throughout the country, not only in Flanders and Brabant, but also in Holland, for example in the dunes near Overveen, in the jurisdiction of Henry of Brederode. Calvinism had one advantage over the other Protestant religions: a well thought-out and efficient organization. The congregations were governed by a church council or consistory, and the representatives of the consistories came together regularly at the meetings of the classes and the synods. The preachers were thoroughly educated – if not by Calvin himself, then by his followers in Geneva – and travelled around the country zealously trying to attract converts. The Calvinists saw the government as a servant of God, which thus also had to be converted. On 15 July, representatives of both the nobles and the consistories came together in Sint-Truiden, in the neutral territory of Liège, where they may already have discussed the possibility of organized, and even armed, resistance.

The advent of Calvinism in the extreme south of the Netherlands was not only related to the proximity of France or the fact that Artois and Hainaut were French-speaking. The rural areas of Artois and the south-western corner of Flanders had become heavily industrialized by the production of textiles. Thousands of people earned a meagre living in this industry and, even in prosperous times, lived hardly above the poverty line. When a trade conflict with England caused the supply of wool to dry up, the result was widespread unemployment. The military conflict between Sweden and Denmark had even more severe consequences, when the Øresund strait was closed to shipping in 1565. That cut off the supply of vital grain from the Baltic. This, together with the failure of the harvest in the Netherlands itself and the exceptionally harsh winter, caused widespread hunger in 1566. That had not been seen in the Low Countries in living memory. The wealth of the Catholic Church aroused feelings of jealousy where the misery was at its most acute, and there, too, Calvinism found its most ardent support. The Marquis of Bergen op Zoom blamed the religious troubles on the thousands of wage labourers in Valenciennes.[61] In Tournai, the situation was so extreme that the poor were referred to as the *Tous-nus*, the 'completely naked', because they hardly had clothes to cover their bodies. This ragged folk wanted not alternative dogmas but food, and in their misery, every form of violent protest seemed to offer a way out. Viglius wrote to a friend in Spain that, due to the stagnation in trade and commerce around Oudenaarde, more than 8,000 people were without work. They were normally employed by the merchants, but there was now no work and they had to find other ways to survive.[62]

The Iconoclastic Fury

Preacher Sebastiaan Matte, originally a hatmaker, spoke the language of the common folk. On 10 August 1566, the feast day of St Lawrence, he gave a rousing sermon outside the St Lawrence monastery in Steenvoorde, a village then in the extreme southwest of Flanders but now just across the border in France. When he had finished speaking, twenty members of his audience – led by another preacher – entered the monastery and started destroying all the statues. Three days later, the same thing happened in the monastery of St Anthony in nearby Bailleul. The following day, Matte preached in Poperinge, a short distance away to the north, and a crowd of around 100 people smashed everything in the church. From there, groups of several dozen people went on the rampage through Flanders and Brabant wreaking destruction in churches, monasteries and convents. It is actually impossible to see this iconoclastic fury, known as the *Beeldenstorm* (Destruction of the Statues) in the Low Countries, as a single coordinated movement. In some places, the destruction was caused by angry groups of unemployed and hungry people who had been living below the poverty line for some time; in others, it was more disciplined and efficient, conducted by groups whose main aim was to 'purify' the churches.

The fury thus varied from village to village and from town to town. As the centre of government, Brussels remained unaffected. In many towns, the situation depended on the civic militia, an organized group of armed citizens whose task was to preserve law and order and who had to be available in the event of military attacks on the town. If the militia did not support the destruction in the churches – as was the case in Leuven, Lille, Bruges and many other cities – then it did not happen. But Antwerp (20 August), Ghent (22nd) and Valenciennes (24th) suffered the full force of the fury. In Ghent, it was a direct consequence of the shortage of food. After a good harvest at home, people expected prices

18 Portrayal of the *Beeldenstorm*, the iconoclastic fury. The artist has left the front of the church open, to give a good view of what is happening. Inside, people are destroying statues, paintings, tombs, glass windows and items used in Catholic worship. At bottom right is a man with a burning candle in his hand, intended to show that the events took place at all hours of the day and night. On the right in the background we can see someone making off with a large sack of loot. Engraving by Frans Hogenberg (1535–1590).

to fall quickly; when that did not happen, there were food riots on 21 August and the poor set their own prices. The following day, already in a state of heightened agitation, they directed their fury at the churches, monasteries and convents.[63] Chronicler Marcus van Vaernewijck noted that fathers took their children with them to the church to bang away at the statues with their small hammers.[64] The villages around these cities also felt the fury of the protestors, but above the major rivers the destruction was more isolated. To prevent worse, some cities – for example, Leeuwarden on 6 September and Groningen on 18 September – authorized statues to be destroyed in orderly fashion. On 14 September, the Count of Culemborg had all the statues in his town removed, and Brederode did the same in Vianen on the 25th.

Countless works of art were destroyed during the iconoclastic fury, as a result of which only a few churches in the Low Countries still retain their pre-1566 atmosphere. These relatively brief but severe incidents in August and September 1566 were extremely dramatic, but the systematic purification of church buildings in the years that followed was at least of equal importance: most statues disappeared and most murals were painted over after the triumph of the Reformed movement in the 1570s.[65] In some cases, ecclesiastical or secular authorities were aware of the potentially double value of their costly altarpieces: for religion and for art. The *Adoration of the Mystic Lamb*, the altarpiece in St Bavo's Cathedral in Ghent created by the Van Eyck brothers, was moved to a safe place. In Leiden, the city authorities ordered Lucas van Leyden's *Last Judgment* to be removed – which is why it can now still be seen in the city's De Lakenhal museum. In Alkmaar, the new Reformed city leaders did not want to keep the large altarpiece by Maerten van Heemskerck in the church but realized that it was a waste of money to destroy it. So they sold it to the (Lutheran!) cathedral in Linköping in Sweden.[66]

And yet, only a small percentage of the population was involved in the destruction of the statues; most people watched in silent resignation. It is fascinating that, in the Netherlands – unlike during the religious wars in France – the majority of the population simply let the activists

19 Marianum (double-sided statue of Mary and the Christ Child) in the church of St Leonard in Zoutleeuw, in the Belgian province of Flemish Brabant. The 16th-century interior of the church has been carefully preserved intact. Mary and Jesus are surrounded by five coats of arms, showing the five wounds suffered by Jesus on the cross: his heart, hands and feet.

go about their destructive business. This has been interpreted in widely varying ways. It is safe to say that the first, severe wave of destruction in the summer of 1566 took loyal Catholics completely by surprise. Many chroniclers of that time, at least, express their indignation, their amazement and their inability to do anything about it. As simple believers, it had always been impressed upon them that they should follow their priests, their shepherds, obediently. But what should they do now? Arm themselves and fight? That could have led to terrible civil wars, like those in France. Some suggested letting Protestants build their own churches. There were priests who called on the government to intervene, for instance in conservative cities like Leuven and Lille, where the iconoclastic fury did not occur. In most places, the municipal authorities wanted to restore order and therefore did not organize prosecutions. In France, however, the majority of Catholics believed in the ideal of *une foi, une loi, un roi* – one faith, one law, one king – and everyone who opposed that was a sinner against the sacrosanct unity of the people. The king was king by the grace of God, crowned and anointed by the Church. That was not the case in the Netherlands. There, because of the composite nature of the land, the ruler was four times a duke, six times a count and seven times a lord. To pronounce death sentences in his name was completely out of the question.[67]

Nevertheless, the response among Catholics was fierce enough. They may have felt sympathy for the poor wretches who went to their deaths at the stake so bravely, singing and praying, but now that the dissenters had become so powerful that they were able to smash statues in the churches, a reaction was inevitable. The Catholic nobles distanced themselves from the dissenters, explaining how relatively easy it proved to restore order. The situation was tense enough: the governor-general was initially desperate after the fierce iconoclastic fury in Antwerp and Ghent on 20 and 22 August, but she was saved by the high nobles. After consulting with Orange and Egmont, the Compromise of Nobles decided to disband, in exchange for which Margaret consented to allow preaching where it had already taken place up to that point. Egmont responded to these events by saying 'eerst de staat, dan the godsdienst' (first the state, and then religion) and restored order in Flanders. As Viscount of Antwerp, Orange restored peace in the city and had a few of the ringleaders strung up. The inhabitants of Culemborg submitted a petition to their count, asking him to put an end to the Protestant preaching and to enforce the placards,[68] but he took no action.

The ferocity and scale of the *Beeldenstorm* made a deep impression on both the secular and religious authorities in the Netherlands, Catholics, Lutherans and Calvinists alike. But they should have been warned by the events in France. It was only four years since churches, monasteries and convents in large parts of the country had been divested of their statues and paintings.[69] The government could thus have foreseen that these events could also happen in the Netherlands. Nevertheless, the king and the Spanish court were in shock.[70]

On 3 October 1566, Egmont, Horn, Orange and Louis of Nassau met in Dendermonde, in Flanders. Tradition has it that they discussed the possibility of armed resistance. But for what purpose, against whom, and how? Had a number of them thought about taking over strong cities and presenting the king with the fait accompli of a society where different religions lived alongside each other? In short, what would later be achieved – with great difficulty – in 1572? (See Chapter Three.) Egmont was too loyal a servant to the throne to consider such an option. Brederode, on the other hand, wanted to fight and fortified his small town of Vianen, to the south of Utrecht. Orange supplied him with a number of cannons. In the south, Valenciennes and Tournai chose for Calvinism and refused to admit the soldiers sent by the government to be garrisoned there. The trial of strength that followed may not have been on the scale of the tragic years to come, but it was a first, bitter struggle. The governor-general had tried to get both cities to make their peace with the king on several occasions but, after they had refused to do so at each opportunity, she ordered her general, Philippe de Noircarmes, to take them by force. Tournai fell in January 1567. This gave Margaret fresh courage and, on the advice of Viglius, she demanded a new oath of loyalty from the nobles to see whom she could trust and who not. Orange, Horn and Brederode refused. Lesser noble

20 Henry of Brederode, initiator of the Compromise of Nobles and the only noble who wanted to resort to military action as early as 1566–7. By Hans Liefrinck I (*c.* 1518–1573).

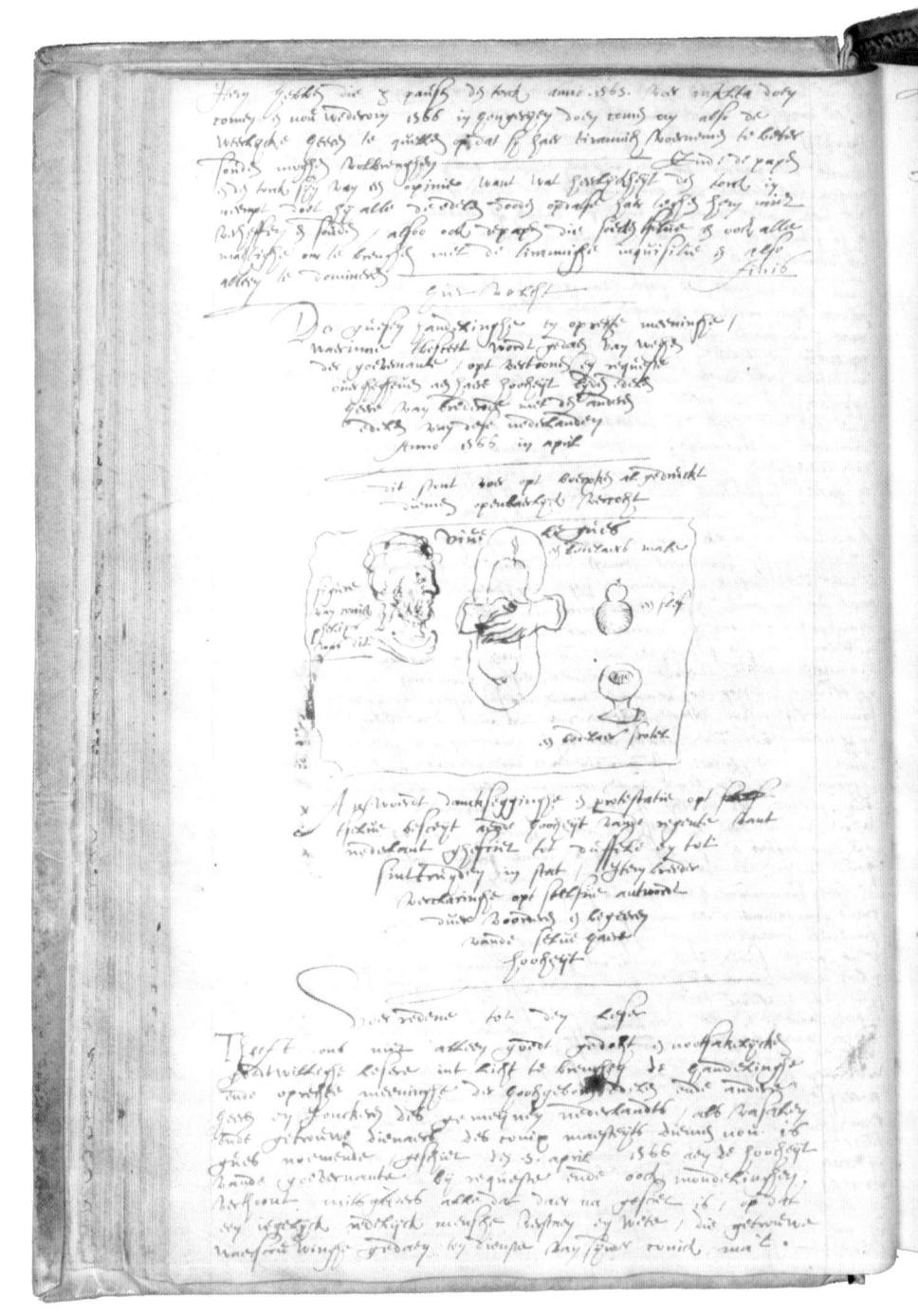

21 The symbols of the Compromise of Nobles. Quick sketch by Godevaert van Haecht in his *Chronicles* of 1565–74.

Willem Blois van Treslong submitted a request for religious freedom for the third time and threatened armed insurrection if it were not honoured this time. The governor-general rejected this outright, but at the end of February she wrote a concerned letter to the king saying that Brederode's troops were as strong as hers. Another month later, her generals succeeded in dashing the rebels' last hopes. On 13 March, at Oosterweel, to the north of Antwerp, a small Calvinist army led by John Marnix of Toulouse was decimated without mercy.[71] Heart-rending scenes were played out on the city walls, from where the beggars' supporters were pressing to attack the government troops. Orange stopped them from doing so, as they would have been no match for the trained soldiers and would face certain death. Eleven days later, the government army took over Valenciennes, extinguishing the last significant hotbed of resistance. In Spain, however, the king had already ordered that the rebels in the Netherlands be punished, to set an example.

22 The *Wilhelmus*, as written down by Willem De Gortter. De Gortter was an orator from Mechelen who died in 1620. He wrote down a large number of poems and songs, illustrating them with splendid coloured drawings of military figures of the time.

3

Loyalty Tested
Under Alba's Repression: 1567–1573

The Arrival of Alba and his First Actions

The Duke of Alba thought it would take six months to gain control of the Low Countries. During the nobles' opposition to the king, allowing a few heads to roll seemed to him the best way to assure greater respect for royal authority. At the court in Spain, Alba was a member of the hawkish faction and had advocated a hard line even before the iconoclastic fury known as the *Beeldenstorm*. The king rejected the restraint and moderation that the governor-general of the Netherlands had promised after the nobles had submitted their Request. This enraged Montigny so much that he stormed angrily into the king's rooms. Philip, always concerned to retain his composure, became a little hot under the collar.[1] On 3 September 1566, letters arrived from the governor-general bearing news of the destruction of churches, monasteries and convents. Many of those at the court were literally sickened by the reports and the king took to his bed for several weeks. Alba himself was felled by an attack of gout. This was the first time he had suffered from the complaint, but it was to recur many times when fate turned against him.[2]

The royal Council of State did not meet in Madrid to discuss the situation in the Netherlands until 22 September. Opposing Alba and his fellow advocates of the hard line were a number of nobles who had been rivals of the Alba clan for many years. Ruy Gómez da Silva, Prince of Eboli, was a boyhood friend of Philip II. He was a member of the king's Spanish Privy Council, also when Philip was in the Low Countries, and was his most influential adviser. He was even known as Rey (King) Gomez. His faction was known as the 'Ebolists', while Alba's supporters were called 'Albanists'. A prominent follower of Eboli was Francisco de Eraso, one of the king's secretaries.[3] The Ebolists were advocates of decentralized rule of the Habsburg Empire, and thus of a

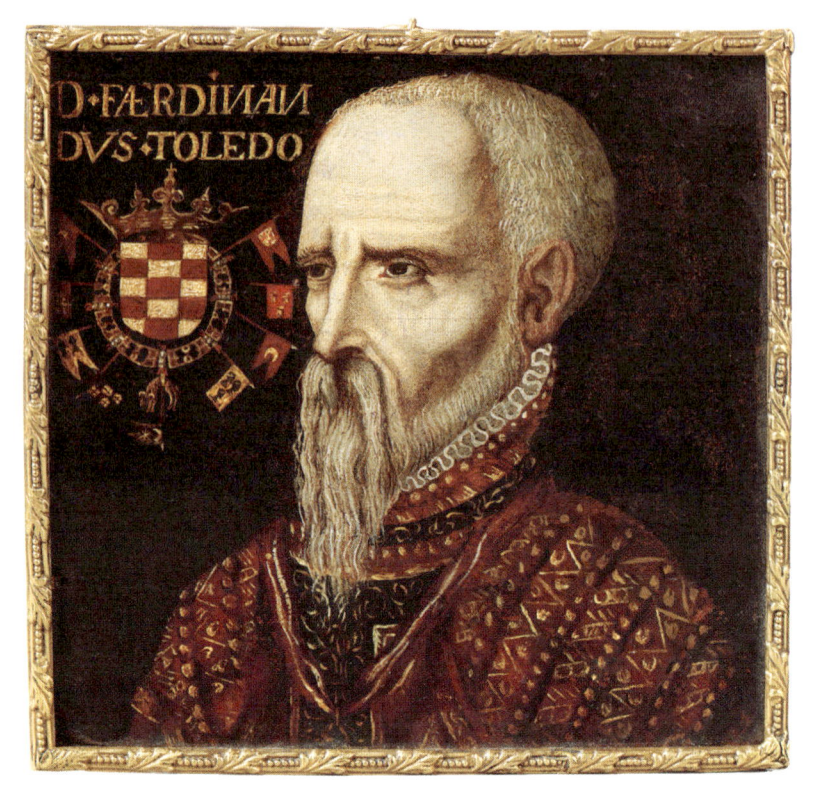

23 The Duke of Alba. Portrait by an unknown artist, probably from the time that the Duke was in the Netherlands.

moderate approach to the problems in the Netherlands, while Alba and his supporters felt that the empire should be ruled directly by the king from Castile, the natural centre of power.[4] The Low Countries' nobles were therefore in favour of Eboli coming to the Netherlands himself to restore authority and trust with a soft hand. Alba did not think this possible; first an army would need to impose order, and he thought that 800 executions would be required. Only then could the king himself travel to the Low Countries to act as a good and merciful ruler and grant pardons. In other words, a period of short, hard action was required, followed by restoration of normal relations. They had to set an example, or the Italian territories would also rise up against the king's authority. The Council appointed Alba himself to put his proposals into practice. The duke had talked himself into the job and he had little choice other than to accept, albeit very much against his will. The faction of Eboli and Eraso were pleased that he would be absent from the court for a long time, which was very convenient for their own ambitions.[5] Alba's many years of service as an excellent military commander in the field had made him an indispensable pillar of support for the throne, and that experience and reliability now made him the obvious choice to restore order in the Netherlands. But his rivals were working to undermine him, even before he left the court. It is important to remember this, as we shall see later that the representative of the most powerful man in the Western world proved unable to repress the rebellion in the Low Countries.

A major expedition to the Netherlands could not be mobilized before the end of 1566. The troops were stationed in Italy and had to cross the Alps and then pass through neutral territory to the Low Countries – a gigantic operation that required months of preparation. Just before Alba was due to leave the Spanish port of Cartagena for the passage to Italy, he received a final message from Eraso informing him that he was to be allocated fewer troops than planned and that his own fee had been reduced.[6] This illustrates how divisions among the Spanish administrators led to irritations and mismanagement. Although Alba did not allow this to put him off, he was already regretting the undertaking.

Looking at a map of present-day Europe, we see that his route passed through what is now eastern France: Savoy, Franche-Comté and Lorraine. In the time of Philip II, Savoy and Lorraine were allies of Spain, while Franche-Comté was Habsburg territory. Since the classic study by Geoffrey Parker this has been known as the Spanish Road,[7] and it remained in use until 1622. To the west of this Spanish corridor, the French armies kept a very close eye on the situation. On the other side, Swiss pikemen guarded their cantons, like a hedgehog rolling up to protect himself when a fox comes too close. Alba could have taken advantage of the situation to smoke out the heretic's nest in Geneva on his way past, but the duke imposed strict discipline and did not allow his troops to deviate from the route by a single millimetre. On the way, he received letters from the governor-general, informing him that his presence was no longer necessary as she had already succeeded in restoring order. The duke ignored the message; the king had given him carte blanche to do what he felt was necessary. Moreover, he thought that Margaret had only been able to restore order because of the threat of his impending arrival.[8]

Alba arrived in Brussels on 28 August 1567. Margaret soon realized who was in charge in practice and decided to step down. Philip II approved her resignation on 13 September, and at the end of the year she left the Netherlands to return to Parma. Alba, who had thought that, as captain-general, he would only be required to restore order, now found himself appointed governor-general, with the concomitant governing tasks. His appointment meant that, for the first time in history, the Netherlands had a non-royal representative acting for the king. In the first weeks after his arrival he showed himself to be benevolent and courteous, but this was only to capture as many members of the former opposition in his net as possible. In a few cases, he was successful – the Counts of Egmont and Horn allowed themselves to be lured to Brussels. They both realized too late that their loyalty was to be their downfall, as on 9 September, Alba had them arrested. He clearly enjoyed the consternation that this caused at home and abroad. Around the same time, Montigny was arrested in Spain and interned in the state prison in Simancas.

Other opponents had no such illusions and had gone into voluntary exile in good time: Henry of Brederode stayed in the Duchy of Cleves, and in April 1567 Orange had returned via Breda to Dillenburg Castle, his ancestral seat in Nassau. In September, the prince wrote Alba a letter offering his services pro forma to the duke, a sham that neither of them would have believed genuine. This pretence earned the prince the nickname 'William the Silent'. The name by no means suggested that the prince was silent by nature – he was in reality very talkative and an excellent orator. After William's flight, inquisitor Pieter Titelmans had said (in Latin): 'If sly William has escaped, the joy will be short-lived.'[9] 'Sly' (*astutus*) was translated incorrectly into Dutch as 'silent'. Consequently, what Titelmans – as an enemy of Orange – had intended as a negative slur on the prince's character, gradually acquired a positive interpretation, especially in the nineteenth century – as if the prince's tendency to be a man of few words made him an astute politician. During his lifetime, William was never called 'the Silent'.[10]

Besides these few leading figures, tens of thousands of ordinary people who practised the new religion left the country. Most went to

24 A translation of the New Testament from the Greek, 1556. One of the many publications printed in Emden. The translator's name is written by hand on the title page.

the neighbouring countries, Germany or England. There they settled in exile, in Norwich, Emden, Cleves, Frankfurt or Heidelberg. In some places, there were so many of them that they outnumbered the original inhabitants, but with their numbers and their professions, they also contributed to the economy. At the same time, they set up publishing houses to produce religious and political works in their own language. Emden became the main publishing centre, bringing out more than 200 books between 1554 and 1574.[11] Many books were also published in Norwich, which the Dutch settlers called Noordwijk, including the Heidelberg catechism in Dutch.[12]

Besides these law-abiding citizens, who wanted to continue to practise their religion in the diaspora and were able to pursue their professions, there were others who sought refuge in the forests of Flanders or on the open seas: these were known as the *bosgeuzen* (beggars of the woods) and the *watergeuzen* (sea beggars). They were forced to make a living by illegal means. The *bosgeuzen* were usually easy prey for the government, which was strong on land, and they were of little further significance after 1568.[13] But the sea beggars would mark the beginnings of a radical change. They are known historically as a rough bunch, but they came from all layers of society, from nobleman to beggar. As pirates, they survived by capturing ships, including those owned by their own countrymen. If they fell into the hands of royalists, their fate was sealed and they were hanged on the gallows or a mast, or were shipped off to Brussels for interrogation and inevitable execution.

The Council of Troubles

Faced with the problem of ruling an entire country, Alba could call on the support of the three advisory councils (see p. 45), but had no central bureaucracy. The States General had always resisted such a move. Alba had brought a small number of bureaucrats with him from Spain because he did not trust the local officials. His own officials, however, did not speak the language and were thus dependent on local sources for information. Consequently they were often informed incorrectly or not at all. Furthermore, the bureaucracy was understaffed and divided by internal argument.[14] Under these circumstances, corruption was rife. Alba simply accepted it as par for the course. He did not concern himself with finances, as long as the army was paid on time.[15] If he had adopted the same strategy towards religion as had Parma ten years later – forcing dissidents to toe the line or emigrate – the conflict would have taken a completely different course. But Alba not only held on resolutely to the Roman Catholic faith, but also banned any form of emigration.

The duke wasted no time in setting up the Council of Troubles, only a week after his arrival in Brussels. The subsequent arrests were in reality political, as were the trials. By accusing those involved in the unrest of the previous year of high treason, he legally justified the establishment of the Council, which did not have to concern itself with privileges. Officially, Alba himself chaired the Council, which was of course composed of Catholics from the Low Countries loyal to the king. But in reality, power lay in the hands of two Spanish advisers. One, Luis del Río – who had a Flemish mother – was the willing servant of the other, Juan de Vargas, whose orders he carried out to the letter. Vargas was nothing but a common scoundrel, who had been accused of abusing his stepdaughter in Spain and had come to the Low Countries to escape Spanish justice.[16] Those who like to emphasize Alba's noble gentility and culture never mention the name of Vargas, who would not have got so far without the duke's protection, and who left again in Alba's wake. One thousand and thirty-seven executions were performed and 11,130 rulings were issued confiscating property.[17] The number of death sentences was much higher, but many of the accused had left the country and were sentenced in their absence. The property of all those who had fled was confiscated. The rules were strictly observed during the trials, but the large number of confiscations was partly due to the new regime's need for funds. The fact that, after Alba left, no more death sentences were issued is evidence of the prejudices that governed the judgments and decisions of the councillors.

Among the wider public, the court soon became known as the 'Blood Council'. The number of victims was grossly exaggerated and, in the popular imagination, the horrific methods employed by the Council knew no bounds. The Counts of Egmont and Horn were only the two most highly ranking victims. There was no question of a normal legal process. The counts were not given pen and paper to defend themselves and were hardly allowed to speak to their lawyers. The sentence may not have been set in advance, but the accusation of lese-majesty, causing injury to the crown, made a death sentence inevitable.[18] Egmont's secretary was put to the rack to force him to reveal his master's political plans. Antoon van Straelen, mayor of Antwerp, who had quelled an uprising in his city on 14 March 1566 at the risk of his own life, was horrifically tortured and executed. On 4 October 1567, the Council of Troubles sentenced Montigny to death. The sentence was carried out ten days later in his prison in Spain. Not with a sword, as was the privilege of a nobleman, but in secret, by strangulation. Was his furious outburst against Philip a factor in this ignominious end? Philip II announced that Montigny had died a natural death.

Alba emphasized that all of these repressive measures were aimed not at those who practised a different faith, but at 'rebels'. By doing so, he wanted to avoid his victims in the Low Countries invoking the sympathy of the German Lutheran princes. Alba maintained a cordial, but very resolute, correspondence with the German princes, both Protestant and Catholic, assuring them of his good intentions.[19] Towards the end of his period as governor-general, he increasingly saw his mission as a fight against heresy.

Alba showed no clemency for Orange. He had the prince's twelve-year-old son Philip William, who was studying at Leuven University, arrested and sent to Spain as a hostage. There, he was allowed to continue his studies at the University of Alcalá and enjoyed a certain freedom of

25 A remarkably serene painting from a time of fierce religious warfare: the investiture of Godfried van Mierlo as bishop of Haarlem by Franciscus Sonnius, bishop of Antwerp. The ceremony took place not in Haarlem but in St Paul's Church in Antwerp.

movement. He would not be given permission to return to the Netherlands until 1596, after an enforced absence of thirty years.[20]

By contrast with the widely detested Council of Troubles, one of Alba's positive achievements was the codification and humanization of criminal justice. Given what has been described above, it is not something we would immediately associate with the duke. He had been contemptuous of the customary passage of justice in the Netherlands, saying that 'justice can be bought in the Low Countries as meat from the butcher.'[21] He instructed his jurists to bring unity to criminal law and the administration of criminal justice, a process that culminated in the introduction of the Criminal Ordnances in 1570.[22] This achievement is actually to the credit of the Low Countries' jurists, who had felt for a long time that analysing and harmonizing the widely varying legal rules would help promote centralized government in the Netherlands. But Alba was very much in favour of this and encouraged it. Both the Council of Troubles and the Criminal Ordnances were abolished in the Pacification of Ghent and, in practice, the new and very humane criminal law legislation of 1570 remained in force in the royalist Low Countries.

For the Roman Catholic Church and the Catholics, the strong arm of Alba was necessary to finally install the bishops, who had been appointed long before but not officially installed. Moreover, the duke also ensured that bishops appointed in Dutch-speaking regions also spoke Dutch themselves.

Orange's Campaign of 1568

If someone had to take the initiative for armed resistance, it would have to be the Prince of Orange. As the highest-ranking noble and one of the country's most prominent leaders, he was expected to defend traditional privileges and the interests of the people. His honour was at stake and, of course, he wanted to regain the domains that had been taken from him. He maintained contact with the sea beggars, to whom he granted letters of marque to fight the enemy, and with the Calvinist consistories, to acquire financial support for his initiatives. He recruited an army, mainly funded with Nassau family capital, and drew up an ambitious plan of action: his brothers Louis and Adolf of Nassau were to lead an invasion in the north of the Low Countries. Orange himself would lead a large force into the centre of the Netherlands, attack the centre of government in Brussels and try to lure Alba into engaging in open battle. He was hoping that, after a year of rigorous rule, the people of the Low Countries would have had enough of Alba and would support him, actively or passively.

Did Orange really believe that he could defeat Alba, and had he given any thought to what policy he would pursue if he were to succeed? The governor-general represented the country's lawful ruler and maintained the Catholic faith. A majority of the people would have been in agreement with that and would have tried to make the best of it under the 'Iron Duke'. Was the prince nothing more than an agitator? Alba certainly portrayed him as such, and he impressed on his commanders that the armies of the Nassau brothers did not represent a foreign power. Their troops were therefore not soldiers but rebels and should be shown no mercy. Any of them who fell into the hands of the royal army were to be killed immediately. Orange was well aware that he was being branded as a rebel and sought to justify his actions with a remarkable argument: he was not fighting the legitimate authorities, but those who advised the king badly and had violated the laws of the land. His fight was not with King Philip but the Duke of Alba. He adopted the motto *Pro rege, lege et grege*, 'For the king, the law and the people'. In April 1568 he published a *Justification* in several languages, explaining the reasons for his actions in the past and present. It was the start of a sixteenth-century propaganda war, in which he was advised by a number of preachers and others who were deft with the pen. Orange's battle on paper was intended to justify to the people of the Low Countries, as well as to foreign rulers, the battle he was now waging in the field.

His brothers Louis and Adolf of Nassau invaded Groningen to divert attention from the major attack on Brabant. At first, everything went as planned. On 23 May 1568 Louis defeated the Spanish troops in the first battle, at Heiligerlee, though Adolf was among those killed. William had ordered Louis to lead his army under the banner of freedom of religion and conscience. It was to become the fundamental moment in the Revolt.[23] Since the Peace of Münster, signed in 1648, was the actual and legal end of the conflict, it has gone down in history as the Eighty Years War. If the Peace had been signed a year earlier, the Battle of Oosterweel in 1567 may have been seen as the start – and it would probably still have been called the Eighty Years War, simply to end up with a round number. Dirck Janszoon, a prosperous farmer in Sint Annaparochie, Friesland, who recorded everything he experienced in his *Memorijen*, notes the start of the 'Netherlandish war' as 1566.[24]

No historian will defend by fire and sword the claim that the war really started on 23 May 1568.[25]

The victory at Heiligerlee was an isolated success, perhaps a stroke of luck. There was an unsavoury tint to the defeat on the royalist side. The royal stadtholder Jean de Ligne, Count of Arenberg, a high-ranking noble of whom Philip II was especially fond, had died in the battle. Alba had expressly ordered him not to engage with Louis's army with only his own troops, but to wait for reinforcements from Gelderland, which were on their way under the leadership of the stadtholder, the Count of Megen. However, Gonzalo de Bracamonte, a Spanish officer under Arenberg, allegedly urged him to take the risk. After Arenberg replied that he was only following orders, Bracamonte apparently asked him whether he was afraid to go it alone. An Arenberg who didn't dare go into battle? Jean wasn't prepared to let that pass and engaged with Louis's troops, with disastrous consequences.[26] If Spanish commanders treated those loyal to the king in the Low Countries with such disdain, what did they think of the rebels?

Alba was disappointed at Arenberg's death, as he was one of the few higher nobles who had served the king without reservation. But he did feel that Arenberg should have had the good sense to ignore Bracamonte's taunts, and that his immensely rich widow should now marry a Spaniard. He also took immediate punitive measures, issuing orders on 28 May for the Count of Culemborg's palace in Brussels to be razed. The fact that this was where the Compromise of Nobles had been agreed was sufficient reason for this symbolic act. In accordance with Old Testament tradition, Alba had salt scattered on the ground to prevent anything from growing.[27] On 1 June 1568, he had the first nobles who had been sentenced to death beheaded on the Paardenmarkt square in Brussels. Egmont and Horn shared the same fate on 5 June, on the more prominent Grote Markt. Egmont remained naïve to the last, believing even as he stood on the scaffold that he would be pardoned. It was an event that – as Montaigne reported in his *Essays* – made the whole of Europe shudder.[28]

After that, fear struck the people of the Low Countries. Alba himself went to the north, where Louis of Nassau had tried in vain to lay siege to the city of Groningen. That the people of the city did not want to let him in did not necessarily mean that they were friends of Alba. When the duke's army was looking for the enemy near the town of Slochteren, suddenly no one seemed to know where they were.[29] Once Louis's troops had been tracked down, they proved no match for Alba's army and were decimated without quarter at the Battle of Jemmingen (or Jemgum) on the River Eems. Louis himself escaped only by jumping into the river. This was as far north as the Castilian duke had ever been and he quickly returned to Brussels to prepare for the Prince of Orange's invasion.

In the summer of 1568, Orange very efficiently mobilized a large army of 30,000 men, but its size also made it very expensive and his financial resources were limited. He had gained experience as a general during Charles v's war against France, leading two campaigns. But they were of minor importance compared to the two resounding victories against the French that Egmont had chalked up against his name at Saint Quentin and Gravelines. Furthermore, Orange was facing one of the most successful generals of his time, who had pacified Italy and defeated the Protestant rulers in the Holy Roman Empire. And yet Alba had not dared, in either of Orange's campaigns, to engage directly with the prince, because the latter – through efficient organization – did not give him the opportunity.[30] Alba now avoided a battle in the hope that Orange would not be able to pay his troops for longer than a few weeks. He was later criticized for this by his officers.[31] He shadowed the invasion army and was surprised to see that the prince, at the start of the march, had succeeded in getting his army across the River Maas. Near the village of Stokkum, where the river was fordable, Orange had strung the cavalry out across the river on a long rope, breaking the force of the current. Behind this living dam of horses and men, the troops crossed the river with their equipment.[32] The prince then passed through the neutral territory of Liège, but when he arrived in Brabant, none of the towns were willing to open their gates for him, knowing that Alba had the strongest army, the strongest credentials and the strongest position. So the prince, without justification, laid siege to Liège.[33] The siege failed, and in December, after marching in vain through Namur and Hainaut, Orange disbanded his army in France. 'Orange is now a dead man,' Granvelle wrote to the king. But he was mistaken.

After the failed invasion, an anonymous poet wrote a song about the prince's deeds, known as the *Wilhelmus* (see illus. 22), more an almost biblical glorification of his actions than a historical portrait. In 1932 the *Wilhelmus* was officially adopted as the national anthem of the Netherlands. Who may have written the song has long been a matter of dispute. Philip Marnix, Lord of Saint-Aldegonde (1540–1598), is seen as the most likely candidate, especially in the Protestant tradition. He was the younger brother of John Marnix, Lord of Toulouse, who had died at Oosterweel. Both were Calvinist lesser nobles and had studied under Calvin in Geneva. After that, Philip had emerged as a pamphleteer. His *De Bijen-corf der H. Roomscher Kercke* was a biting satire on the evils of the Roman Catholic Church.[34] But the Mennonites, too, found themselves at the sharp end of his pen. During his years of exile from the Low Countries, he worked as a secretary for Orange and soon became his right-hand man. Are the *Bijen-corf* and the *Wilhelmus* not mutually exclusive? The intolerant, aggressive tone of the former is in stark contrast to the solemn serenity of the latter. That is one good reason why Marnix is unlikely to have written the *Wilhelmus*. Wishful thinking apart and on the basis of critical examination of other remaining texts, experts place the still unknown author in Orange's German – and more specifically Nassau – environment.[35] In Belgium, however, Marnix is seen in a more favourable light. He was popular among nineteenth-century liberals for his anticlericalism. In 1998 his portrait appeared on a Belgian postage stamp, and in 2012 a modern sculpture of Orange and Marnix together was unveiled in Antwerp, where the latter is revered for the honourable terms under which he surrendered the city to Parma in 1585.

26 The statue of Alba, which he commissioned to be made from the bronze cannons captured at Jemmingen. Opinions about the statue continued to be divided. Most commentators see it as illustrating Alba's pride and self-glorification. Others claims that the duke wanted to deflect blame from the king and take it upon himself. They see his extended arm as a gesture of friendship. Alba's successor had the statue removed.

While the *Wilhelmus* became a lasting monument to Orange, Alba had a statue of himself cast from the bronze of the cannons he had captured at Jemmingen. His main biographer saw this as a sign that his political judgement was beginning to desert him.[36] Orange and Louis of Nassau continued their fight in 1569 at the side of Huguenots Coligny and Condé in the French religious wars. They did this on the basis of a reciprocal arrangement: the French had declared their willingness to fight with the Nassau brothers in the Low Countries. Coligny would always remain grateful for their support and consider the agreement a debt of honour.[37]

A General Pardon and the 'Tenth Penny'

After the military threat had been averted, Alba could further consolidate the government apparatus in the Netherlands. It had become clear to everyone that Philip II would not be coming to the Low Countries himself after Alba had pacified them, to bring reconciliation and clemency. Every time, the king was prevented from making the journey by domestic problems or his international commitments. It therefore fell to the duke to grant clemency. That was irregular and his heart was not in it. But it was part of the policy he himself had recommended and he had a General Pardon drawn up. This step was welcomed by those loyal to the king as a sign of the government's good faith. But there were so many exceptions to the pardon that it had hardly any effect in practice and almost no one in exile from the Netherlands dared to return. There was of course a formal ceremony in Antwerp to announce the pardon, in which the bishops also played a prominent role, but even supporters of Alba felt that it was too little, too late.[38]

In 1569, Alba wanted to make a start on reforming the tax system.[39] This was urgently necessary because, with the king requiring all his funds for his international policies, the Netherlands would in the future have to pay for its own government and defence. Alba now had no choice but to convene the States General – not to ask their permission, but to inform them of what he had already decided. On 21 March 1569, to prevent the States from organizing themselves and, as usual, expressing criticism, the duke called them together for one day in Brussels. His message was simple, whether the lords and gentlemen would agree to the following three tax proposals: 1) a one-off levy of 1 per cent on all possessions, in other words, a capital tax; 2) a turnover tax of 5 per cent, known as the *twintigste penning* (twentieth penny) on the sale of real estate, like houses and estates; and 3) a turnover tax of 10 per cent, the *tiende penning* (tenth penny) on all movable goods, and especially daily necessities and goods. If the first two taxes were hard to swallow, the third – the tenth penny – was met with dread. Contemporaries believed that, in a trading nation like the Netherlands, such a tax would mean the end of trade. The king had already met with flat refusal when trying to introduce such a form

27 The Revolt in the Netherlands, or the Eighty Years War, was also a propaganda war fuelled by printed texts and pamphlets. At the centre here is William of Orange. To the right are his coat of arms and a lamb; to the left, the arms of Alba and a wolf. In the shield bearing the ten pennies, there is a cross on the tenth penny. The significance is abundantly clear.

of taxation on several occasions before, and his representative would endure the same fate. The resistance against Alba's tenth penny was a major element of the 'loyal resistance' during the years from 1569 to 1572. It was enough to convince Alba not to push for it to be introduced in the early years of his government. From 13 August 1569 to 13 August 1571, he settled for a fixed sum by way of compensation. But when that period had expired, he ordered the tenth penny to be collected, for good or bad. That provoked widespread resistance, even in a royalist city like Amsterdam and no less in Brussels, the centre of government. Although the tenth penny was never collected, it set a lot of people thinking about change. The only question was: what kind of change?

Orange's Campaign of 1572

In 1572, Orange wanted to risk another invasion, hoping that more people now found Alba's continued regime intolerable than had been the case in 1568. Moreover, in the intervening years, he had strengthened his contacts with the Protestants in France, the Huguenots. He could now count on the support of Condé and Coligny and, with French military assistance, his second invasion over land – together with an attack from the sea – should be successful. The attack by sea was to be undertaken by the sea beggars. The beggars were nobles, burghers, merchants and fishermen from all provinces in the Netherlands. As there were no Spaniards at all serving on Alba's ships, the beggars would find themselves fighting against crews and troops that were also from the Low Countries. On 10 July 1568, on the River Eems, the beggars had defeated a fleet from Holland under the leadership of Admiral Boschuysen. During raids on land, the sea beggars would severely assault clerics and government officials, and steal from their fellow countrymen.[40] They repeatedly targeted the Frisian island of Terschelling, for example. On 2 and 3 March 1571, they raided Monnickendam, a port town north of Amsterdam, and a month later they looted another thirteen villages in the north of Holland. The coast of Flanders was also a regular target for their raids. They attacked neutral ships and sold their booty in Emden, La Rochelle or English ports.

Orange tried in vain to create some form of order among these undisciplined pirates, with the aim of building up a reliable fleet. An attack from the sea would hit Alba's weak spot, as he lacked a naval force of any significance. In his guise as lord of the sovereign principality of Orange, the prince issued the sea beggars with 'commissions to wage war'. As a mark of distinction, he gave them his flag in three colours: red, white and blue – the same as in the arms of his principality, which showed a hunting horn in these colours on a golden field. Just as they had taken Monnickendam by surprise the previous year, the beggars were now capable of capturing another town, Brill for example, or Enkhuizen. The big problem for Orange – besides financing his own troops – was coordinating all the beggars' activities with his own. On 27 March 1572, he appointed his brother Louis commander of the beggars' fleet.

Before Louis could do anything, the sea beggars had already undertaken an audacious operation. On 1 March 1572, under pressure from Alba, Queen Elizabeth of England had ordered them all to leave English ports. Drifting around on the open seas, they nevertheless launched yet another raid, this time in the small port of Brill, on the island of Voorne in the Maas estuary, a little over 20 kilometres west of Rotterdam. Led by Willem II van der Marck, Lord of Lumey, and Willem Blois van Treslong, the beggars appeared at the gates to the town on 1 April and claimed it in the name of the Prince of Orange. Blois van Treslong had presented the signet ring of his father (who had been sheriff of the island) to reassure the townspeople. Some fled, while others stayed.

Because the Spanish troops had left, the beggars decided – unusually – to remain in the town and to strengthen the wall defences with their cannons. On 6 April the beggars also captured another important port, Veere, on the island of Walcheren in Zeeland. This was a stroke of luck, as the port housed the arsenal of the Burgundian-Habsburg fleet. The beggars could now help themselves to the abundant supplies for their ships, armaments and ammunition.

Where the beggars had, until now, captured towns by force, the events of a few days later in Flushing saw the beggars being welcomed in to the town by its inhabitants. When Catholic worshippers left church

28 The arms of Veere and Flushing. From a rare book, *Hoe en wanneer Holland tot een graafschap is afgezonderd* (Arnhem, 1647), of which only one copy has been preserved, in the University Library at Leiden.

on Easter Sunday, they encountered three quartermasters who had come to arrange billets for Spanish infantry regiments. After earlier experiences with Spanish troops billeted in the town, the townspeople objected, said they were loyal subjects of the king, but would only allow troops from the Low Countries to be stationed there. It was 22 April before Flushing agreed to admit a fleet of beggars' ships to the port, and when they came they flew the flags of both the king and the Prince of Orange.[41]

Alba allegedly responded to the loss of the town with the words 'No es nada', 'it means nothing'.[42] The stadtholder of Holland, Maximilien de Hénin-Liétard, Count of Boussu, led an army to Brill, but was unable to retake the town because the townspeople had flooded the surrounding land. The beggars mounted a counterattack, sacking Delfshaven, but Boussu drove them out again. Rotterdam refused to grant Boussu right of transit but after negotiations the Spanish troops were permitted to pass through in small groups. Once inside, however, they overpowered the city militia and broke their word, looting, killing and raping.[43] This scenario would be repeated over and again: towns that only managed to defend themselves by flooding the surrounding land, and Spanish troops breaking their word, killing and looting, and thereby alienating the largely royalist population from the king's authority. The sea beggars, in their turn, were also guilty of a number of lynchings. Lumey was the worst in this respect, antagonizing both friend and foe with his hard-handed reprisals. In Gorinchem he had twenty members of the clergy arrested, maltreated and sent to Brill. Although Orange wrote to him requesting that he do the men no harm, Lumey considered himself a high-ranking noble and therefore worthy of a handwritten letter from the prince personally rather than one that had only been dictated and signed by Orange. On 9 July he threatened to hang the clerics if they did not renounce their faith. All except one refused. Those who died are now recognized by the Catholic Church as martyrs to the faith.[44] It is therefore no surprise that most towns were not very keen to admit the beggars as liberators.

Orange was initially irritated that the sea beggars had struck so early in the year, as his planned attacks could no longer be launched at the same time. And yet, at first, his plan seemed to be successful: on 23 May, French Protestant noble and army commander François de La Noue captured Valenciennes for Orange. A day later, Louis of Nassau mounted a surprise attack on Mons. With these two Hainaut towns in rebel hands, it was now a matter of waiting for the invasion of Orange himself and

29 Government troops drive the beggars out of Delfshaven. To the left and above in the narrow street, the government troops with the cross of St Andrew in their flags. To the right, in the square, the beggars with their red, white and blue flag.

the help of the French Huguenots. In June, when the reinforcements took too long to arrive, Enkhuizen decided on its own initiative to support the prince. After that, his supporters succeeded in taking over most towns and cities in Holland and Zeeland. In both the north and south of Holland, towns admitted the sea beggars so that they once more had access to the sea and could trade and fish in freedom.[45] Only Middelburg, Amsterdam and Goes remained on the side of Brussels.

In July 1572 Dordrecht, as the oldest town in Holland, took the initiative to call the States of the province together. Strictly speaking, it did not have the right to do this, as only the king or his representative, the stadtholder, could convene a meeting of the States. That is what made Dordrecht's summons such a revolutionary act – even though the meeting of the States General in 1477 on the initiative of Brabant could be seen as a precedent (see p. 21). At the meeting of the States, Marnix acted as Orange's representative. The States took the memorable decision to recognize the prince as the king's stadtholder, based on the assumption that his old appointment in 1559 was simply still valid. Like Orange, they claimed to be fighting not the king but his representatives, whom they considered bad. The prince himself confirmed this interpretation, claiming that he had never broken with the king but, according to provision 58 of the Joyous Entry, had stopped working with the government because of dissatisfaction. Now he was, as it were, resuming his responsibilities.[46]

Importantly, the States also voted at the meeting to provide Orange with funds to start his second campaign. In the Achterhoek, the eastern region of Gelderland, the prince's brother-in-law William van den Bergh took possession of large parts of the land, including the towns of Zutphen and Deventer. Almost all of Friesland, too, declared its loyalty to the prince, who immediately appointed a representative in the province. In August, with less hesitation than the previous time, Orange invaded the Low Countries, taking Roermond on the fourth day of the month. Now it was his men who were guilty of murdering a number of monks.[47] A few weeks later, on 30 August, the prince had success in Brabant when Mechelen opened its gates to him. The city and university of Leuven avoided capture and looting by offering a tribute of 16,000 guilders. That was followed by a successful attack on Dendermonde.

The advantage of capturing these towns in the heart of Brabant was, however, tempered by bad news from France: in the early hours of the morning on 24 August, St Bartholomew's Day, the French king had many of the Protestants in Paris murdered in cold blood, including their leader, Gaspard de Coligny. Several thousand Huguenots had come to the capital a few days earlier to celebrate the marriage of the king's sister Margaret to the Protestant Henri of Navarre. The Catholics took the opportunity to kill them en masse. It was political murder, and it was repeated in many other French cities.

After what became known as the St Bartholomew's Day massacre, Orange could no longer count on support from France and therefore had to go to Mons himself to relieve his brother and his troops. He and his army got close to the town, but Alba had surrounded it not only with an inner siege line facing the city walls (known as a 'circumvallation' line), but with a second outer ring to repel relief attempts from outside (a 'contravallation' line). This method would be used repeatedly in the Low Countries in the decades that followed. Orange's attack foundered on this external ring. After the prince had set up camp 5 kilometres to the south of the town, Alba ordered one of his commanders, Julián Romero, to attack the camp at night. This was known as a *camisade*, after the white shirts that the attackers wore over their armour so that they could recognize each other in the dark.[48] In total panic, Orange's men fled or were killed. The prince himself barely escaped with his life; legend has it that he was awakened by his dog. Without French help, the two brothers had to give up the fight. Louis managed to negotiate an honourable retreat, which Alba respected. Orange withdrew through Mechelen and Roermond, travelling on to Kampen, where he crossed the Zuiderzee to Enkhuizen so that he could, in his own words, 'find his grave' in Holland.

Haarlem and Alkmaar

Philip was delighted at the elimination of the French Huguenots. Furthermore, for a year, he had had a free hand in the Mediterranean region. On 7 October 1571 his half-brother John of Austria had defeated the Turks decisively at Lepanto, allowing the king to devote all his money and attention to subjugating the rebellious provinces in the Low Countries. Alba decided to apply the method of the 'deterrent example', choosing the town of Mechelen to serve as an object lesson for the whole of Brabant. He organized a punitive expedition under the leadership of his son Fadrique. The royal troops were given carte blanche to loot and pillage, or force the townspeople to pay to prevent it, and to cause all the other havoc to be expected from soldiers running amok. The reprisal unleashed such fierce indignation that Alba now, for the first time, issued a printed declaration justifying his actions.[49] The other towns in Brabant immediately opened their gates to the troops voluntarily, as did Roermond. In Gelderland, Zutphen was the target and thousands of townspeople were slaughtered, directly putting a stop to any further thoughts of resistance: the whole duchy undertook to obey Alba immediately.

The small town of Naarden was the first in Holland to feel the duke's wrath. If the town had admitted stadtholder Boussu on 20 August, most probably nothing would have happened. But a band of beggars had arrived the same day, just before Boussu. They had even fired shots from the town walls. Boussu went, via Muiden, to Amersfoort, which the beggars had just left. From there, on 19 November, he again sent a troop of cavalry to Naarden to try and change their minds. This time, a shot was fired at the Spanish trumpeter. A final warning on 30 November was also ignored. These incidents must have sealed Naarden's already inevitable fate. The garrison, which consisted of only 100 men, realized the impossibility of defending the town, whose walls were easily breached. On 1 December, seven men went to Don Fadrique's camp near Bussum to negotiate. There, they encountered the Spanish army commander Julián Romero, who already knew what fate was to befall the town. But three times he assured them nothing would happen to the townspeople. Together, they all returned to Naarden, where the town leaders offered Romero a feast in the town hall. After the meal, the men of the town were summoned with drum rolls to the town hall. After the doors had been closed, a priest told them to prepare themselves for their deaths. The Spanish soldiers carried out the executions with muskets, swords and clubs. No one escaped. But, here too, memory or propaganda has increased the number of victims. Anyone who sees the small building, with a relief on the front gable to commemorate the heinous deed, will find it difficult to believe that 500 men were gathered together here and murdered. Later prints also show the building, which had formerly been a church, to be much bigger and higher than it was in reality. In the town itself, soldiers hunted down men who had ignored the summons to the town hall. They were then free to loot the town and abuse the women. Last, they set fire to a number of buildings. In the days that followed, people from surrounding villages came to buy looted goods from the soldiers. We know all this from the account left behind by the priest and rector of the Latin school, Lambertus Hortensius, who was probably one of the few to be spared, because of his status as a member of the clergy.[50]

The Spanish armies now moved on, via royalist Amsterdam, to Haarlem, which Don Fadrique expected to capitulate as quickly as the other towns. But the newly stationed garrison and the people of the town, including the women, had other ideas. Since they knew that they would suffer the same fate as the inhabitants of Rotterdam, Mechelen, Zutphen and Naarden, they decided to fight to the bitter end. The town put up a stubborn resistance. Led by Orange, now based centrally in Delft, the other towns of Holland helped the people of Haarlem to withstand Don Fadrique's siege by providing them with a constant supply of food and weapons via the Haarlemmermeer, the large lake adjoining the town. Haarlem held out until, eventually, a beggars' fleet was defeated on the lake by a royalist squadron that included ships from Amsterdam. It had taken the Spanish seven months, from the middle of December 1572 to the middle of July 1573, to bring the town to its knees. The town managed to avoid being sacked by negotiating a compensation payment during the negotiations on its surrender. Hundreds of the men in the garrison were executed, with the exception of a number of Germans, to avoid problems with the Germans serving in Alba's army. The royal troops had, however,

30 Kenau Simonsdochter was a dynamic woman who urged the garrison and the people of Haarlem to stand firm against the enemy. She may well have been one of the brave women who are reputed to have stood on the walls to fight against Don Fadrique's troops.

suffered thousands of deaths, either directly in the fighting or to the daily hardships of cold, rain, mist and frost. King Philip was allegedly enraged when he heard how many victims had fallen, some 8,000. Even Julián Romero wrote of the horror with which people spoke of the house of Alba (and thus not the duke alone): 'Cursed be the Tenth Penny and he whoever invented it, since it is the cause of all this.'[51] Haarlem became known as the graveyard of the Spaniards.

31 This rare German map of Haarlem during the siege shows how the progress of the battle was closely followed abroad. Note how much water there is in the area around the city, and the triangular fort in the centre, which never existed in reality. Nuremberg, 1575.

Alba was seriously concerned about the small number of Spaniards in the royal army. Historians and other sources generally speak of the Spanish army and Spanish troops, but genuine Spaniards usually only accounted for some 10 per cent of the total. The others were Italians, Germans, Walloons and so on. The Spaniards did make up the hard core, especially among the high-ranking officers, who were generally nobles, but even this had been reduced by death and desertion.[52] The many long months of hardship had demoralized the Spanish troops, and their commanders, too, had doubts about the value of the whole undertaking: if taking every town cost so much time and money and so many lives, where would it end? Did all the towns in Holland and Zeeland, most of them surrounded by water, really have to be recaptured with such great loss of life?

After the capture of Haarlem, the Spanish troops began to mutiny against their own commanders. That was the first time this had happened in the Netherlands. They chose a spokesman (*eletto*) to negotiate with their commanders for their back pay. A mutiny like this was a genuine act of desperation. It was impossible for soldiers from Spanish or Italian

TOT EER VAN HAER GESLAGT TOT LOF VAN DESE DAAD
DIE KLAMPEN HEM AEN BOORT DIE WETEN NOCH WEL RAEDT
HIER IS EEN HOORNS HOP, DAER GAET 'T OP EEN VEGHTEN

lands to desert. Where would they have gone? Back to their homelands, on foot, in the midst of a hostile population? Desertion was therefore no option and, for soldiers, mutiny was their only way to go on strike. The two sides were reconciled after the army leadership agreed to the soldiers' demands. Haarlem was a unique case, as, after this first reconciliation, the ringleaders of the mutiny were hanged after all, but that was ordered by the high-handed Don Fadrique.[53]

There was no military alternative, and on 21 August 1573 the Spaniards laid siege to Alkmaar. Before the siege started, an incident occurred that perfectly illustrated the division within the town council and among the burghers. At one gate to the town there was a unit of royalist troops, and at the other a detachment of beggars; both demanded to be admitted. The large majority of the townspeople were Catholic, but also disliked the Spanish. While the town council was meeting to discuss the situation, two bold supporters of the prince allowed the beggars' detachment to enter, and the die was cast. Alba boastfully swore to leave no man, woman or child alive in the town.[54] The siege lasted more than a month and a half. Then, on

32 The 'House with the Bullet' at Appelstraat 2, in the centre of Alkmaar. The cannonball that hit the wooden house during the siege of the town can be seen in the rear facade, which overlooks the canal.

ER SIET MEN 'T EENE SCHIP VAST AEN 'T ANDER HEGHTEN
ER SIET MEN REGHTE LIEFDE DAER DOET MEN ONDERSTANT
ER VEGHT MEN SONDER GELT VOOR 'T LIEVE VADERLAND

33 Part of the relief on the gable of the *Bossuhuizen* in Hoorn, one of the most beautiful sites in the Netherlands commemorating the war. The relief depicts the victory over the royal fleet.

the prince's initiative, his representative in the north of Holland, Diederik Sonoy, ordered the dykes to be breached, flooding the land around Alkmaar. On 8 October the Spanish gave up the siege and their army, which had seemed invincible, withdrew. Three days later, in sight of the Zuiderzee coastal port of Hoorn, the beggars' fleet under the command of Cornelis van Monnickendam won a resounding victory over a government squadron of ships from Amsterdam, led by Boussu. The stadtholder himself commanded a ship called the *Inquisition*, which was asking for trouble. An ordinary seaman called Jan Haring climbed onto the ship's mast and succeeded in bringing down the commander's flag. Boussu was taken prisoner and held in what has since been called the *Bossuhuizen* (Boussu Houses) in Hoorn. The battle is portrayed in words and images in a magnificent relief on the wall of these houses. One verse of the text reads, 'Here men fought without reward for love of the fatherland'. But that is not strictly true. A few days after the battle, Captain Cornelis was accosted in the street by a number of members of his crew who were still waiting for their pay.[55] The 'Golden Age' of the Netherlands, and all the wealth it brought from cattle-raising, fishing, trade and shipping, did not dawn until many years later.

Nevertheless, the first victories on land and sea had the effect of raising the rebels' morale. That did not mean, however, that Holland to the north of the IJ was now free of Spanish troops. Amsterdam remained a solid royalist stronghold.[56] But other places, like the village of Assendelft, between Zaandam and Beverwijk, remained loyal to the king. Nearby

34 Lambert Melisz. takes his mother to safety across the ice.
Carved and painted facade relief from the period.

Westzaan was, however, sacked by the Spanish in 1573. In those cold winter days, the Spaniards caught sight of a simple young man pulling a sled across the ice. Suspecting that he was transporting precious booty, they pursued him. But they found no gold or silver – the boy was dragging something much more precious to him, his mother, and managed to reach the safety of Hoorn. This moving tale did not, however, go down in history under the name of the real hero, but of Lambert Melisz., who claimed that it was he who had saved his mother. The real hero himself was forgotten. In this way, the great struggle went together with petty meanness. To this day, the ice rink and the home for the elderly in Westzaan are named – unjustly – after Lambert Melisz.[57] The folklore of many villages and towns in Holland preserve memories of the years of Spanish rule.[58]

Three days after the defeat on the Zuiderzee, the appointment of Alba's successor, the Catalan Don Luis de Requesens, was announced. He arrived in Brussels on 17 November and power was transferred on 29 November, seven years to the day after Alba had accepted the appointment himself. The French delegate reported that Alba remained indoors, not only because of his gout, but also because he was afraid to show his face in public. If the people had dared to, they would have celebrated his departure with fireworks.[59] Alba had said that six months and 800 deaths would be enough for him to teach the Netherlands a lesson. It eventually cost him six years, untold amounts of money and countless lives. And when he left, the situation was worse than when he had arrived. Philip II himself would later say that Alba had cost him the Low Countries.

4

The Netherlands, or *Belgium Nostrum*
From War to Pacification: 1573–1576

Holland as a Military Training Ground

By the time the Spanish gave up their siege of Alkmaar, the towns of Holland and Zeeland had managed to keep their heads above water against a much greater power for a year and a half. After this first success, the situation remained precarious. There was little hope for the rebels of expanding the territory where they held the upper hand. They could do little more than defend themselves as well as possible and wait and see where the axe would fall next. The Revolt was very different now from how it had been in the late 1560s. Contemporary historians on the side of the king were already speaking of a Second Revolt.[1] In the first phase of the Revolt, the high-ranking and lesser nobles had taken the initiative. The main critics among the high nobility had already fallen prey to the executioner (Egmont, Horn, Montigny and many from the lower ranks) or had died a natural death (Bergen and Brederode). The others had conformed to the new regime, either from conviction or necessity. The only high-ranking noble who supported the cause of the rebels from Holland and Zeeland was the Prince of Orange. Since his last campaign, Orange had remained permanently in the coastal provinces to lead the resistance to the royal regime.

In the second phase, the prince and his supporters gained a solid foothold in Holland and Zeeland. The driving force of the rebels were the Calvinists: they had risked their lives and property for their faith, often had several years of exile under their belts, and were prepared to go to the very limits. Orange also finally joined the Calvinist church publicly in December 1573, taking part in the celebration of the Lord's Supper, which is customary in the Reformed church. That did not mean that he had made a complete U-turn. The prince was not a man for religious dogma. During the discussions preceding his marriage to the Lutheran countess

35 Poem by Jan van Hout in Janus Dousa's friendship album on the friendship that developed between them during the siege; dated 2 December 1575. Roughly translated, the poem says that friendships made in times of peace are easily forgotten, while those forged in war last forever.

36 Dordrecht surrounded on all sides by water. Large parts of Zeeland and Holland looked like this.

Anna of Saxony, he had irritated his prospective in-laws by saying that, in his view, everyone could enjoy holy salvation in their own way. There is no reason to assume that his opinion had changed after he had 'converted' to Calvinism. Other than this, we can only guess at the nature and content of the prince's beliefs. He remained a supporter of freedom of religion and conscience, both out of principle and for practical reasons, and rejected anything that restricted that freedom. Time and again, the ideal of religious freedom proved a serious stumbling block in the practical reality of the war: whenever either the Catholics or the Calvinists gained the upper hand, they banned the practising of their enemies' faith, but did not make holding the faith alone punishable by death.

What else had Orange and his supporters learned from the years of conflict? In the first place, that the beggars and the prince's troops needed greater discipline, which was no easy task.[2] That started with withdrawing all letters of marque and commissions to wage war. Privateering had already been banned. Outrages against monks and priests, like those in Brill, Roermond and many other places, had to cease. The notorious Lumey, who had been responsible not only for the killing of the martyrs of Gorinchem but also the gruesome death by torture of Delft prior Cornelius Musius, was first arrested and then, at the end of April 1574, sent out of the country.[3] The beggars' units and armed militia groups had to be transformed, step by step, into an official armed force on land and sea. The precondition for achieving this was cooperation between Orange and the towns of Holland and Zeeland, with the prince leading the political and military fight, and the towns providing the funding and all other required support. Giving the towns shared responsibility for policy – which was traditional in the Low Countries – and their willingness to take it, meant that the problems could be addressed fundamentally. Another essential requirement was a clear hierarchy: authority lay with the prince and the States, to whom the armed forces had to pledge their allegiance. And so it happened. Orange created legislation in Holland relating to military matters in 1574 and extended it to the States General as a whole in 1578.[4] In this way, with his knowledge of the situation and his organizational skills, he laid the basis for the regular armed forces of the later Dutch Republic.

A first improvement was punctual payment of soldiers' pay, initially every few weeks and then every week.[5] The towns helped by providing accommodation for the troops. These two measures ensured that the soldiers could pay for what they needed, so they no longer needed to beg or loot. Paying for their accommodation meant that people who could hardly keep their heads above water earned a little more on the side. Orange reduced the size of infantry companies by half (from around 300 to 150 soldiers), to make them more manageable and deployable. The next step was to check whether these regiments actually contained all the men on the payroll. That was achieved by inspecting the troops at set times, in the presence of controllers not only from the military but also from the towns, to make sure that the public money was being spent correctly. Giving every town and province shared responsibility in this way increased their engagement with the armed forces.

The troops then had to be trained to obey orders and form up in battle order, and so on. That included how to dig trenches and build fortifications, for which they sometimes received extra pay. And rules were introduced for their equipment. Independently of the Revolt but around the same time, stone city walls were replaced throughout Europe – starting in Italy – by stone fortifications. They were laid out in the shape of a star, the bastions forming the points, which protruded into the surrounding land to enable the flanks to be defended too. A whole network of these fortifications gradually emerged across the whole of the Low Countries, from Bourtange in the north via Naarden and Heusden in the centre, to Lier and Gravelines in the south. Their construction and maintenance were contracted out locally, so that the towns' economies benefited.

Out of necessity, shared responsibility also applied to the fleet. The idea of a central policy and arsenal based in a single port – the prince had designated Rotterdam – foundered because of practical difficulties and jealousy on the part of other port towns. As a result, in practice, five admiralties emerged: in Zeeland (Middelburg), South Holland (Rotterdam), North Holland (Amsterdam), in the northern tip of North Holland (Hoorn and Enkhuizen in turn) and in Friesland (first Dokkum, and then Harlingen). Through interaction with urban and regional networks, the system eventually worked better than a centralized, national one would have done. This whole package of measures, introduced by Orange and of course put in place over a number of years, meant that the war in Holland and Zeeland, rather than bringing decline and ruin, actually brought progress and profit. Orange's later successors, his son Maurice and his cousin William Louis, were able to build on the foundations that he had laid.

What cannot be emphasized enough is the complete change in mentality of Orange himself. Where very many nobles turned their noses up at burghers – even if they were wealthy merchants or bankers – he saw that the people of Holland and Zeeland, as well as those of Brabant and Flanders, were capable of great things. The French nobleman who claimed that anyone who resists a monarch always comes off worst was proved wrong in the case of Orange. Of course, the prince remained a high-ranking noble even though, due to force of circumstance, his household was much simpler than he had been accustomed to in Brussels.[6] But he now became the prince of merchants and craftsmen, even of fishermen and farmers. In the States of Holland, traditionally, only the six large cities (Dordrecht, Haarlem, Leiden, Amsterdam, Delft and Gouda) had a vote. Under his rule, that was increased to eighteen, expanding the support base for his policy.[7] On 11 July 1575, the States of Holland and Zeeland expressed their appreciation of the prince by offering him the Supreme Authority (*Hoogste Overheid*) in their provinces so as to give him greater leverage in governance.[8]

The Siege of Leiden

After the departure of Alba in December 1573, the prince found himself having to deal with another opponent, the Catalan Don Luis de Requesens, who was more of a diplomat than a general. He had a pleasant appointment in Italy and had no desire to move to the difficult – and cold – Low

Countries. He knew of course from Alba the thorny situation he would find himself in. He put it off for such a long time that Philip II eventually had to summon him officially to travel to his new post. After his first acquaintance with the geographical – or, rather, hydrographical – situation of the Low Countries, he exclaimed, 'They are all islands!' And they were, too, in a certain sense. Unlike Alba, during his term of office, Requesens would make serious attempts to reach agreement with the rebels, but at first, for the time being, the fight continued to be waged by military means. In the same month as the debacle at Alkmaar, the Spanish troops laid siege to Leiden. The siege of Haarlem had cost the Spaniards many lives, something the army leadership could not allow to happen twice. So they adopted a new strategy, sealing off the city completely from the outside world in the hope of starving its people into submission. It was also an emergency measure, as they had no cannons. The other towns in Holland did not have the manpower to mount a successful attempt to relieve the city. The siege of Leiden continued into the early months of 1574, while the rebels had two successes in Zeeland. On 27 January, they defeated a royal fleet on the Eastern Scheldt near Reimerswaal, which, like the victory on the Zuiderzee, proved their superiority at sea. As a result, in February, Middelburg surrendered to Orange in person. Under tough Spanish commander Cristóbal de Mondragón, the royalist town had held the beggars at bay for several months. Typically, Orange had given orders that the town not be looted – after all, its inhabitants had to be respected as fellow countrymen and -women. This angered the soldiers, who had been looking forward to sacking the town. During the subsequent reorganization of the town authorities in Middelburg, there was another typical example of the prince's aversion to hair-splitting. The Mennonites refused to confirm their allegiance to the town by swearing an oath. The town authorities would not agree to this, but Orange ordered that the Mennonites could not be forced to make an oath against their own convictions and that a pledge of allegiance would be sufficient. This may now seem like a storm in a teacup but, given the standards of the time, it was highly exceptional. It was yet another example of the prince successfully expanding his support base.

In the meantime, the siege of Leiden continued. The only way to relieve the city seemed to be a successful diversionary attack from outside the country. Once again, it fell to Louis of Nassau to take this task upon himself. With financial support from his brother John of Nassau and a French donation, he recruited an army from across the Holy

37 Luis de Requesens, the third governor-general of the Netherlands, representing the Spanish king, 1573–6. After Alba's hardline policy, he tried to govern more moderately.

Roman Empire to make an attempt to break the siege. And, as planned, the besiegers left their positions to engage the invading army in open battle. But they did not need to fight: it was the troops of Sancho Dávila, captain of the citadel of Antwerp, who met the invaders on the heathland at Mook, to the south of Nijmegen, on 14 April 1574. The Battle of Mookerheyde became a second Jemmingen. As then, the Spaniards showed no mercy, and this time Louis did not escape. He and his younger brother, Henry of Nassau, were among those who were killed or unrecognizably disfigured on the battlefield, or perhaps died trying to escape through the marshes. Louis of Nassau had always been Orange's right-hand man, and the prince was devastated. After their victory, Dávila's troops wanted to be paid and mutinied to get their money.

But there was no way back: Holland and Zeeland had to rely on their own resources, and unfortunately, the people of Leiden had failed to take advantage of the Spanish withdrawal by stocking up on food and munitions. They only just had time to catch their breath before the Spaniards were once again outside the city walls. Their commanding officer now tried to win them over with tempting offers and promises of favourable conditions of surrender. The king would do this, he said, the king would do that . . . The only answer he received from the city was *Fistula dulce canit, volucrem dum decipit auceps* (Sweet are the notes of the flute, when the fowler lures the bird to his net).[9] This learned and witty reply came undoubtedly from Jan van der Does, Lord of Noordwijk, who held a leading position in the defence of the city. Van der Does was also renowned as a writer of neo-Latin poetry, under his Latinized name Janus Dousa. Other leaders of the resistance included mayors Dirck Bronckhorst, who was to succumb to the deprivations of the siege, and Pieter van der Werff, who was to rather exaggerate his part in Leiden's defence. He allegedly declared that he would rather chop off his arm and let it be eaten than surrender the city. Another official who played a decisive role in the defence of freedom was the forbidding city secretary Jan van Hout. During a tumultuous meeting at the town hall between supporters and opponents of continuing the fight, he ordered everyone to be quiet, so that he could record each speaker's name and opinion. That silenced those who favoured negotiating with the Spanish.

Another famous anecdote has since been proved false. During the siege, as was the case everywhere, there was disagreement about

38 Louis of Nassau, the Prince of Orange's brother and right hand.

whether the fight was about *haec libertatis causa* (the cause of freedom) or *haec religionis causa* (the cause of religion). The preachers of course claimed the loudest that it was about saving the Calvinist faith. When one preacher announced this from the pulpit, Jan van Hout apparently drew his pistol and said to the mayor, who was sitting next to him, 'Shall I enlighten him?' But Van Hout did not even attend the service, and the preacher had been quite mild in expressing his opinions.[10]

The hardships in Leiden were not caused by bombardments and assaults, but by hunger and disease. Of the 18,000 inhabitants, 6,000 died, mostly the poor, as the rich always knew how to get hold of food.[11] The only way to relieve the city was to flood the surrounding countryside, as had happened at Alkmaar. It would cause great damage to all the farmers in the wider surroundings, but there was little choice.[12] The States of Holland only decided to employ such drastic measures after much discussion, and the prince needed all his powers of persuasion to convince them.[13] But water does not yield easily to coercion, either, and it was two full months before the water level was high enough to force the Spanish to abandon their siege for the second time, this time for good: on 3 October 1574, Leiden opened its gates to the beggars as liberators. The prince heard the news in Delft while attending Mass in the Walloon Church – even in Holland he retained his preference for

39 This lion bears the arms of Leiden and the feathers in its helmet are in the colours of Orange. It is fighting against a basilisk, a mythical creature that is half-dragon, half-snake. The lion is also driving wild boar out of the Garden of Holland. Objects from the Catholic Mass lie in the mud – a goblet and host, an aspergillum for sprinkling holy water, and a rosary – together with a crook and a tiara, symbols of episcopal and papal dignity. Contemporary coloured drawing.

French – and ordered the good news to be announced from the pulpit. When he visited the city the following day, he criticized a number of leaders for their negligence and made a few changes to the municipal government. Later that same year, he launched an initiative to set up a university and proposed locating it in Leiden. The foundation deed specifies that the prince and the States established the university in the name of King Philip, again making the point that their quarrel was not with the monarch, but with bad Spanish government. The actual setting up of the university was entrusted to Jan van der Does and Jan van Hout, whose cooperation during the siege had laid the foundations for a close friendship (see illus. 34).

Futile Attempts at Peace

New governor-general Requesens made a number of attempts to bring the warring parties together. Besides the human suffering it brought about, the war also caused great damage to trade. Requesens took a number of measures to try and gain the favour of public opinion. He disbanded the Council of Troubles and now officially scrapped the Tenth Penny, which Alba and Philip had already abandoned a year earlier. He announced an amnesty for those who opposed the regime, but, since it excluded some 300 'heretics', it had little effect. In the meantime, the army was costing enormous sums of money and the Spanish coffers were once again nearly empty. As an emergency measure, in June 1574 – still during the siege of Leiden – Requesens called the States General together in Brussels, primarily to obtain permission to levy new taxes. As always, the States took the opportunity to vent their criticisms: of the misbehaviour of the Spanish soldiers, of the regime's policies and of the violation of privileges. The States of Brabant in particular urged the governor-general to honour the rebels' demands. It was decided to send a delegate to the prince to see how he felt about possible peace terms. And, through the mediation of Emperor Maximilian II, peace talks indeed started in Breda on 3 March 1575.

That did not mean that both parties actually sat together around the table. It was far beneath the dignity of the royal delegation to negotiate with such rebels directly. The mediators, including Günther von Schwarzburg, a brother-in-law of the prince, spoke separately with the representatives of both sides. The differences regarding religion proved insurmountable: the Brussels delegation demanded by order of the king

40 Symbolic depiction referring to the peace talks in Breda. The caption reads: 'It pleased God to give us peace, but with violence envy chases away charity.'

that the Protestants leave the rebellious provinces and surrender all arms and fortifications. The king would then, in his good mercy, accept all the people of Holland and Zeeland as his obedient subjects. Not only was that unacceptable to Holland and Zeeland, but they too made unacceptable demands: the new bishops were to leave the Netherlands. Needless to say, the negotiations broke down.

Requesens had no other choice than to continue the armed conflict, despite his limited resources. It was to become a hot and bloody summer in the border zone of Holland and Utrecht. On 8 August 1575, the royal troops captured the small town of Oudewater and committed horrendous atrocities, the details of which I will spare the reader but which contemporaries described in detail.[14] The prince had advised the town to flood the surrounding lands, but the hay was drying there and, as it was indispensable as food for their cattle, the townspeople had ignored his advice. It was a miracle that the same fate did not befall the people of Schoonhoven when the town was captured, while nearby Woerden successfully withstood a siege of no less than eleven months. The town was once again relieved after the prince ordered the surrounding land to be flooded. Woerden's ordeal was as bad as that of Leiden, but has received far less attention in the literature.[15]

In Zeeland, Mondragón was not daunted by water. The tough Spaniard wanted to mount an attack on the town of Zierikzee, on the

41 Pro-Spanish interpretation of how the royalist soldiers cross the Zijpe, accompanied by heavenly phenomena.

island of Schouwen-Duiveland. To do that, he would have to cross the Zijpe, the strait separating Schouwen-Duiveland from the neighbouring island of Sint Philipsland. That would mean either a pontoon bridge or wading across at low tide. He settled for the latter and, with their courage and discipline, the royal troops gave their opponents a lesson in warfare on their own terrain. Up to their ankles in mud and to their waists in water, their weapons held high and dry above their heads, they waded through the Zijpe, hurrying to beat the tide and with the sea beggars' fleet firing on them from the other side.[16] Once the Spanish reached Schouwen-Duiveland, the beggars' troops gave up the fight prematurely when their leader was fatally wounded.

The defence of Zierikzee against the Spaniards gives us yet another telling glimpse of the relations between the different parties in the Netherlands. The town's inhabitants had suffered so much at the hands of the prince's troops that they preferred to accept Mondragón's peace terms and surrender the town without a fight. Here, we are a long way from the 'national struggle' against Spain. Only the fanaticism and the bold actions of one of the garrison's commanders prevented the immediate surrender of the town. He managed to get reinforcements into the town, arrested seven councillors who had irritated him with their lax attitudes, and sent them under guard to Middelburg. The Spaniards then laid siege to the town, which they executed with precision. They successfully frustrated a relief attempt by water, and Mondragón – sweet revenge for the loss of Middelburg – forced the town to capitulate.[17] That put the rebels in a very perilous position: the Spanish victories had divided the rebel area into three. The capture of Haarlem had cut off the north of Holland (above the IJ) from the rest of the province. The capture of Schouwen-Duiveland and Zierikzee had now driven a wedge between the islands of Holland and Zeeland. In Zeeland, Walcheren was the only remaining rebel stronghold.

Seeking Support from Abroad

In these thorny circumstances, it became increasingly necessary to seek the support of a foreign ruler. Orange had already tried that in 1573, without success. At first sight, Elizabeth I, the Protestant queen of England, seemed the most obvious choice. But Elizabeth was extremely cautious, wanting above all to avoid war with Spain. Like her father, Henry VIII, she pursued the traditional policy of maintaining close contacts with the

Netherlands in the interests of English trade. She may have been a Protestant, but she was no champion of the Protestant cause. She feared France more than Spain and, in the divided world of French politics, clandestinely supported the Huguenots, but not from principle. The French Catholics, led by Henri I, Duke of Guise, wanted to free her rival Mary Stuart, the Catholic queen of Scotland whom Elizabeth was holding prisoner, and help her to take the English throne. That was one reason why Elizabeth mistrusted especially French attempts to gain more influence in the Netherlands. Elizabeth and Alba had maintained good relations, until she seized a number of ships carrying gold intended for his government. The conflict led to a trade war, which Elizabeth lost, but both Elizabeth and Alba made sure it did not lead to real war. When the rebels captured Flushing in 1572, Elizabeth successfully justified the presence of an English regiment by saying that she was taking custody of the town for the King of Spain. After Alba's departure, she also had a good relationship with Requesens, and in April 1575 they agreed that they would expel each other's rebels from their countries. She followed the conflict in the Netherlands with great interest, but stuck to her tried and trusted recipe of providing support in secret, and not intervening officially for as long as possible. With that cautious policy, she secured the safety of England and of her crown for half a century.[18] The delegation from Holland that visited her in January 1574 would therefore return home empty-handed.[19]

Because the later Dutch Republic was to become such a great power in the seventeenth century, it is difficult to imagine that, in the 1580s, its predecessors had to go looking for a foreign ruler to support them. For contemporaries, however, it must have seemed impossible for the rebels in the Low Countries to defeat the Spanish enemy on their own. No assistance could be expected from the Lutheran German princes; their aversion to the Calvinists was greater than their hatred of Catholics. The only other option was France. The same applied on the other side, too: if 'Brussels' had to defeat Holland and Zeeland using only its own resources, a ceasefire or peace treaty would have been agreed in no time. The people of the present-day Benelux might then have found themselves living in a '*Confoederatio Belgica*', along Swiss lines, with Catholic and Protestant cantons, and with the cars in the Netherlands, Belgium and Luxembourg having registration plates bearing the letters 'CB' (in Latin to avoid the language problem). But Brussels had the Spanish war coffers (which were usually empty) and a reservoir of

42 Queen Elizabeth I of England, who was prepared to provide the rebels with covert support, but not too openly.

trained troops at its disposal, and Holland and Zeeland therefore needed to find a comparable ally.

In France, the latest in a series of civil wars between Catholics and Protestants was in full swing. Perhaps the Duke of Anjou, brother of the French king and religiously neutral, would come to the aid of the Netherlands? He had already successfully brokered a peace settlement between the two religious factions in France and was ambitious enough to be interested in a role on the European stage.[20] And was he not a contender for the hand of Queen Elizabeth? But no one is willing to support a losing cause – patrons only offer their protection when success has already been assured. Anjou was no exception: if he wanted to rule the Netherlands, it would be better to marry a daughter of Philip II and ask for them as a dowry. So official assistance from abroad was no option. Nevertheless, between 1572 and 1576, English, Scottish, French and German companies did serve in Orange's army. Their governments turned a blind eye to them being recruited and there were always enough volunteers willing to take part in the rebels' struggle.

The Netherlands United in Resistance

The situation was not much better on the royal side. At one point, Requesens complained that he had not heard anything at all from the king for seven months. On 1 September 1575, the Spanish king – for the second time in his reign – had to announce that the state was bankrupt. When Requesens died unexpectedly on 5 March 1576, there was not even enough money in Brussels to pay for his funeral. Furthermore, Requesens had not named a successor, so the Council of State automatically took temporary control of the government. The Spanish troops, meanwhile, brought the uncertainty to an end by simply surrendering their advantage. They had not been paid for some time and it was a miracle that they had been prepared to continue fighting for so long. After their capture of Zierikzee, they had had enough of a life without prospects and decided to seek their own compensation. At his advanced age, Mondragón was to see the royal troops rise up in mutiny – which must have been unprecedented for him – and go on the rampage in search of booty. The whole army in the Low Countries rebelled. The mutineers chose the town of Aalst, in Flanders, as a robbers' den, and from there they set out on their raids. Under the *elettos*, leaders elected from their own ranks, they ravaged towns and countryside. That was too much for the Council of State. With one exception, all the Council members came from the Netherlands and were fierce defenders of their country's interests. The Council declared the Spanish troops enemies of the land and empowered the States of Brabant to recruit troops to fight the rampaging bands of mutineers. The Council of State itself, however, fell prey to the radical mood in Brabant and its members were all arrested on 4 September 1576.

The following day, the Council was deposed as temporary head of state, and, the day after, the States of Brabant showed that they could play a leading role now the worst had come to the worst. As in 1477, they convened the States General.[21] And once again, the States General decided to negotiate with the rebellious provinces: they all considered themselves citizens of the Netherlands and the rebels in Holland continued to insist that they recognized the king as their sovereign lord. Why, then, should they not be able to reach agreement, even if it were only to join forces to fight the Spanish troops? Again, representatives of Holland and Zeeland met a delegation from the States General, now in Ghent. Unhampered by a governor-general who upheld the will of the king, they reached a 'satisfactory' provisional agreement, known as the Pacification of Ghent. As in previous negotiations, the agreement addressed two areas of policy – politics and religion. As far as politics was concerned, all the provinces had the same old demands of the crown: withdrawal of Spanish troops and government of the Netherlands for and by their own people. They would only accept the new governor-general, appointed by the king in the meantime, if he endorsed the Pacification. Religion remained a prickly issue and it would be up to the States General to come to a definitive decision. The provisional solution was essentially to apply a double standard: the representatives of Holland and Zeeland wanted freedom for Protestants in the other provinces, while forbidding Catholics to practise their religion freely in their own. Consequently, Catholics would remain the disadvantaged party in Holland and Zeeland, while elsewhere no action could be taken against the Protestants. The placards against the Protestants were suspended. In theory, since Catholics were not prosecuted in Holland and Zeeland, this meant freedom of conscience for everyone, everywhere. The political accord was most important; they hoped to reach agreement on religion at a later stage.

A day after this agreement had been reached, the need for a united front became abundantly clear: on 4 November 1576, Spanish troops entered Antwerp and, for the following four days, went on the rampage, looting, killing and committing arson. The city had already suffered much. For the previous four years, shipping had been severely hampered by the rebels based in Flushing, who had only allowed ships through on payment of a toll. Royal bankruptcies had twice caused great damage to Antwerp's trade and industry. In 1574, the city had to resort to lending money to satisfy mutinous soldiers.[22] And now, the murderous scenes that had played out in Mechelen, Rotterdam, Zutphen, Naarden, Haarlem

43 During the 'Spanish fury', the sacking of Antwerp, the town hall also went up in flames.

and Oudewater were repeated in Antwerp. Two and a half thousand of the city's inhabitants fell victim to this 'Spanish fury'.[23] The Renaissance town hall went up in flames, along with some thousand other buildings, and the soldiers were occupied for many more days piling their loot onto carts. Anyone who had harboured reservations about making a deal with the rebels now abandoned them, and on 8 November 1576 the Pacification of Ghent was ceremoniously signed.

The awareness of belonging to the same federated state now meant that instead of speaking of the Netherlands as a collection of separate domains, it now signified a single entity embracing all seventeen provinces. This is reflected in a linguistic change in Dutch from the plural *de Nederlanden* to the singular *Nederland*. The same happened in French, changing from *les Pays-Bas* to *le Pays-Bas*. In Latin, the whole country (and thus not only the southern provinces) was referred to as *Belgium nostrum*. These names were used interchangeably.[24]

Although the country was now unified in name, it proved difficult in the political and military actions that followed the signing of the Pacification of Ghent to translate that unity into joint action. As with Holland in 1572, each town had to fend for itself and acted without consulting the others. On 9 November, Ghent successfully drove out the Spanish troops. The following year, the people of Utrecht tore down the Vredenburg, the coercion castle in the city. The inhabitants of Antwerp did the same to their citadel in August 1577. In the meantime, Orange issued warnings about the intentions of the new governor-general, Don John of Austria. Don John was a natural son of Emperor Charles V. He had grown up in Spain, had defeated the Turks at the famous battle of Lepanto (1571) and, since then, had become too big for his boots. The order to succeed Requesens in the Netherlands seemed to him the perfect opportunity to achieve his great ambition: he would defeat the rebels, cross the Channel to England with his army and free Mary Stuart from her prison, dispose of Elizabeth and, together with Mary, ascend to the throne of England.

His experience in the Low Countries would have a sobering effect on Don John. On 3 November 1576 he arrived in Luxembourg, with no money and no authority over the mutinous Spanish troops. He had to make the best of the situation, which was not one of his strong points. Nevertheless, the States General sought a way to make his life as easy as possible. On 7 January 1577 they concluded the first Union of Brussels with the Council of State. In the Union, the States endorsed the Pacification of Ghent, emphasized once again their loyalty to the king, and pledged to preserve the Catholic faith. This final point was interpreted by some as a plea for the free practice of Catholicism in Holland and Zeeland, causing that discussion to flare up again. In reality, the first Union of Brussels was a Catholic Union and therefore contained no limiting provisions for Don John.

Against Orange's advice, the States General passed a resolution known as the Perpetual Edict recognizing Don John as governor-general. In return, Don John endorsed the Pacification of Ghent as laid down in the Union of Brussels. It was agreed that the Spanish troops would leave the country, for which the States General had to pay 600,000 guilders. On 6 April, King Philip also approved the Pacification, but not with full conviction; he simply had no other choice.[25]

Opposition was so widespread that, on 28 April, Philip even agreed to the withdrawal of the Spanish troops, and they left. A little over a week later, Don John held his Joyous Entry in Brussels and took his oath. But the new governor-general, bursting with energy to act, could not contain his impatience; by 24 July it had already run out, and he took the citadel of Namur by force. This military coup had no impact at all and he had to

44 The people of Antwerp take to the streets en masse to demolish the hated citadel, 1577.

negotiate again with the States on new conditions for further cooperation. Neither the king nor his governors-general seemed to have learned much from the political situation or the criticism from all quarters: the people of the Netherlands had been making the same demands for ten years, but the crown never seriously considered any response other than military action. Their modus operandi was always the same: concede when there was no other choice and seize power when the opportunity presented itself. A month later, the king dithered once again about whether to send his troops back in, on 28 August he ordered them to stay in Italy, only to send them back to the Low Countries on the 31st.[26]

In the meantime, more militant groups had taken over in the towns of Brabant: in Brussels, a radical people's committee known as the 'XVIII' or 'Eighteen Men' had taken power. These agitators, supporters of the prince, forced the States General to invite Orange to Brussels.[27]

45 Prince William of Orange on board the boat on which he made his entry into Brussels on 23 September 1577. Atop the lavishly ornamented vessel are the arms of Philip II. Below, to the left, are the prince's own arms. In the trees are the arms of the provinces of Artois and Hainaut. The flag at the stern shows St Michael, the patron saint of Brussels, and the dragon. Woodcut by A. van Leest in Jan Baptist Houwaert, *Declaratie van die triumphante incompst* (Declaration of the Triumphant Entry) (Antwerp, 1579). The original woodblocks for this engraving can be seen in the permanent exhibition in the Plantin-Moretus Museum in Antwerp.

5

The Netherlands Divided
The Short-lived Success of the Moderate Centre: 1576–1584

Orange's Finest Hour

The Pacification of Ghent succeeded in holding all the provinces of the Netherlands together for less than three years. To conclude, however, that the agreement was doomed to failure would be to use the benefit of hindsight. It would be all too easy to leap forward as quickly as possible from the Pacification in 1576 to 1579, the year in which the Netherlands divided into two, with the southern provinces united in the Union of Arras and the northern (roughly speaking) provinces in the Union of Utrecht. That would give the impression that the Dutch and the Belgians were 'in their rightful place'. But that is looking back from where we are now. We could just as easily say that it is a miracle that the Union of Utrecht, originally intended as a temporary alliance, has prevailed for more than two centuries.

The Pacification had left a definitive settlement of the religious question to a future meeting of the States General. It is therefore not surprising that, every time the States came together, religion was once again on the agenda. At a meeting of the States General in December 1577, Orange would take the opportunity to amend the First Union of Brussels, agreed earlier in the year and deliberately focused on freedom for Catholics to keep governor-general Don John happy. The resulting Second Union of Brussels also guaranteed Protestants freedom to practise their religion. In July 1578, Orange tried to persuade the States General to approve a Religious Peace, under which, in places where at least 100 families requested it, they would be allowed to practise their own religion. But that had met with resistance from both the Protestant States of Holland and Zeeland and Catholics in the other provinces. Nevertheless, no fewer than 27 towns dared to put the law into practice, though it was not to last long in any of them. The prince was way ahead of his time in introducing the new rules.[1]

46 Matthias of Austria and Prince William of Orange with the arms of the Seventeen Provinces between them. Engraving by Johannes Wierix (1549–c. 1620).

It is typical of Orange that he first asked the States of Holland and Zeeland for their permission to accept the invitation to go to Brussels – as if the seeds of a constitutional ruler were already starting to grow within him. When he arrived in Antwerp, he was first the guest of honour at three days of feasting. After that, his journey continued by boat along the Willebroek canal, an impressive feat of hydraulic engineering at the time, to the capital. Outside Brussels, three boats were awaiting the prince and his entourage, decorated with small beech trees bearing the arms of the seventeen provinces. In the first boat, musicians played the *Wilhelmus*. In the last boat, painted in the prince's colours (orange, white and blue), Orange sat under a canopy ornamented with coats of arms. In pride of place on top were the arms of the king, showing that everything was supposedly still hunky-dory between the monarch and the Netherlands. Below, to the left, were the arms of the prince. Orange's glorious entrance in Brussels took place on 23 September. It was ten years since he had last seen the city. Now he was received by an enthusiastic crowd as a liberator, the man who warned them against the policies of the crown from the very beginning. The bells rang out, cannon salutes resounded, people cheered and were moved to tears. It was a day of triumph, the likes of which Orange was not to see very often. The English ambassador, in principle a neutral spectator, reported how the people welcomed the prince as if he were an angel descended from heaven.

Among those who officially welcomed the prince was Philip de Croÿ, Duke of Aarschot. Aarschot had gradually emerged in the preceding years as the leader of the opposition in Brussels. If the rebels had a tendency towards radicalism, this did not mean that those more favourable to the crown danced completely to the tune of Alba or Requesens. Before Alba arrived, Orange and Aarschot had been rivals, but now that, under the repressive regimes of the two governors-general, Aarschot had become an opposition leader, they sought contact again. Although Aarschot seemed jealous of Orange's current success – Belgian historian Henri Pirenne was also less than complimentary about Aarschot, calling him a half-crazy, presumptuous braggart[2] – they worked closely together during the years that the Pacification was in force. Their political aims were, after all, the same: to see the Netherlands governed by indigenous nobles in accordance with national interests. They seriously discussed a marriage between Orange's eldest daughter and Aarschot's son, Charles of Chimay. While he was in Brussels, Orange did not attend Protestant services and allowed Mass to be read in his Catholic domain of Breda. This was enough for the wider public in Brabant to believe that, in his heart, he was still a Catholic.[3] In short, all parties tried to reach agreement and avoid extreme standpoints.

What could now be better than a return to the old situation, with the Netherlands ruled by a 'natural prince', a legitimate descendant of the house of Austria? 'Legitimate' was a reference to the illegitimate birth of Don John, who was still trying to prove that he was a rightful son of Charles v. John wrote an angry letter to Philip stating that Orange was now determining policy. The Catholic nobles also refused to cooperate with Don John. Two weeks after Orange arrived, Aarschot made it known that Archduke Matthias of Austria, a younger brother of Emperor Rudolf II and a nephew of King Philip, was willing to take on the job as governor-general. Matthias was twenty years of age, was up for an adventure and had said yes to the invitation. He had already travelled to the Low Countries, without first asking permission of the king or the emperor. With no experience at all of politics, he proved no match for Orange, who, with his affability, soon won the confidence of the young Austrian.

Mathias, who liked to walk around in a replica antique suit of armour, quickly saw Orange as a second father. Orange had him eating out of the palm of his hand, to such an extent that the new governor-general was soon known as 'the prince's clerk'. The appointment of Matthias showed just how possible it was, in sixteenth-century circumstances and despite the enormous distances, to respond and make decisions quickly – if the will was there. The distance to Vienna was not much shorter than to Madrid and yet the invitation and its acceptance by Matthias were arranged within four weeks. The conditions on which Matthias had accepted the governor-general's position were also extremely interesting. Compared with those of the Joyous Entry, they restricted his governing powers to such an extent that they as good as established a constitutional monarchy *avant la lettre*.[4]

Just as they had when Granvelle departed, the high-ranking nobles now had to prove again that they were capable of running the country. Orange was at the pinnacle of his power, especially when the States of Brabant also appointed him *ruwaard* (protector) of Brabant, the equivalent of stadtholder in the other provinces. Aarschot, in turn, was appointed stadtholder of Flanders. As a high-ranking noble, however, he had little to do with the burghers – unlike Orange – and, when he left for Flanders, said very little about them. Once he arrived in Ghent, he found the situation there very different from what he was used to.

Radicalization of the Opposition in Flanders and Brabant

The revolt of Brussels and the south in 1577 was different from the two earlier revolts of 1568 and 1572; rather than just Holland and Zeeland, almost all the provinces now took part. The only exceptions were the arch-Catholic Luxembourg, Limburg and Namur. In most provinces, the fight was not about religious freedom, but liberating the country from the Spanish soldiers. The majority of the population were Catholic and wanted nothing to do with Calvinism. That makes it even more surprising that, in 1578 and the years that followed, the Calvinists gained the upper hand in the larger cities of Brabant and Flanders. This radicalization went so far that, on 1 May 1581, Brussels banned the Catholic religion, followed by Antwerp on 1 July 1581.[5] As late as June 1577, a young mason in Ghent was sentenced to a flogging and fifty years in exile simply for keeping his cap on when the procession bearing the Real Presence passed.[6] A little over a year later, the situation was completely reversed and radical

Calvinists were in control of the city. Orange had promised Ghent a return to the situation before 1540, the year in which Charles v had withdrawn most of the privileges of the proud city. When Aarschot arrived there as stadtholder in 1577, he made a bad start by sweeping this restoration of privileges from the table. The militants wanted the old privileges back, including the influence of artisan guilds on the city government and restoration of Ghent's control of the surrounding countryside.

That led to a veritable reign of terror over the city and the surrounding area. The two leading figures were Jan van Hembyze, an alderman who had lost his son in the troubles and was now ready and willing to introduce draconian measures, and the young nobleman François Rijhove, a supporter of Orange. On 27 October, Rijhove went to Antwerp to propose to the prince that a number of leading Catholics be arrested. The prince did not give his permission, but did not advise against it either. Rijhove and his supporters took the prince's refusal to come down on one side or the other as tacit approval. During the night of 28 October 1577 they arrested none other than their stadtholder, Aarschot; the bishops of Ypres and Bruges; the grand-bailiff of the city; and a number of other nobles and city officials. A day later, they set up a Calvinist city militia by taking on 300 vagabonds and issuing them with arms.[7] On 1 November, a radical Committee of Eighteen Men was set up. When Orange arrived in Ghent on 29 December, he succeeded in settling the differences and getting Aarschot released. Consequently, he could once again allow himself to be feted as the man who brought reconciliation, while it would have been better if he had stopped Hembyze and Rijhove from committing their rash deeds in the first place. Their radical actions set the Catholics against them and, as in 1566, the indifference of the Catholic nobles was now tinted with the aversion aroused in them by the Calvinist activists.

In January 1578, Alexander Farnese – prince of Parma and son of former governor-general Margaret – arrived with new troops to help Don John regain power. On the 28th of the same month, Farnese easily defeated the army of the States General at Gembloux, halfway between Brussels and Namur. The people of Brussels were already afraid of a siege and the army of the States General seemed unable to recover after the defeat. But in early August, the two armies once again faced each other on the battlefield, now near the village of Rijmenam, to the east of Mechelen. Parma had advised Don John not to engage, but the latter ignored the advice and was defeated.

It was and remained a matter of every man for himself; the States General proved incapable of devising a joint strategy. Now the other provinces were finally in agreement with Holland and Zeeland, these two provinces continued to collect convoy and license money.[8] *Convooien* were a form of duty, the proceeds of which were used to pay for armed escorts at sea. *Licenten* were a sort of additional export duty on food and other goods (excluding arms and ammunition) supplied to the 'enemy'. At first sight, it seems unthinkable to supply your enemy – with whom you are engaged in a life and death struggle – with goods, but the profits were indispensable to trade, and if you did not supply them, the enemy would simply buy them elsewhere abroad.[9] The duties raised valuable revenue for the defence of Holland and Zeeland, and especially for the admiralties. The people of Antwerp, however, were very angry about what they saw as sabotage on the part of their 'fellow countrymen'.[10] Instead of contributing to the common interest, the States of Holland and Zeeland seemed to prefer to secure the interests of their own provinces first. By means of a 'satisfaction', a written guarantee, they forced those towns that were still loyal to the king – Amsterdam and Haarlem in Holland, and Goes in Zeeland – to join them. Officially, there was nothing to stop Catholics practising their religion, but in reality it proved a dead letter. That Orange was either unwilling or unable to do anything to protect the Catholics in Holland and Zeeland increased criticism of the prince in the other provinces.

In the months that followed the defeat at Gembloux, there were two different offensives, both of which were unfavourable to the moderates in the centre. On the one side, there was a royal offensive from Namur and Luxembourg, led by Don John and Parma. They captured Leuven, forcing the States General to move to Antwerp. At the same time, the radical Calvinists initiated revolutionary change in Flanders. Orange had hardly left Ghent on 15 January 1578 when the Committee of Eighteen Men resumed their aggressive policies. Instead of contributing to a national army to defeat the troops of Don John and Parma, Ghent troops took control of the most important towns in Flanders: Bruges, Kortrijk, Ronse, Oudenaarde, Axel, Hulst, Sint-Niklaas and Ypres. From Ypres they advanced to Dunkirk, Sint-Winoksbergen, Veurne and further.[11] Other towns, like Dendermonde and Deinze, followed Ghent's example and chose militant Calvinism. Everywhere where this radical change occurred, revolutionary Committees of Eighteen took power, there was violence against monks and priests, and iconoclastic fury was unleashed in churches, monasteries and convents.

It is not easy to explain this aggressive Calvinist revival. There had been severe Calvinist activism earlier, in the 1560s. Perhaps an aversion to such militant behaviour and fear of Alba had kept the cities of Flanders and Brabant out of the conflict in 1572 and the years that followed. But the memory of the chaos of 1566 would surely be no less strong than in 1572. So why did Brussels, Ghent and the other towns with their Eighteen Men pursue such a polarizing policy in 1577? The memory of 1566 seems to have encouraged the Calvinists to take action, rather than discourage them. Under Alba's regime, any form of military resistance in the royalist Netherlands was simply unthinkable, but the end of the Spanish governor-general's strict rule had removed some of the pressure. Returned Calvinists and those who had practised their faith in secret now introduced the same radical measures in many towns in Flanders and Brabant as in 1566. And, as in 1566, the Catholics were so accustomed to leaving their religious and political leadership to the clergy that they did not, as yet, offer any resistance. The towns led by Committees of Eighteen Men in Flanders now hardly paid anything to the central government in Brussels because they wanted to use the money for their own defence. But they would be no match for the armies of Don John and Parma.

The Unions of Arras and Utrecht

In the extreme southwest of the Netherlands lay the provinces of Artois and Hainaut (see Map 1, p. 215). Compared to Brabant and Flanders, or Holland and Zeeland, they were still very rural. The nobility had traditionally held political power here and were a major supplier of army commanders for the royal army. In Hainaut, only the capital city of Mons sent a representative of the burghers to the States. In Artois, there were only three major towns, Arras, Béthune and Saint-Omer. On 1 March 1578, the States of Artois, dominated by the nobles, proposed that peace be made with Don John. On 6 March, the States of Hainaut expressed support for the proposal, but the people of Béthune, Aire, Saint-Omer and Douai opposed it and immediately protested. They were, however, no match for the powerful nobles.[12] In Arras, as in Flanders, a minority of fanatical Calvinists took power, hoisting the orange, white and blue flag of the Prince of Orange to show their political colours. Their people's council consisted of fifteen rather than eighteen men, and they referred to themselves as *les Quinze*.

During the troubles under Philip II, nobles from Artois and Hainaut had also taken part in the Compromise of Nobles, but after Alba's arrival in 1567 they had either withdrawn or adapted. Consequently, the group that remained was much more homogeneous, politically and religiously: the radical elements had disappeared and the supporters of reconciliation with crown and altar were united. Serving the crown in governing bodies or in the armed forces was often the nobles' most important – if not only – source of income. The status-conscious Catholic nobles were irritated by the militant actions of the Calvinist burghers in Ghent. Known as the Malcontents, these dissatisfied nobles preferred to be governed by their sovereign lords than by burghers and decided to take action. The States of Hainaut declared themselves opposed to the 'more than barbarian brutality and tyranny of the sectarians and their supporters, which exceed those of the Spaniards'.[13] The Malcontents then put a stop to the Calvinist regime in Arras and had the leaders put to death on the scaffold. That was a victory for the nobility and the wealthy burghers. On 6 January 1579 in Arras, Artois and Hainaut concluded a union.

The Union of Arras was in the first instance a Catholic union, an extension of the First Union of Brussels. Four months later, on 17 May 1579, Artois and Hainaut reconciled themselves with the king in the Peace of Arras. With the Peace, they essentially achieved political ambitions that largely recalled the old resistance ideals of the 1560s: the country free of foreign troops, the king ruling with the agreement of the nobles, and Parma replaced by a governor-general of royal blood. The Union of Arras was therefore not 'treason', betraying the common political cause. Nevertheless, its signatories were not interested in talking about greater freedoms for Protestants. In Tournai and the Tournaisis, the social situation was completely the reverse: here the balance of power was in the favour of the city's burghers. Consequently, supporters of reconciling with the king – the clergy and the rural population – lost out and Tournai chose the side of the Revolt. The fact that Tournai was French-speaking was no reason to join the Union of Arras. The city did not succumb until forced to its knees by Parma.[14]

In the Protestant provinces of Holland and Zeeland, the situation was in some ways simpler, because the town authorities had a firm hand on the reins. Unlike in Artois and Hainaut, the nobles did not play a leading role here or constitute a forceful opposition. There was also far less jealousy between the towns than there was in Flanders and Brabant. The town councils consisted of Protestants who had, as it were, 'channelled' Calvinism and had a strong aversion to fanaticism. Mennonites and Catholics were tolerated without putting pressure on them to convert to Protestantism.

Many people in a large number of towns to the north of the major rivers were still devoted to the Catholic Church and the king. Parker illustrates this clearly with the numbers of communicants in the town of Kampen at Easter 1579: 67 at the Calvinist church compared to 8,000 at the Catholic churches.[15] It is debatable whether this is a fair comparison, since the Protestants imposed strict conditions on who was permitted to take part in the Lord's Supper, while for Catholics it was compulsory to take communion at Easter. In their fight against the Spanish, the Netherlands could possibly look to Switzerland for a precedent. There, Protestant and Catholic cantons had united in a military confederacy, while each canton continued to organize its own affairs, including religion.

In the same month as the Union of Arras, January 1579, the Union of Utrecht was concluded. It was initiated by John of Nassau, stadtholder of Gelderland from 1577 to 1580. The members of the Union were Gelderland, Holland, Zeeland, Utrecht and Friesland, together with a number of large cities in Brabant and Flanders. The Union left much unsaid: there was nothing about the king or the Catholic religion. Each province was permitted to make its own rules regarding religion, as long as no one was prosecuted for their religious beliefs. Orange actually opposed the Union, because it distracted attention from the old ideal of uniting the whole of the Netherlands in the fight against the Spanish. He finally signed a formal document assuring his support on 3 May. Overijssel pledged its support in the same way. There were now therefore different groups of territories in the Low Countries: those provinces still loyal to the king (Luxembourg, Limburg and Namur), those united in the Catholic Union of Arras, those signed up to the Union of Utrecht, officially neutral but Protestant in practice, and a number of towns in Brabant and Flanders which had not formally signed either treaty. The territory covered by the Union of Utrecht very soon, however, coincided with that of the rebellious provinces.[16]

Parma

The option of making a choice is always precarious for those in the middle who do not want to choose, because of the very fact that they can be forced to do so. That is why the States General accepted the invitation from Emperor Rudolf II to go to Cologne for peace negotiations in May 1579. Don John had unexpectedly died of the plague on 1 October 1578 and had designated Parma as his successor. Parma was a courteous nobleman who, like Orange, had a talent for dealing with people, was an astute politician, and possessed a degree of patience that Don John could never summon. He acquired great fame as a general despite being regularly forced – without the Spanish millions to back him up – to refrain from military action. In June 1579, he captured the city of Maastricht. That was a sensitive blow to Orange's prestige. In the eyes of the public, the prince was to blame. As the man with the greatest influence on the States General, he should have forced them to relieve the city. Emboldened by the capture of Maastricht and the return of the Union of Arras under the authority of the king, the royal camp in the peace negotiations in Cologne intensified their demands. They again wanted all Protestants to leave the country (though they were given time to do this) and for the political situation to return to how it was in 1559, with the States having little effective influence on the royal government.[17] The Spanish did not expect this to be acceptable to the rebels, but hoped that it would persuade other nobles, cities or provinces to abandon the revolt.

And that is what happened, at least to some extent. In March 1580, the stadtholder of the northern provinces, Georges de Lalaing, Count of Rennenberg, chose, together with his southern Catholic family members, to reconcile with the king. In 1576, the year of the general revolt against Spain, he had served the government of the States General and a year later was appointed stadtholder of Friesland, Groningen, Drenthe and Overijssel. In 1578, he had captured the towns of Kampen and Deventer from the Spanish, but in the year that his family reconciled with the king, he also decided to return to the royal camp. Just as his southern kinsfolk were irritated by the spread of Calvinism in Flanders, he was offended by the efforts of the fanatical John of Nassau to enforce Calvinism in Gelderland. The Catholic inhabitants of Groningen were loyal supporters of Rennenberg, and on 3 March the city and the surrounding lands (*Ommelanden*) once again pledged obedience to Philip II. Forewarned by Rennenberg's susceptibility to Parma's offers, the rebels had taken control of Friesland in good time. But they lost large areas of the provinces of Drenthe and Overijssel, where Rennenberg captured the towns of Coevorden and Oldenzaal. When the count died suddenly in July 1581, Parma appointed Francisco Verdugo as his successor. Verdugo was a seasoned Spanish military leader who, through his marriage to a natural daughter of the Count of Mansfeld (who was stadtholder of Luxemburg), was considered at least half a native of the Netherlands. He had already served at Saint-Quentin in 1557 and would distinguish himself exceptionally in the service of the royal government in the northernmost provinces.[18]

Parma would have to be satisfied with these successes for the time being. The scenario changed yet again in 1580 and 1581, because Philip gave priority to the conquest of Portugal. Rather than supporting Parma's offensive, Philip now consented to Granvelle's proposal to declare Orange an outlaw. In the ban of outlawry, the prince was called everything under the sun: an atheist, a bigamist, a drunkard, the man who was sacrificing the Netherlands to satisfy his own ambitions, and the man without whom there would long have been peace between the king and the Netherlands. Parma opposed the declaration, considering it a dishonourable tactic in the fight against the prince, and held it up as long as possible. Although it was dated 15 March 1580, he did not publish it until 15 July.[19] In response to the ban, Orange's staff – in consultation with the prince – wrote the *Apology*, justifying his deeds. The *Apology* was just as slanderous as the ban and was primarily intended as propaganda. Its main objective may have been to justify the prince's actions, but it did not mince words in denouncing his opponents. It described Spain, the Spaniards and the Spanish regime in the darkest of terms. King Philip and the Duke of Alba were tyrants whose only aim was the downfall of the Netherlands. The prince gave his anti-Spanish feeling full rein but, as propaganda designed to defame the enemy in a time of full-scale war, the time for nuances and for respecting the rights of the opponent was past. On the contrary, the sharply worded anti-Spanish sentiments expressed in the *Apology* were intended to persuade all those still in doubt in the Netherlands to abandon their loyalties to the Spanish crown. That there were still those in the States General who hesitated to go over to the rebels completely is illustrated by the fact that they did not want to publish the *Apology* on their authority. The document was finally published in four languages, and on the authority of the States of Holland, whose members provided Orange with a bodyguard.[20] The prince concluded the *Apology* with his motto *Je maintiendrai*, 'I shall maintain'. The motto originally read as *Je maintiendrai Nassau*, to preserve his honour, his family and his domains. Gradually, the prince omitted the word Nassau, as can be seen in a portrait from 1578. In later years, he used the words with a wider meaning, for example in a letter to the States of Holland which ends with the words *ce qui par vous sera résolu, je le maintiendrai*, 'I will maintain [i.e. uphold] what you decide'. In this wider sense, the motto appeared under the coat of arms of the later Kingdom of the Netherlands.

Parma's success in 1579 was, paradoxically enough, the reason for his stagnating progress in 1580. In the Peace of Arras, he had to pledge to send the foreign troops out of the country and he had the political and military courage to fulfil that promise in April 1580. This was a bonus for

47 Abraham de Bruyn (attrib.; c. 1538–1587), portrait of William, Prince of Orange, with his motto *Je maintiendrai*, 'I will maintain'.

Philip, as he was able to use the 5,500 Spaniards to conquer Portugal.[21] Among the Spanish troops was Sancho Dávila, the hero of Mookerheyde, without whom Alba – who had been given command of the troops – refused to leave. Parma also dismissed the Italian and German troops, so that he indeed ended up with an army consisting entirely of men from the Netherlands, mostly Walloons. Due to the conquest of Portugal, he received no financial support in 1580 and 1581, meaning that for two years he could do very little. He did not capture Tournai until 29 November 1581, after a long siege,[22] but his attack on Bergen op Zoom a week later was foiled. After two years of squabbling, the nobles and the States in the Union of Arras accepted that they could not defeat the rebels without foreign troops. To Parma's amazement, they themselves requested the return of the Spanish and Italian troops.

Orange's French Policy

At the same time, the States General had called in foreign assistance. On 29 September 1580 the States signed a treaty with the Duke of Anjou, the brother of the French king Henri III. Anjou was given the grand title of 'Defender of the Liberties of the Netherlands' and undertook to supply 10,000 troops to support the States. If the States also wanted to offer sovereignty over the Netherlands to Anjou, they would have to repudiate their allegiance to Philip. That occurred on 26 July 1581 when, in the Act of Abjuration, they officially renounced the king as their ruler. The States did not, therefore, renounce the king with an oath; it was a decision taken at a regular meeting of the States General, with no pomp and circumstance. Anjou did not, however, arrive in Flushing – the town from where Philip II, the legitimate ruler, had left for Spain for good – until 10 February 1582, more than a year after the treaty had been signed. Orange was the first to go down on his knees

48 The Reformation Wall in Geneva. The relief shows the meeting of the States General in which Philip II was repudiated as the sovereign lord of the Netherlands. To the right of the relief is a passage (in French) from a letter from Orange to the States of Holland ending with the words 'Ce qui par vous sera résolu, je le maintiendrai' (I will maintain whatever you decide).

49 Symbolic depiction of the repudiation of Philip II as sovereign lord of the Netherlands: in the otherwise almost empty chamber of the States General, there is a herald bearing the arms of the provinces on his tunic. There are not seven, as is usual, but eight: the county of Zutphen, normally included under the duchy of Gelre, is shown here separately (a lion above a cross).

and acknowledge Anjou as the new sovereign, and the latter was invested as Duke of Brabant on 19 February in Antwerp. This French policy was not popular; after all, the French were traditionally the enemy and Anjou was a politically indifferent ruler, interested only in his own fame and benefit; an untrustworthy rogue whose appearance – due to his excessive lifestyle – required much use of the powder box. The burghers of Holland and Zeeland wanted nothing to do with a Catholic ruler. They had already recognized Orange as the Supreme Authority in 1575 and requested an exceptional status for themselves. To keep Anjou outside the door, they insisted that Orange accept the title of count of Holland, but the prince had declined the offer. When Orange was the victim of an attempted assassination on 18 March 1582, most people believed that Anjou was behind the attack. The would-be assassin, a Basque Catholic named Juan Jauregui, shot the prince through his jaw. The wound refused to heal and it took several months for Orange to recover, during which time Anjou did not show his face. The ordeal was clearly more exhausting for Orange's third wife, Charlotte de Bourbon, and she – rather than the prince – died, on 5 May 1582.

That summer, Parma reopened the offensive: he had his Spanish elite troops back and, on 4 July, he captured the town of Oudenaarde.[23] A little later, while Anjou and Orange were in Ghent for Anjou's investiture as the Count of Flanders, a daring attempt by Parma to take that city, too, was only narrowly repelled. However, in the autumn, the long-awaited French army arrived in the Netherlands and the balance seemed to tip in favour of the rebels. It looked as though Orange's French policy would finally bear fruit: he now had an extra 10,000 men, including well-trained Swiss troops, to throw into the fight against Parma's armies and – who knows – there might soon be a war between France and Spain. Parma read the situation the same way and was suddenly aware of his minority position. On 8 January 1583 he wrote to the king that, without immediate financial support, country and faith would be lost to the crown.[24]

The Spanish were saved by an unexpected change of tack by Anjou and the French troops. The duke had had enough of his subordinate position and planned to capture Antwerp and a number of other Flemish towns, to make himself lord and master of the country. The people of Antwerp were, however, warned at the last minute and, on the morning of 18 January 1583, gave the dumbfounded French troops a thorough beating. During this 'French fury', more French soldiers died than citizens of Antwerp. Although the events discredited Orange's French policy even further, the prince still attempted a formal reconciliation with Anjou, even after the latter left the Netherlands for good in June 1583. Orange continued to hope for French intervention and in April 1583 married Louise de Coligny, daughter of Admiral de Coligny, the French Huguenot leader killed during the St Bartholomew's Day massacre. Louise was to become the mother of the future stadtholder, Frederick Henry. With confusion reigning in the States camp, the initiative passed once again to Parma, who would retain it for the coming few years: in July 1583 he captured almost all the towns along the Flemish coast, in preparation for the enclosure of the cities of Ypres, Bruges and Ghent. His successful surprise attack on Zutphen in September showed that he was planning to continue his campaign of conquest in the north, too.

The Death of the Prince of Orange

As a result of his blunder with Anjou, Orange's French policy had made him a politically isolated figure. Though some shared his belief that the revolt could prevail only with foreign assistance, the critics had the upper hand. He had even lost the long-standing support of his brother, John of Nassau. Yet nothing could change the prince's mind and he wrote resolutely to his brother that the best policy was the one his enemy feared the most. And Spain would mostly fear the increase of French influence in the Netherlands.[25] After Anjou's departure, Orange and the States of Holland again negotiated the transfer of sovereignty to the prince himself: the States wanted to promote him to count, under strict conditions, to which Orange agreed on 12 December 1583.[26] In June 1584, the negotiations were still under way, because Amsterdam and Gouda had lodged objections.[27] In the end, Orange's promotion did not go ahead, not because the prince was assassinated but because, on 10 June 1584, Anjou died. Orange and the States General consequently decided to offer sovereignty to the French king, and a delegation was immediately sent to Paris. Sovereignty over the limited area in the hands of the rebels would, of course, be less attractive to the French monarch if Orange had already been made count of Holland.[28] The French king declined the offer and the murder of the prince shortly afterwards put an end to any further discussion of his sovereignty.

Balthasar Gérard, from the Free County of Burgundy (Franche-Comté), had decided to take on what he considered the blessed task of assassinating the Prince of Orange. After careful preparation,

50 William, Prince of Orange. Above him, on the frame of the painting, his final words.

51 The simple grave of the Prince of Orange in the New Church in Delft. The States General did not commission a more fitting tomb for the prince until much later.

he succeeded in getting close to the prince and, on 10 July 1584, shot him on the stairs of his home in Delft, now known as the Prinsenhof. Wounded in the chest, the prince collapsed and is reputed to have said, 'Mon Dieu, Mon Dieu, ayez pitié de moi et de ce pauvre peuple' (My God, my God, have pity on me and this poor folk). His sister Catharina asked if he committed his spirit to Christ, to which the prince answered 'yes', and died.

The same caveat applies to the prince's last words as to all 'last words' – we have to be careful in believing that they really were the final words uttered before the victim expired. These words may have been attributed to Orange for their propaganda value. They implied that the prince's last thoughts were with his people and that he died a pious man. One portrait of the prince has a frame bearing these words, while many authors point out their resemblance to earlier writings and statements by the prince.[29] That is indeed true – his last words are almost identical in their content and meaning to the closing sentences of his *Apology*. Yet this is not in itself proof of their authenticity: after all, the court chaplains and text-writers had also played their part in writing the *Apology*. So why not now, too? One argument in favour of the authenticity of the prince's last words is that there was almost no time for them to be falsified. They are recorded in the minutes of a meeting of the States General, also in Delft, only a few hours after his murder. The possibility that the representatives present at the meeting fabricated the words themselves must be ruled out: there was so much criticism of Orange in those years that his opponents would certainly not have wanted to present the events in a more favourable light. We will never be absolutely sure what the prince said as he lay dying on the stairs in Delft. Here, too, the wish is the father to the thought, both among those who believe the words to be authentic and those who do not.[30]

Generally speaking, the phrase *pater patriae*, 'father of the fatherland', is a cliché and has been said about practically every ruler who has remained in power for any length of time. As early as 1558, when he had been king for only three years, there was a portrait of Philip II in a stained glass window in Gouda with the letters 'p.p.' – for *pater patriae* – below it. Calling the Prince of Orange the 'father of the fatherland' must first be seen within this humanist tradition. Second, it also appeals to the feelings of solidarity and belonging of the man and woman in the street. The people of North Holland would say 'Willem-Vader is gekomen' (Father William has come) when the prince went on tour around the province in 1577.[31] Finally, the name 'father of the fatherland' has been preserved in the history books, and especially in more popular accounts. But the Protestant republic that emerged under his guidance in the northern Netherlands was not the fatherland that the Prince of Orange had in mind, geographically or religiously. In geographical terms, the territory controlled by his supporters was less than half of the Netherlands as a whole. And ideologically, too, only part of his ideal had been achieved: freedom of conscience was assured, but his contemporaries had shown themselves not to be open to full religious freedom. The real fatherland comprised all the Low Countries, as left to Philip II by his father Charles V: the fatherland that Orange had served in the emperor's army and in the Council of State in Brussels.

6

An Offensive War
The North against the South: 1584–1609

The Fall of Antwerp

Belgian historian Henri Pirenne called the assassination of Orange a superfluous criminal act.[1] In his latter years, after all, the prince had proved incapable of resisting Parma's offensive campaign. On 7 April 1584, after a siege of six months, Parma captured Ypres. A month later, he surrounded Bruges. The city did not wait for the attack before capitulating. Every town and city that surrendered was offered honourable, even favourable conditions. Initially, Parma had also chosen a hard-line approach. His strategy was strongly focused on the economic base. As he did not have the money or manpower to lay siege to all the towns, he had his cavalry drive out the rural population. The towns then not only lost their supply of food but also had more hungry mouths to feed. A blockade was then usually enough to make them surrender more quickly.[2] In 1578, Parma captured the small town of Zichem, in the Oranges' domain of Diest, and had all the men killed.[3] The capture of Maastricht in June 1579 was the last time Parma allowed his men to loot and kill, and that was probably because he lay ill in bed. After that, the towns he captured were spared such atrocities. Former opponents were offered pardons, and Protestants who did not want to return to the fold of the Mother Church were given ample time – sometimes years – to sell their possessions and leave the country. It was thus a thorough religious purge but it soothed the wounds in the towns, where Catholics were still in the majority. After the capture of Dendermonde and Vilvoorde, Ghent capitulated on 17 September 1584. Apart from its 40,000 inhabitants, the city also accommodated 20,000 refugees. After that, Parma moved on to the major cities in Brabant. On 28 February 1585 he started talks with Brussels, and only ten days later the city was once more under royal rule.

52 *Alexander Farnese*, Prince, later Duke of Parma, governor-general of the Netherlands. By Otto van Veen (Otto Vaenius; *c.* 1556–1629).

53 Parma kneels before the Virgin Mary, to whom he dedicated the capture of Antwerp. Tympanum from 1869 above the entrance to Our Lady in Gaverland Chapel in Melsele, Beveren, west of Antwerp.

The masterstroke of Parma's talent as a politician and strategist was to be the capture of Antwerp. He set up his headquarters in Beveren, in the Land of Waas, on the left bank of the Scheldt, to the west of the city. There, a relief in the wall of one of the churches commemorates how he dedicated the capture of the town to the Virgin Mary. Parma's mildness in religious matters was driven purely by political motives. He showed no mercy to obstinate Protestants. In Beveren he had the preacher Johannes Florianus killed by drowning in a well.[4] As with earlier sieges, Parma had brought a select group of engineers along, whose technical interventions made his military operations possible. An ingenious pontoon bridge closed off the Scheldt to the north of Antwerp, preventing the supply of food and munitions to the besieged city. Part of the land had been flooded, but the water was by no means deep enough everywhere, and the dykes that were still above water became the scenes of bitter fighting. The most hard-fought battle was on the Kouwenstein dyke; Orange had given orders for it to be breached so that Antwerp would have an open connection with Zeeland and could not be surrounded. But the city's butchers, who let their cattle graze there, had prevented it. Once the battle on the dyke was over, after fierce fighting in which the royal troops – led by Parma himself – emerged victorious, the city's fate was sealed.

Parma's success led Queen Elizabeth of England to make a political U-turn. Since Don John had devised serious plans to depose her and

Spain also proved to have a hand in other plots against her, she did not want to see the Spanish acquire too much power in the Netherlands. She was alarmed by Parma's successful advance, and though she condescendingly rejected the offer of sovereignty over the rebellious provinces, she did send her confidant the Earl of Leicester with 8,000 troops to support the rebels. In return, she demanded a number of strategic positions as collateral: Brill in South Holland, and Flushing and Fort Rammekens on the island of Walcheren in Zeeland.[5] In Elizabeth's time, Antwerp was already seen as a pistol pointed at England's chest. It is therefore not surprising that she chose as guarantee of repayment positions from where – if it came to it – she could defend herself against an attack from Antwerp. But Zeeland continually held up the negotiations, and when the reinforcements finally arrived from England, it was too late for Antwerp.[6] The city had capitulated on 17 August 1585, after being promised on generous terms. We will never know if Zeeland deliberately held up the agreement with England to ensure that Antwerp fell into Parma's hands, giving them the opportunity to further sabotage the city's trade. In this case, the authority of a stadtholder like Orange could have been decisive and led to a more favourable outcome.

Some months after the fall of Antwerp, Parma had to abandon his siege of Bergen op Zoom because he had been unable to seal off the town's access to the adjacent waters of Zeeland. If only that had been the case at Antwerp, too! This made the shortcomings of Parma's military capabilities painfully obvious: like Alba, he had no fleet. Inland, however, he remained dominant. A year later, he laid siege to Grave, a small, fortified town on the Maas, and enclosed it as tightly as he had Antwerp by closing off its access to the river. The town capitulated on 7 June 1586.

The Union of Utrecht preserved the position of stadtholder. It was still considered necessary to have someone who stood above the wrangling within a province and who could settle conflicts between provinces. A year after the death of Orange, Johan van Oldenbarnevelt, the pensionary of Rotterdam, argued forcefully for Maurice, Orange's second son, to be appointed stadtholder of Holland and Zeeland, and on 13 November 1585, his eighteenth birthday, Maurice was duly invested. On 16 March 1586, Oldenbarnevelt himself was appointed Land's Advocate of Holland. He was then 39, very young to hold that office. Together, he and Maurice had the task of ensuring that Leicester, after being invested as governor-general, did not intervene too much with the internal affairs

An Offensive War

of the Union. In their eyes, Leicester was there purely to lead the military defence of the northern alliance.

As governor-general, Leicester was not a success, despite his best intentions.[7] His vanity and the fact he spoke no French, only Italian – at that time, no one in the Low Countries spoke English – made communication difficult, but not impossible. More problematic was that he wanted to pursue a principled Calvinist policy and chose Utrecht as his seat of government. Try explaining to someone from outside that the fight may also have been about the Protestant faith, but that policy was determined by Holland – and Holland was not willing to sacrifice too much to defend Protestantism. As a Calvinist, Leicester saw the solution to the conflict in banning trade with the enemy. But the absurd truth about trading with the enemy was that the war was financed by the revenue from that very convoy and licence money, together with many other levies. Furthermore, Leicester had made unfortunate choices when selecting his political advisers and staff. He picked a number of fanatical Flemish officials – foreigners in the eyes of the northerners – some of whom, to make things worse, had been found guilty of financial irregularities. This circle of Flemish advisers looked down on the burghers in the government of Holland. They referred to them disparagingly as 'the sovereign lords Hans Crap-pepper, Hans Pedlar, Hans Brewer, Hans Cheesemonger and Hans Miller'.[8] The man who was to succeed Leicester as commander of the English troops, Lord Willoughby, also had great contempt for the burghers. He said that it was better to be a stable boy for Queen Elizabeth than a captain in the service of a burghers' regime.[9]

Leicester then took the liberty of being absent in England for more than six months, during which time the Council of State could make no decisions. On top of that, the town of Deventer and the redoubts at Zutphen were lost in 1587 as the result of betrayal by English and Irish officers. Although Leicester brought an army with him when he returned to Flushing, on the other side of the Scheldt Parma captured the port town of Sluis, in preparation for the arrival of an Armada from Spain. This 'invincible fleet' which, according to spies for England and Holland, was in the process of being built alarmed Queen Elizabeth so much that she started wooing the Spaniards again. She had secretly given Leicester orders to persuade the rebels to make peace with Parma. Once this became known, Leicester lost all his credit among his Calvinist supporters, the only support he still had. He even tried, by means of a coup, to wrest control from Maurice and Oldenbarnevelt and to attack Amsterdam and

Leiden. When these plans failed, his position became untenable and, in December 1587, he left the country.

After so many negative experiences with French and English governors-general, the States decided that, from then on, they would govern themselves without foreign support. After the monarchs of France and England had rejected the offer of sovereignty, the States took it upon themselves. To justify that legally and politically, they had François Vranck, the pensionary of Gouda, set out their standpoint. In his *Deduction*, he argued that sovereignty had traditionally resided with the States and that, in the distant past, it had been entrusted to a count. Since that count – Philip II – had been renounced in 1581, sovereignty returned to the States. Queen Elizabeth was astounded to hear this and declared that she had never heard anything like it and didn't believe a word of it. But in the political reality of Holland and its allies, that is exactly what happened: the States claimed sovereignty for themselves and retained it until the end of the Dutch Republic in 1795. As always, theory followed practice. For the record, the States never referred to themselves as the Republic of the United Netherlands, but used the term 'United Provinces'. After Leicester's departure in 1587, the United Provinces stood on their own feet. In April 1588, the necessary reforms in domestic government were introduced. In the same month, as evidence of how self-assured the young Republic already was, the States of Holland provided Henri of Navarre with a grant of 12,000 guilders. He was the Protestant brother-in-law of Henry III of France and a forceful opponent of Catholicism.[10]

The Armada

Queen Elizabeth had not only irritated Philip II with her clandestine support for the rebels. English privateers, notably Francis Drake, had carried out successful raids on Spanish domains in America and attacked Spanish ships on the high seas. Officially, of course, the queen knew nothing of these activities. Philip believed that the best way to stop them was to mount a punitive expedition against England. He ordered a magnificent fleet to be built and equipped which would enable him – in one all-out military offensive and working together with Parma – to defeat England and then punish the rebels in the Netherlands. Ever since Alba's arrival, the Spanish governors-general were handicapped by their lack of a well-equipped and well-commanded fleet. In 1574, Philip had tried to put together a fleet to send to the Netherlands in the port towns

An Offensive War

of northern Spain – Santander in particular. A large number of ships, men and supplies had been gathered together and the admiral had been selected. But lack of money and the outbreak of the plague led to death and desertion. Nothing came of the whole venture, but the king had at least tried it before.[11] The invincible Armada was a new undertaking to turn the situation around in favour of the Spanish. No expense was spared: 130 ships set to sea, with 30,000 men aboard, two-thirds of them soldiers rather than seamen. The flower of the nation jostled for the honour of helping to do God's work – none of them expected to be rewarded with anything more than fame and honour.

Shiploads of books have been written about the spectacular history of the Armada, though mostly from a nationalist English perspective.[12] The admiral, the Duke of Medina Sidonia, had successfully organized the ships' supplies on shore, and had accepted command of the fleet reluctantly because he had no experience at sea. Yet, even with more experience he would have been no match for the English seadogs Francis Drake and Lord Howard. At the end of July 1588, completely at home in their own waters and taking advantage of the tide and the winds, the English harried the heavy Spanish galleons in the Channel with their lighter, more manoeuvrable ships. They had the additional advantage that they could reload their cannons more quickly than their Spanish counterparts. When the battered Armada ran for port and dropped anchor off Calais, English fire ships caused great panic and damage. The anchor ropes were cut through and the ships sailed northeastwards in search of refuge. There was no chance of being united with Parma's army, first because communication between the fleet and the continent was difficult and both sides were waiting in vain for news from the other, and second, because Parma's ports – Dunkirk and Sluis – were being blockaded by ships from Holland and Zeeland, commanded by Justin of

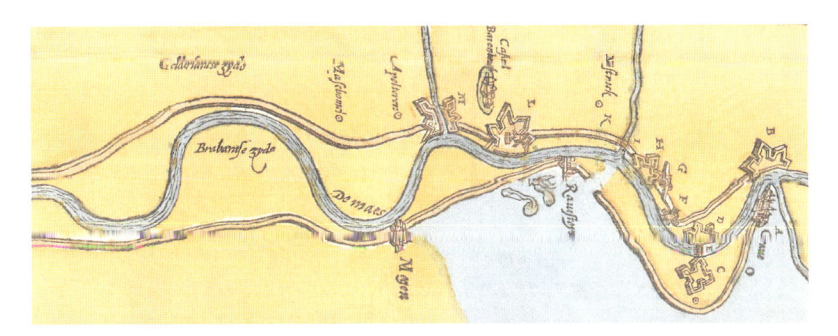

54 The capture of Grave by Parma. Note the river closed off at E.

Nassau, the only extramarital child of the Prince of Orange. Furthermore, Parma's fleet consisted mainly of transport ships, which could not take his troops to England without the cover of the Armada. That was completely out of the question. Off the coast of Gravelines, where Egmont had once been victorious for his king on land, no amount of Spanish bravery could bring them victory at sea. Dispersed by the enemy's cannon fire, the remnants of the supposedly invincible fleet beat a retreat through the North Sea, around Scotland and Ireland and back to Spain. The voyage proved as disastrous as the attacks by the enemy: heavy storms and unfamiliarity with the currents caused many a ship to founder on the Scottish or Irish coasts. By August, the prayers for the dead outnumbered those of thanks for a safe return. The Spanish – keen to blame a foreigner – pointed the finger at the Duke of Parma, accusing him of not being ready or willing to carry the troops to England.[13] A year later, when Elizabeth ordered her fleet to engage with the enemy in Spanish waters, the English ships suffered the same fate. The defeat was almost as dramatic as that of the Armada, but did not receive as much attention in historical accounts.[14]

The Crucial 'Ten Years': The 'Garden of Holland' Closed

Once again, developments abroad were to affect the situation in the Netherlands. The unpredictable French king Henri III, who had been offered sovereignty of the Low Countries, had had Catholic leaders the Duke of Guise and his brother the Cardinal of Guise murdered, on 23 and 24 (Christmas Eve!) December 1588.[15] On 1 August 1589, King Henri himself fell victim to an assassin. Philip II felt compelled to order Parma and his armies to Paris to prevent the city and country falling into the hands of the Protestant successor to the throne, Henri of Navarre. A Protestant king in France, after already having had to acknowledge a Protestant queen in England, was too much for Philip. When he became king, Philip had been compared to King Solomon, whose father David had also still been alive when he was succeeded by his son. Philip's nickname, *el Prudente*, was therefore first taken to mean 'the Wise', by analogy with Solomon, but this was later translated as 'the Prudent'. Philip was certainly very prudent in the early years of his reign. Later, however, he was determined to be the champion of the Catholic faith at any price, not only in his own domains but also in the international arena. By then, he had thrown all prudence to the wind and devoted all his military and financial resources to defending the faith.[16] Although Parma had advised the king first to defeat all the remaining rebellious provinces in the Netherlands now that he was making such good progress, thwarting the danger of a Protestant France was much more important to Philip. On the king's orders, Parma conducted two successful expeditions against France and on 19 September 1590 entered Paris. That gave the rebels above the major rivers in the Low Countries an opportunity they could not afford to ignore.

In his classic study *Tien jaren uit de Tachtigjarige Oorlog* (Ten Years from the Eighty Years War), first published in 1857, Robert Fruin gave a proud and still breathtaking account of the history of the young Republic from 1588 to 1598.[17] He strongly emphasized the independence and enterprising spirit of the still small Union. But he also stressed that, without Parma being tied up in France, such a success would never have been possible. In 1588, Maurice was stadtholder of Holland and Zeeland, and in the years that followed he also became stadtholder of Utrecht, Gelderland and Overijssel. His cousin William Louis had already been Orange's deputy as stadtholder in Friesland and had succeeded him after his death. William Louis preceded Maurice in studying classical warfare, as was customary in Europe at that time. Both continued the reorganization and professionalization of the army of the States, which Orange had initiated. Both also continually favoured an offensive war as the best form of defence. In 1589, William Louis had passionately argued at a meeting of the States General that war should be waged 'with the greatest strength and pugnacity; not, as has been the case up till now, to protect territory against the enemy, but to invade lands that the enemy has under its control'.[18] This shifts the fighting – with all the consequences that brings – to enemy soil and spares one's own.

After the decision had been taken to conduct an offensive war, the Revolt became a 'normal' war. The religious and political motives remained the same, but there was no longer a confusion of parties. On one side was the Union, or Republic, and on the other, the royalist Netherlands. From then on, the conflict became a military confrontation, all the gains and losses of which do not need to be noted individually.[19] The weaker the financial position of one side, the greater the chances of success of the other. The war continued to be primarily a series of sieges; the number of battles remained small, although relief attempts often led to hand-to-hand fighting.[20] The successes of Maurice and William Louis started with 'the surprise of Breda'. Once again, it was Orange who had first pointed

55 The siege and capture of Geertruidenberg in 1593, seen from the north, by Maurice and William Louis. Here, too, the city is shut off on the water-side by a pontoon bridge of ships roped together.

out the possibility of smuggling soldiers into the castle by concealing them in a ship.[21] Maurice approached bargeman Willem van Bergen, who delivered peat to the castle and was therefore familiar with the situation. Oldenbarnevelt designated Charles de Héraugières, a nobleman from Cambrai, as captain of the seventy soldiers who were to perform the risky task. The plan succeeded: on 4 March 1590, they overpowered the garrison and opened the outer gate to allow the prince's army to enter. Because it was the first victory achieved purely with their own forces and without any outside help, it was a great boost for the rebels and the bells rang out throughout the Republic. Héraugières was made governor of Breda by way of reward.

The conquests of the following year were spread over the whole country: in the east Zutphen, Deventer and Nijmegen, in the north Delfzijl, and in the southwest Hulst, in Flanders. In the capture of Hulst, Maurice made clever use of the major rivers. After the fall of Nijmegen, the enemy expected no new attacks because it was too late in the season, and the troops had been sent to their winter quarters. But Maurice loaded his men on ships, sailed down the rivers to Flanders and appeared unexpectedly before the gates of Hulst. The town surrendered without a shot being fired – a story that I found endlessly exciting as a schoolboy.[22]

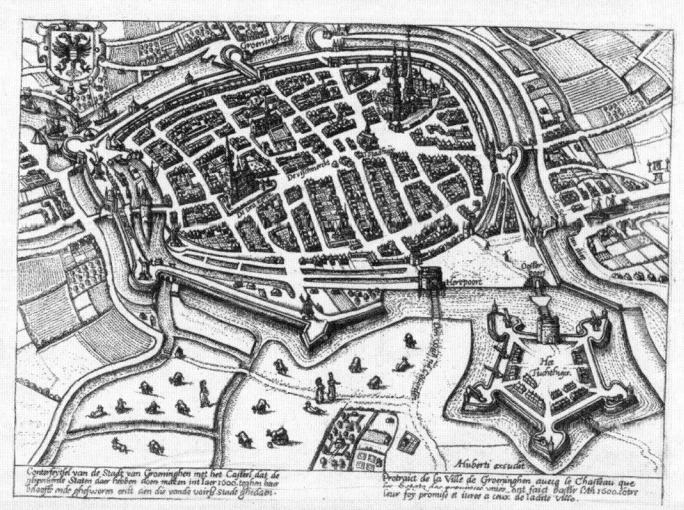

56 Rare print of Groningen, with a report in two languages stating that, since being 'liberated', the city has been worse off. Antwerp, 1600.

In the years that followed, it became clear that the stadtholders had to be careful which towns they attacked. In 1592, Zeeland was angry because the Republic forces had first captured Coevorden and Steenwijk, which the Spaniards used as bases from which to mount raids in Overijssel and Friesland,[23] and promptly withheld all its financial contributions. A year later, the exact opposite occurred: Maurice captured Geertruidenberg, angering Friesland, which wanted the prince to take Groningen first. The stadtholders and Oldenbarnevelt thus had to make sure that everyone got their turn. The stadtholders still had a score to settle with Geertruidenberg as, during the siege of 10 April 1589, the garrison had defected to Parma and had sold the town.[24] It was now payback time for the traitors. The town was not only completely closed off on the landward side, but also from the water. In addition, Maurice entrenched his troops facing away from the town to repel any relief attempt (the same method used by Alba at Mons; see p. 87). When the royalist army indeed approached the town, they saw that the prince's troops were too strongly entrenched to risk a fight. The town capitulated on 25 June 1593, but the traitors were shown no mercy. William Louis observed with satisfaction that expert policy and patience were more powerful weapons in war than brute force.[25]

The siege and capture of Groningen was the climax of the field campaign of 1594. All the captured towns were restored to their previous status in the provinces to which they had previously belonged. Under the terms of the capitulation, known as the 'Reduction', Groningen became the seventh province of the Republic. The capture of the city was the last victory for Maurice and William Louis for some time. The sieges and consolidation of the captured towns and cities throughout the whole Republic had taken too great a toll on the Republic's financial resources. Serious attempts were made to bring Brabant into the Union as a full-fledged, independent province, but they failed. As Marquis of Bergen op Zoom and Baron of Breda, Maurice was in favour of that,[26] but the States General held on resolutely to the idea that they also represented the provinces of Brabant and Flanders and that they should govern the captured territories until the provinces had been completely 'liberated'. The captured territories, known as Generality Lands, were little more than a military buffer zone for the Republic. The Catholic population generally experienced the regime of the States as oppressive.

On some occasions, the Republic's attempts to capture a town would go seriously wrong. On 2 August 1582, betrayal led to Lier, a small but

57 Lier, where the beggars were defeated after they thought that they had captured the town.

fortified town to the south of Antwerp, falling into the hands of Parma's troops. The fall of Lier was later referred to as the 'Spanish fury'. On 14 October 1595, the commander of Breda, Héraugières, led a surprise attack on the town. After successfully recapturing it, his States troops immediately started looting. The townspeople called in reinforcements from Antwerp and Mechelen and drove the enemy out, putting some 300 of them to the sword. This response, which they proudly referred to as the 'Lier fury', can be found only in detailed Dutch histories of the Netherlands.[27]

The States army achieved a spectacular victory – spectacular because it was daring and successful – at Turnhout at 1597. The cavalry – without Maurice, who arrived later with the infantry – surprised the royalist field army while it was on the march and put them to flight. English regiments played an important role in this first victory in the field since the Battle of Rijmenam nearly twenty years earlier.[28] The battle, fought in the winter season on 13 January, did not lead to a counter-offensive in Brabant.

58 The young brothers Frederick Henry (1584–1647) and Maurice (1567–1625). Above them are the arms of the Seven Provinces, topped by the red lion of the Republic, with a sword and a bundle of seven arrows.

Later that year, Maurice led a field campaign in Gelderland, mainly in the Achterhoek region of the province. For the first time, he was accompanied by his younger half-brother Frederick Henry, a youth of fourteen who was very eager. The first priority was to secure the Republic's back door. During the whole of the Eighty Years War, the small town of Rijnberk (Rheinberg) on the Rhine to the south of Wesel was a bone of contention between the royalists and the rebels. From there, it was possible to control the trade on the river and supply the troops with provisions. For that reason the town had changed hands between the Republic and the royalist Netherlands six times. Maurice then captured all towns to the north of the major rivers that were still under royal rule: Meurs and Lingen in the Holy Roman Empire, Grol and Bredevoort in Gelderland, and Enschede, Ootmarsum and Oldenzaal in Overijssel. These victories represented a milestone in the Revolt. It was described in more affectionate and symbolic terms as 'The Garden of Holland was closed.'[29]

These domestic successes began to receive appreciation abroad. Now that, under the statesmanship of Oldenbarnevelt and the military leadership of the Nassau cousins, the Republic had proved its right to exist and its resilience, the surrounding countries were willing to strengthen – and benefit – from this potential. On 31 October 1596, a Triple Alliance was agreed between England, France and the Republic. It would only survive for a few years, but most importantly, by concluding the alliance, the two other partners recognized the sovereignty of the Republic.

The internal situation in the royalist south of the Netherlands was completely different. A spent force, Parma fulfilled his duty to the end, unaware that he had fallen from grace in Spain, which showed no gratitude for his achievements. His death on 6 December 1592 was a release for both him and the king. What followed was a succession of various governors-general and no less than forty mutinies by the Spanish troops. The first to act as temporary governor-general was the already aged stadtholder of Luxembourg, the Count of Mansfeld.[30] He continued Parma's fight against the French, but only kept shop until Archduke Ernest of Austria, second son of Emperor Maximilian II, took over as a prince of royal blood. Ernest, however, died within a year, on 20 February 1595. One of the Spanish members of the Council of State, who was also commander-in-chief of the Spanish troops, the Count of Fuentes, then appeared to have received secret instructions to become deputy governor-general. This revival of Spanish influence was too much for the Duke of Aarschot, who had been an opponent of Orange but had worked together with the prince from 1576 to 1579. It was after all completely in violation of the agreements made in the Peace of Arras: government of the Netherlands by people from the Netherlands. Aarschot was so aggrieved by his minimal influence on government and felt treated with such contempt by the Spanish nobles that he left the country, embittered, and spent his remaining days in Venice. This was yet another example of how the Spaniards treated their allies. Aarschot's half-brother, Charles Philippe de Croÿ, Marquis d'Havré, had better fortune: he was appointed head of the Council of Finance and urged that peace be made with the United Provinces. This proposal was blocked by Madrid. Aarschot's son, who was to have married Orange's daughter Maria, became stadtholder of Hainaut in 1593, knight of the Golden Fleece, and succeeded his uncle as president of the Council of Finance. In 1596, those finances went completely wrong yet again, and for the third time, the king announced his bankruptcy.

New Opponents – the Archdukes

Philip II wanted to eventually preserve the Netherlands for his dynasty by giving them to his daughter Isabella Clara Eugenia as a dowry, under strict conditions. Her cousin Ernest of Austria had been the first choice for her husband, but after he died unexpectedly, that honour passed on to one of his younger brothers, Albert.[31] Albert had grown up at Philip II's court and had initially chosen a career in the Church. As cardinal-regent, he ruled Portugal on Philip's behalf. After that, he was appointed archbishop of Toledo, the richest archbishopric in Castile. He hung up his clerical robes after Philip had appointed him governor-general of the Netherlands. After he arrived there in 1596, he had two

59 The capture of Hulst by Archduke Albert of Austria in 1596.

An Offensive War

military successes. In the south, in April, he captured Calais from the French, and in August, in the north, Hulst – only a stone's throw from Antwerp – from the Republic.[32] He also distinguished himself in battle during these encounters.

In religious matters, however, he committed an enormous error in terms of public opinion, possibly sticking too closely to a literal interpretation or slavishly following the policy of his uncle, Philip II. When a Mennonite woman, Anneke van den Hove, was sentenced to death in Brussels because of her faith, Albert had the sentence actually carried out, using the normal form of execution for women: being buried alive. It caused widespread public outrage, and pamphlets and cartoons condemning the decision appeared everywhere. It was to be the last time anyone was executed in the royalist Netherlands because of their religion.

60 Archduke Albert and Archduchess Isabella, sovereigns of the royalist Netherlands.

In the final year of his life, on 6 May 1598, Philip II abdicated as ruler of the Netherlands in favour of his daughter Isabella. The terms of the transfer of power were, however, such that the Netherlands would never be free of Spain. First, Philip had not recognized the independence of the Republic, meaning that, in legal terms, Isabella inherited all of the Low Countries, including the Republic. If she or her husband died without heirs, the Netherlands would return to Spanish rule.[33] If they only had a daughter, she would have to marry the King of Spain or his son. All marriages in the ruling family would have to be approved by the king. The Spanish troops remained in the Netherlands and the Spanish king would appoint all commanders, including those of the citadels. The archdukes would practise the Catholic faith and prosecute heretics.

There were other, secret provisions that essentially meant that the policy of the archdukes was tied hand and foot to Madrid.[34] The

States General in Brussels was informed of all this on 22 August 1598. Seats had been reserved for the northern provinces, but they were – of course – not present. Philip II finally died on 13 September 1598, after a reign of 43 years, in El Escorial, his residence to the north of Madrid. Although his end was gruesome – maggots crawled out of his still-living body – his faith remained unbroken.

Philip II was succeeded by his son Philip III. He is less well known in the Low Countries because Albert and Isabella ruled over the Netherlands. Philip relied mainly on his most prominent minister, the Duke of Lerma. Together, they aimed to pursue an explicit policy of peace, known as the Pax Hispanica. As such, this tied in closely with what the archdukes had in mind. Isabella and Albert were married in Valencia on 18 April 1599, after which they went to the Netherlands. According to custom, they were invested in several cities, where they took the oath on the Joyous Entry and the provincial privileges.[35] The inhabitants of the royalist Netherlands now hoped for a return to the old days of Emperor Charles: a government led by a prince of royal blood, for the people and by the people, and in accordance with old customs. And if people of other faiths were simply forced to leave, rather than being burned at the stake or buried alive, the times of prosperity and piety would surely return. The meeting of the States General in the year 1600 was the litmus test for the new regime. Albert and Isabella found themselves caught in a serious dilemma. They were expected to rule the Netherlands as laid down in Philip II's deed of abdication, but they wanted to rule as they thought the people of the Netherlands would expect them to. The meeting – now of the royalist provinces with government officials – proved to be a repetition of standpoints, reminiscent of the rare meetings in the early years of Philip II's reign. The self-confidence of the royal States General was such that they were vocal in expressing criticism of the regime's policy. They were astounded to see the government official kneeling as he made his speech – they could not see themselves reduced to such sycophantic bowing and scraping. That was the last time the royalist provinces were called together by a ruler. The States would not be convened again until 1632, under severely deteriorated circumstances.

The Battle of Nieuwpoort

Both parts of the Netherlands found themselves facing a crucial test in June 1600. Privateers from Dunkirk, then a Flemish port, were causing

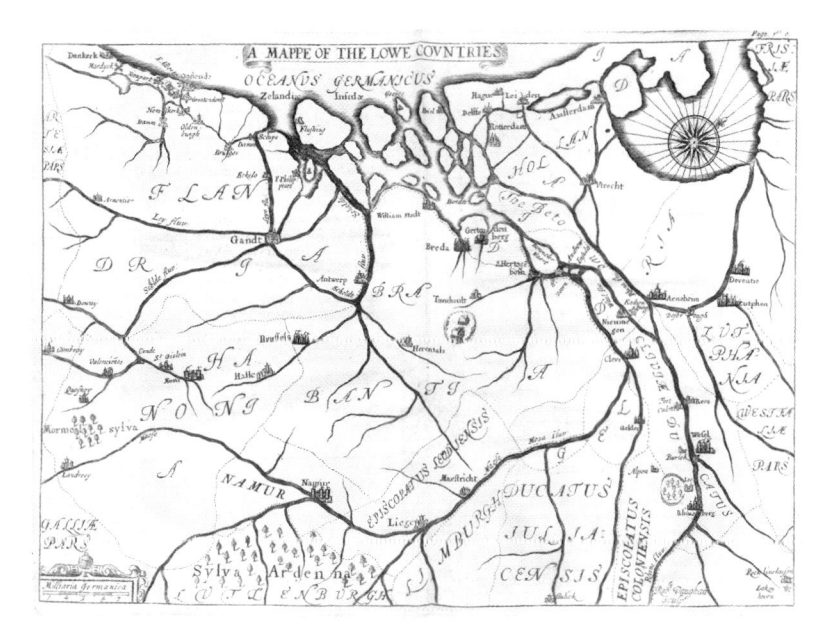

61 The territory where the war between the Republic (right) and the royalist Netherlands (left) was fought. By way of exception, the map shows the two armies at Turnhout (right of centre). From Francis Vere, *The Commentaries, being Diverse Pieces of Service, Wherein He Had Command, Written By Himself in Way of Commentary* (Cambridge, 1657).

the trading cities of Holland serious problems. Johan van Oldenbarnevelt called for Holland's trade interests to be secured by mounting a surprise attack on Dunkirk from Ostend, which was still a Republic stronghold. On paper, it was a justified proposal, but in practice, such a daring military operation so far from the home base was an extremely risky undertaking. In previous years, Maurice had been known as a leader who always used his troops sparingly. He was not averse to taking a risk, as long as it was a calculated one. That had been the case in the surprise attack on Breda, and the capture of Huy (in what was then Liège) – another surprise attack by Héraugières, the same man who had led the assault on Breda.[36] Huy was intended as a springboard into the heart of Brabant, but Héraugières only held the town for five weeks.

The intended operation against Dunkirk could, however, put the entire army of the Republic – and therefore, the Republic itself – at risk. Maurice found the whole undertaking so irresponsible that he did not want to go ahead with it, and William Louis also considered it insanity. The prince, however, continued with the attack, as he had been ordered to. William Louis stayed in Friesland, not so much because he was stubborn but, more likely, to reduce the risk. The operation was thoroughly prepared, with a large number of ships, horses and wagons, arms and provisions.[37] On 20 June, the enormous invasion fleet of thousands of troops on hundreds of ships lay off Flushing, but a headwind stopped them from setting course for Ostend. It was decided that the army would go ashore at Philippine, in the east of what is now Zeeuws-Vlaanderen (Zeelandic Flanders), and make its way to Dunkirk over land. This meant that the element of surprise was completely lost. Moreover, they had no maps to help them find their way on this unforeseen longer trek over land. Initially, the invaders from the north had hoped that the Flemish and Brabant towns would again rise up against foreign domination, as they had in 1576. Oldenbarnevelt, who was travelling with the troops, sent letters to the towns demanding they pay to be liberated or suffer the consequences. But the military and political division of the Low Countries proved also to have taken root in people's minds: the large towns and cities ignored the threat and chose the side of the regime in Brussels, because their inhabitants consciously supported the royal house and the Catholic faith. On the other hand, the Spanish army at first had no desire to fight and, once again, they had not been paid. The Republic's leaders in The Hague knew this, and it was one reason why they dared to undertake the operation. In an impassioned speech, Archduchess Isabella – who had used her jewellery as collateral to raise money – persuaded the troops to fight.

Surprised by the sudden appearance of the enemy, Maurice was forced to engage in battle on the beach and in the dunes of Nieuwpoort. There were heavy losses on both sides. The States finally won, and it was hailed as a spectacular victory – but it had been a very close-fought battle. The victory also did little to further the campaign. Maurice did lay siege to Nieuwpoort, but the townspeople flooded the surrounding countryside, defeating the troops from Holland with their own

62 One Netherlands' lion fighting the other. Cover of one of the many reports published on the siege of Ostend.

tactics. Maurice retreated from Nieuwpoort to Ostend, where the troops boarded ship and returned home. He had a meeting in Ostend with Oldenbarnevelt, who had followed the campaign from the town. Harsh words would certainly have been exchanged, but historians assume that there was no lasting schism between the two prominent leaders of the Republic. Writers and graphic artists presented the victory to those at home and abroad as a glorious triumph.[38] Anyone who doubted the prestige of the Republic was fooling themselves. Albert demanded 3,000 guilders per month from the States of his provinces, but they wanted peace negotiations with the Republic.

The encounter at Nieuwpoort made it clear to Albert that Ostend was an intolerable enclave on the Flemish coast, a thorn in the claw of the Flemish lion. He laid siege to the town, but, as the Republic was able to bring in supplies by sea, the battle was to last for many years. The title page on one of the books on the battle for Ostend shows two lions fighting, representing one part of the Netherlands fighting the other. Maurice twice tried to lure the enemy away from Ostend by laying siege to 's-Hertogenbosch. In 1601, he failed because the early onset of winter raised the possibility of an attack in Holland across the frozen rivers. In 1603, high water prevented Maurice from sealing off the city completely from the outside world, enabling Albert to send a couple of thousand reinforcements to strengthen the garrison.[39] A year later, Maurice tried the same tactics again: taking advantage of the enemy still laying siege to Ostend, he launched an attack deep in the heart of Brabant, penetrating as far as Tienen but not really making any gains of lasting importance. On his way back northwards he laid siege to Grave, which resisted for two months but surrendered on 19 September 1602.[40] Many English troops died there because of the boggy conditions in the trenches. Queen Elizabeth would have preferred to see him mount a diversionary manoeuvre at Ostend. The increasing criticism of Maurice, at home too, meant that he dared undertake sieges but not engage in open battle.[41]

The battle for Ostend took an unexpected turn with the arrival of a war volunteer, the enormously wealthy Marquis Ambrogio Spinola. Spinola was a banker from Genoa with no military experience, but he provided the funds for the campaign and soon displayed a fine command of the art of warfare. On 28 September 1603, Albert wrote to King Philip III that he had put Spinola in command of the siege of Ostend. By applying constant pressure, the new commander increasingly sealed the town off from the outside world. Aiming to compensate for the imminent loss of one port in Flanders by capturing another one, Maurice laid siege to the town of Sluis.[42] Spinola had the courage to send his troops to Sluis without delay in an attempt to end the siege. On 17 August 1604, there was a severe test of strength between the two armies, which ended when Spinola withdrew. The following day, Sluis surrendered to the Republic forces. But Spinola did not let Ostend off the hook, and, after an epic conflict that eventually lasted three years, the town was finally forced to its knees on 20 September 1604.[43] After having shown his talent for warfare, Spinola turned his attention to politics, travelling from Italy to the Spanish court to make his views clear to the king in person. That was something the king was not used to. Spinola demanded command of the troops in the royalist Netherlands, otherwise he would leave – and take his money with him. The crown had little choice, and Philip III appointed him not only commander of the troops but also put him in control of financial affairs in Brussels. He was instructed to return to the court every year for consultations when the winter season caused a temporary suspension of hostilities in the Low Countries.[44]

With Ostend safely in Spanish hands, Spinola had his hands free to devote himself to other plans. In Spain, he had proposed invading the eastern part of the Republic, via the Holy Roman Empire.[45] He moved his armies east and entered Overijssel from the Empire, capturing the border town of Oldenzaal and thus creating a breach in the

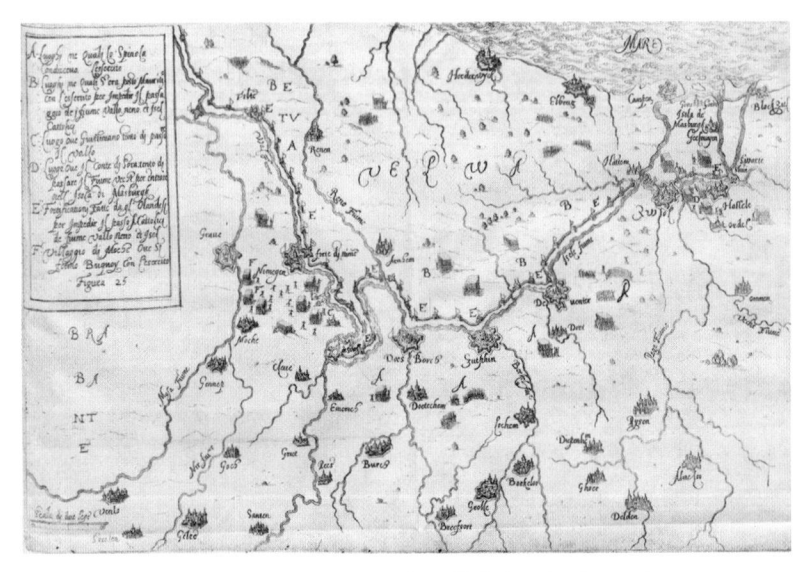

63 Just like China, the Republic had its own Great Wall, though of somewhat more moderate proportions. From Pompeo Giustiniano, *Delle guerre di Fiandra* (Antwerp, 1609).

Garden of Holland. For safety's sake, Maurice strengthened the defences at Coevorden, also on the border.[46] A year later, Spinola's ambitions had grown even larger. He wanted to march with his main army through the Achterhoek region of Gelderland and cross the River IJssel to strike at the heart of the Republic. The water in the river was now at a low level, enabling it to be waded in several places. To enable them to use the IJssel as a line of defence, the Republic had built a series of wooden forts on the western side of the river, at regular distances from each other and linked by an earthwork dyke. The line ran from the Zuiderzee to Nijmegen and then from Nijmegen along the north bank of the River Waal to the town of Tiel. Maurice had posted an army of 15,000 men along this dyke. Spinola succeeded in capturing the towns of Groenlo and Lochem, but the IJssel Line remained intact. Although his main attack failed, the towns captured by Spinola in Gelderland and Overijssel remained under the rule of the archduke for twenty years, and therefore under the Catholic restoration (see Chapter Seven). Consequently, they became Catholic enclaves in Protestant surroundings.[47]

From Sea Beggar to Global Power

As the army was gradually formed over two decades from regular and irregular troops, the same happened to the navy. The most prominent province, Holland, had experience with naval warfare from its Burgundy-Habsburg past. Holland refused to accept the authority of the commander-in-chief of the Burgundy-Habsburg fleet (known as the Admiral of the Sea) unless the position was held by the stadtholder of Holland and Zeeland. The two provinces could then be sure that their interests would be solidly embedded in those of the wider whole. Then all sails would billow in the same direction.[48] Since 1559, that stadtholder had been the Prince of Orange, who had taken advantage of the position to gain experience in naval matters. As we have already seen, he rescinded the letters of marque and 'commissions to wage war' that he had issued as the Prince of Orange once he returned to his position as stadtholder of Holland. When his son Maurice succeeded him as stadtholder in Holland, he also became Admiral-General of the Union. This was the moment at which the States' fleet was born. Both Orange and Maurice had to intervene when internal conflicts occurred, which happened relatively often, especially between Holland and Zeeland. At sea, as on land, there were conflicting interests.[49] The decentralized organization of the navy in the Republic into five admiralties had in practice more advantages than disadvantages. Collecting the convoy and licence money – the levy on trade with the enemy – centrally would never have raised as much as it did when organized separately by the five admiralties. The provision that, if an admiralty had any money left over, it had to be paid to the central government remained a dead letter. Creative bookkeeping enabled each admiralty to ensure that it did not end up with a positive balance.[50]

In 1587, the navy of the royalist Netherlands also took shape when its only admiralty was established in Dunkirk. In reality, the situation was simpler there, because there were fewer port towns and competition was thus less fierce. No matter how severe the fighting would become at sea, the ships from Dunkirk had it in some ways a lot easier than their counterparts in the Republic, as they 'only' had to restrict themselves to privateering and not focus on specific military targets. Their only aim was to accumulate loot, which they did with great success.

The 'Ten Years' would be as successful at sea as on land, until the Republic reached the limits of its potential in that arena, too. We have already mentioned the victories on the Zuiderzee (11 October 1573) and in the waters of Zeeland (27 January 1574). When, after their victory at the Battle of Mookerheyde (14 April 1574), the mutinous Spanish soldiers also went on the rampage in Antwerp, Requesens ordered his royal fleet – still under construction – to sail up the Scheldt to prevent it from falling into the hands of the mutineers. The Zeelanders, always on the alert for an opportunity to gain an advantage, immediately sent out a force to destroy this squadron. Any initiative to try and build a fleet in the inner harbour at Antwerp had to take place under the noses of the Zealanders and was therefore doomed to failure. It was thus not surprising when the government in Brussels transferred these activities to Dunkirk.

Just as the Republic's army had taken the fight to enemy territory, the fleet also found attack the best form of defence. They went after the enemy ships on the Spanish coast, at first together with the English. Their first major success was the attack on Cádiz, where a new Armada was reputably being built. The joint English–Holland fleet did not restrict itself to destroying the enemy ships (on 21 June 1596) but also captured the city the following day. The victorious crews ran rampant until they left again on 5 July.[51] Three years later, the joint admiralties of the Republic dared to send an independent expedition to Spain – that is, without the English. The large fleet of 73 ships, under the leadership of Admiral Pieter van der Does, had been given an overly ambitious mission: to destroy the Spanish war fleet, capture the silver fleet, cause damage to the towns and cities along the coast and, if possible, lay siege to the Canary Islands and the island of São Tomé. The confrontation with the Spanish war and silver fleets never materialized. That made the sacking of São Tomé and the Canary Islands even more ebullient than usual; a museum in the Canary Islands keeps the bad memories of Van der Does alive.[52] After the death of Queen Elizabeth in 1603, not only now had the Republic to rely on its own resources, but the English were equally happy to support the Spanish. Under their then neutral English flag, they transported Spanish soldiers to the royalist Netherlands.[53] The last major operation by the Republic's fleet before the signing of the Twelve Years Truce was the Battle of Gibraltar in 1607, under the command of Jacob van Heemskerck. It was as if forty years of pent-up hatred burst forth in one afternoon. Because the Spanish ships were larger than those of the Republic, each one was hemmed in by two Republic ships and boarded, in the old-fashioned way. Most of the Spanish ships were lost, and not one of those of the Republic. Four thousand Spaniards perished, and only 100 on the side of the Republic, though Van Heemskerck was among them. He was the first commander to be given a state funeral and a modest, state-sponsored memorial stone.[54]

Besides the war fleet, the trading fleet also spread its wings. After the first successful voyage to the Indies, there was fierce competition between the newly established trading companies, all of which had the same goal: to earn as much money as possible from trade in colonial goods. The competition caused prices to fall dramatically. Here, too, the organizing hand of Oldenbarnevelt was indispensable. Through his efforts, the companies all joined forces in 1602 to form the Dutch East India Company (VOC), the world's first joint stock company. In imitation of the tried and tested formula of the state and the admiralties, the VOC had a decentralized form of governance, with 'Chambers' in the various trading centres where it had set up companies: Amsterdam, Rotterdam, Middelburg, Hoorn and Enkhuizen. The world, it seemed, was within the Republic's reach.

64 Adriaen van de Venne, *Fishing for Souls*, 1614, showing the leaders of the Low Countries, each on their own bank of the river but joined by the rainbow. On the left is the Republic, with Maurice and William Louis and the preachers; on the right, the archdukes with the Catholic clergy.

7

The Twelve Years Truce
*Division in the North,
Recovery in the South: 1609–1621*

First a Ceasefire

The history of the Twelve Years Truce shows how sensitive Spain was about even a treaty with the rebellious provinces.[1] Simply entering into official negotiations could be seen as a loss of face, of honour – of *reputación*, as the Spaniards themselves called it. It would be an admission that the conflict could not be solved by political or military means. No matter how well the Republic seemed to be doing, the war was costing them enormous amounts of money, too. Since 1605, it had been receiving financial support from the Palatinate and Brandenburg, two new Calvinist allies in the Holy Roman Empire, but continuing the war on the same footing would be disastrous. In both the Republic and in Spain and the royalist Netherlands, there was increasing awareness that the war could not go on for ever. In Spain, however, there was no desire for peace as such. The king and his advisers hoped that, if they agreed to a peace treaty or a truce, the people of the Republic would return to their trade and commerce, giving Spain the opportunity to rebuild its military power. It could then renew its offensive with renewed strength.[2] But many in the Republic – with Prince Maurice, Oldenbarnevelt and the preachers at the forefront – were prepared for this very eventuality.[3]

The proposals for negotiations had a long history. The first steps had been taken some ten years earlier, with the deliberate, though cautious, peace policy of the archdukes. Immediately after he took office in 1598, Archduke Albert had sounded out the willingness of Queen Elizabeth to enter into peace negotiations.[4] When he started actual talks with the English, on neutral French territory in Boulogne, he could not do that solely on his own authority. The Spanish king specified a number of quite arrogant conditions, including allowing Catholics to practise their faith publicly in England, and the return to Spain of all the places that Elizabeth held in the Republic as collateral (Brill, Flushing and Fort Rammekens). The English found these demands outrageous and peace was never concluded between the two crowns during Elizabeth's lifetime. That did not happen until 1604, one year after her death, after which the Republic seemed to be abandoned to its own fate. It was therefore not surprising that Oldenbarnevelt turned his sights to the east – he could well use the support of the Palatinate and Brandenburg.

After forty years of fighting, the Spanish still had no real name for the rebels and the rebellious provinces, other than *rebeldes* (rebels) and *herejes* (heretics). The Spanish word *Flamencos* (Flemings) may initially have referred to all the inhabitants of the Low Countries, but as the Revolt progressed it came to be used more specifically for the people of those provinces loyal to the crown, while *Holanda* and *holandeses* were used for the Republic and its people.[5] One advisory report for King Philip III stated that Spain was involved in three wars: against the French, the English and the rebels.[6] Because of the many islands in Zeeland and South Holland, and the many inland seas and lakes in Holland itself, Spanish sources often use the term *las Islas*, the islands, to refer to the Republic.[7]

As a neutral between the warring parties, King Henri IV of France saw an opportunity to benefit from the conflict. He remembered that the rebellious provinces had offered sovereignty to the Duke of Anjou and to his predecessor, Henri III. Both had declined, fearing war with Spain. But Henri did not share that fear. He invited the provinces to transfer sovereignty to him, which he would then voluntarily delegate to Prince Maurice. Maurice liked the idea, but Oldenbarnevelt was more cautious. It was one thing to let the French in, but another to get them out again.[8] Henri then wanted to know how the Republic intended to pursue the war and with what resources. That was actually an opening move in a game in which the two great monarchies of France and England, watched closely by the three smaller monarchies of Denmark, Brandenburg and the Palatinate, took the Republic by the hand to bring the talks with Spain to a successful conclusion. The Republic may have achieved much in political, military and economic terms, but how would it fare further without external support, especially from England and France? This is clearly shown by the illustration of the ambassadors of France and England between the negotiating parties. It starts with the Spanish representatives at the top left, then come the ambassadors, followed by the representatives of the Republic.

65 The participants in the negotiations between the royalist Netherlands (top row) and the Republic (bottom row). In between are the French and English intermediaries.

There had been calls for negotiations in both the north and the south of the Netherlands since as early as the turn of the century. In 1606, a number of individuals from the two regions, nobles and merchants, had explored the options for reaching agreement. That paved the way for Franciscan priest Jan Neyen, the head of his order, to go from Brussels to The Hague. He was received in the deepest secrecy in the Binnenhof, the seat of government, where he spoke with Maurice and Oldenbarnevelt on behalf of the archdukes.⁹ The archdukes also sent their most trusted right hand man, commander-in-chief Ambrogio Spinola, to Madrid. The results of these consultations were so encouraging that a ceasefire was agreed. That enabled an official truce to be prepared, which had to respect the Republic's wish that the seven provinces be recognized as free, independent states. The word 'sovereignty' was a little too much for the south to swallow, but when Father Neyen proposed the archdukes leave the seven provinces *liber ende vrij* (liberated and free), that was acceptable to the Republic. On 12 April 1607, they agreed to a ceasefire as of 4 May. Oldenbarnevelt demanded that the king, as well as the archdukes, should approve the truce. Philip did not agree until 25 October, after Spinola had exerted pressure on him by demanding 300,000 ducats a month to meet his military commitments. The crown simply did not have that kind of money. Furthermore, in 1605, the news that the Hollanders had driven the Portuguese out of Amboyna and taken control of the Moluccas had made a deep impression in Madrid.[10] The king and his ministers were inclined to reach a truce in the hope that regaining access to the Iberian markets would stop the Republic from going to the colonies itself. And, to clear his conscience once again, the king had – in violation of the agreement reached so far – made an extra demand: that the Catholics in the Republic would be granted freedom to practise their religion. Maurice and Oldenbarnevelt had no intention of consenting to this. They considered religion a matter that fell under the sovereignty of the state, and since the sovereignty of the Republic was to be recognized, in their view, a future decision on religious freedom would depend on that.[11] It was a smart piece of negotiation, but practical reality forced the parties to reach agreement. On 10 January 1608, Philip III was shrewd enough to authorize Albert and Isabella to negotiate a peace treaty or truce in his name.

A European Conference

The negotiations became a genuine European conference, opening on 1 February 1608 in the Binnenhof in The Hague. Delegates from the north and the south sat opposite each other at a long table. The north was led by Oldenbarnevelt, the south by Spinola. In the same room, but at a separate table, sat representatives of the king of France (his ambassador Pierre Jeannin), the kings of England and Denmark, and nine German states as observers or advisers. If the differences of opinion became too heated, these advisers could take the negotiators to one side and consult with them separately. Each party hoped of course to steer the talks in their own direction. All the foreign delegations had one thing in common: they found it highly unusual that what was under discussion here was the independence of a republic. And not even one with a single head of state, like Venice, but a union of seven small republics. What might that mean for the future of their own countries?

One serious point of contention was the freedom to sail to the Indies, the colonies. The Spanish king wanted to keep this a monopoly for the Spanish and Portuguese, between whom the pope had once divided the world.[12] So as not to sabotage the talks immediately, agreement on the issue was postponed until after the peace treaty had been concluded. Another point of dispute was the Spanish king's demand that Catholics in the Republic could enjoy freedom to practise their religion,[13] which the Reformed governing elite in the Republic opposed. Although the largest part of the Catholic population in the Republic had shown itself to be in opposition to the Spanish regime, if full religious freedom were granted, other Catholic followers might return their loyalty to Spain and thus become a security threat to the States. Like other non-Calvinists – including Mennonites and Lutherans – the Catholics already enjoyed freedom of conscience. But, as mentioned above, the Republic considered this as falling under the sovereignty of the country. The government was the highest authority and was responsible for arranging religious matters as it saw fit. In the context of this issue, Oldenbarnevelt saw independence and sovereignty as the same concept. But others saw them as two separate things. King Henri IV thought the Republic deserved independence, but wanted to be its sovereign. He suggested that, if the war continued, he would provide more support, and less in the case of peace.[14] Because of this insistent friend, Oldenbarnevelt had to play a subtle game, and Father Neyen went to Spain again to discuss the situation with the Spanish king. In the meantime, Oldenbarnevelt took advantage of the presence of the delegations in The Hague to conclude a defensive alliance with England on 6 July 1608, as he had done in January of that year with France.[15] Philip, however, stuck to his demand for religious freedom for Catholics, and on 22 August the States delegation broke off the talks.

Now it became clear how favourable it was that the negotiations involved several parties rather than just two. Pierre Jeannin, an experienced diplomat, conducted consultations with his foreign colleagues and, on 27 August, instead of a peace agreement, proposed a ceasefire lasting twelve years. The terms were less contentious and the scruples on the royal side could be cast aside. The French diplomat avoided using terms like sovereignty and religious freedom, so that no one could take offence. The negotiations were held with the Seven Provinces, 'as with independent states over which neither the Spanish king nor the archdukes would have any claim'.[16] Jeannin added the threat that, if Spain rejected the terms, the war would resume – as of 1 March 1609 – and the Republic would receive support from the rulers represented by all the delegates present.

This new, unforeseen proposal (a truce rather than a peace agreement) first had to be discussed with the home front, so many returned to their countries. On 11 January 1609, the States General of the Republic approved Jeannin's proposals: the provinces were to be recognized as free, religion would fall under their sovereignty and shipping to the Indies would be free.[17] To persuade the Spanish king, Archduke Albert sent his confessor – a tried and tested method if there were moral objections in play. On 25 January 1609, the king also granted his approval, which was announced in Brussels on 8 February. The details could now be thrashed out, which once again caused a lot of commotion, such as determining an appropriate title for the States General in The Hague. And that had to be approved by the regime in Brussels, which did not even want to call together its own States General. It was decided that they were to be called Their High Mightinesses of the States General, or simply Their High Mightinesses.[18]

All the negotiating parties met again on 10 February in Antwerp to resume the talks. On 9 March, the States General of the Republic, the Council of State and the States of Holland moved temporarily from The Hague to the Markiezenhof in Bergen op Zoom so that they could be contacted directly to discuss any issues that came up. It was clear that history was about to be written. The mediating ambassadors, and Jeannin in particular, had prepared the agenda thoroughly. They all agreed on the main points on 9 April, after which they could sign the truce. The mediators signed first, followed in the left column by the representatives of the archdukes and in the right column by those of the Republic. The latter signed not only on behalf of their own provinces, but also of the whole States General of the Republic. The delegations then went to Brussels and Bergen op Zoom to consult with their superiors one more time. On 14 April, all the final details had been ironed out and the texts ratified. Finally, the text of the Twelve Years Truce was officially displayed in front of the town hall in Antwerp.[19] The Spanish king was given three months to ratify the Truce, and although he put it off until the last minute (7 July), he had no choice but to do so, because of financial problems. He was convinced that he would have the Republic back under his own control after the twelve years had passed.

Recognition at Last

The first article of the Truce was a triumph for the Republic: the archdukes pledged, also in the name of the Spanish king, that they would treat the United Provinces as free regions, provinces and states, to which they had no claim.[20] That was followed by the practical details: the Truce would last twelve years and be valid worldwide. It guaranteed the free movement of persons and goods and banned the seizure of goods as an economic and political measure. There was not a word about the position of Catholics in the Republic, the VOC or the River Scheldt, which remained closed off. In effect, the archdukes and the king had to accept the military, religious and economic status quo.

This recognition of the Republic by the Spanish king resulted in considerable loss of face for the Spanish crown. Other European states were not the only ones to recognize the Republic from 1609; countries in North Africa and the Near East did the same. In addition to the ambassadors from England and France, who had been there for many years, other overseas representatives now also came to The Hague, while the Republic sent its own ambassadors elsewhere. It initiated, for example, diplomatic relations in Morocco while, in 1614, Cornelis Haga became the Republic's ambassador in Istanbul. At the same time, however, the people of the Republic itself did not celebrate the Truce with great festivities. There were official celebrations, but because the recognition of the Republic 'simply' confirmed the situation as it had been for many years in practice, there was no dancing in the streets. In the final negotiations on pros and cons, Oldenbarnevelt had proved the smartest. The only small change that the Land's Advocate had been forced to surrender was abandoning the proposal to set up a West India Company (WIC), as counterpart to the Dutch East India Company. The WIC would not be established until 1621, when hostilities resumed.[21]

The Truce could have been jeopardized in 1609, when the Duke of Jülich-Cleves-Berg died. Two German princes, both Lutherans, contested the inheritance; one converted to Catholicism and the other to Calvinism, both to assure themselves of the support of one of the two great power blocs.[22] The Republic could not remain neutral in this dispute just across its eastern border and came to the aid of the Protestant candidate, while Spinola did the same for the Catholic rival. But the Republic had to be very cautious in its military interventions, as it could not permit its participation in the conflict to endanger the Truce. Although Maurice was less concerned about this than Oldenbarnevelt, between 1609 and 1614 they acted in unison on the Jülich-Cleves crisis. One advantage of military intervention was that at least part of the army was not only retained, but also remained in action. Moreover, between 1611 and 1615, the Republic mediated in East Friesland, where Duke Enno and the town of Emden were continually at each other's throats. After Denmark, under King Christian IV, raised the toll in the Øresund strait, the Republic agreed a defensive alliance with Sweden in April 1614 and with the Hanseatic League in June 1616. Although no one as yet claimed that 'the keys to the Øresund lay in Amsterdam', the Republic had steeled itself in the fight against Spain and that experience was now paying off in the period of the Truce.[23]

In 1610, the Republic was alarmed by the assassination of French king Henri IV, who had permitted Protestants a limited degree of religious freedom in his kingdom. On the other hand, his overly persistent friendship had been something of a hindrance to the Republic, and Oldenbarnevelt most probably did not see his death purely as a loss. The new king, Louis XIII, was a minor and his mother acted as regent. Consequently, there was – at least for the time being – little hope or fear of France playing an active part in European politics. That did, of course, mean that the balance of power in Europe shifted once more in favour of Spain.[24]

Recovery of Mind and Body

The Truce brought bitterly needed respite to both the Republic and the royalist Netherlands. The Leo Belgicus, the map of the Netherlands depicted in the form of a lion, was shown in these years not as rampant or passant, but as 'sejant' (sitting). Whole generations of historians have delighted – and continue to do so – in the glorious series of victories by Parma and Spinola on the one hand, and Maurice, William Louis and Frederick Henry on the other, as though the map of the Low Countries were a board game with flags in jolly colours and with little thought for all the bloodshed. In recent decades, however, there has been greater attention to the other side of the coin, the suffering in the countryside. Farmers and artisans in war zones were bled dry and humiliated, tortured and killed. New studies on Flanders, West Brabant, the 'Meijerij van 's-Hertogenbosch' region of Brabant and the farmers' refuges in both parts of Limburg devote considerable attention to the fate of the rural

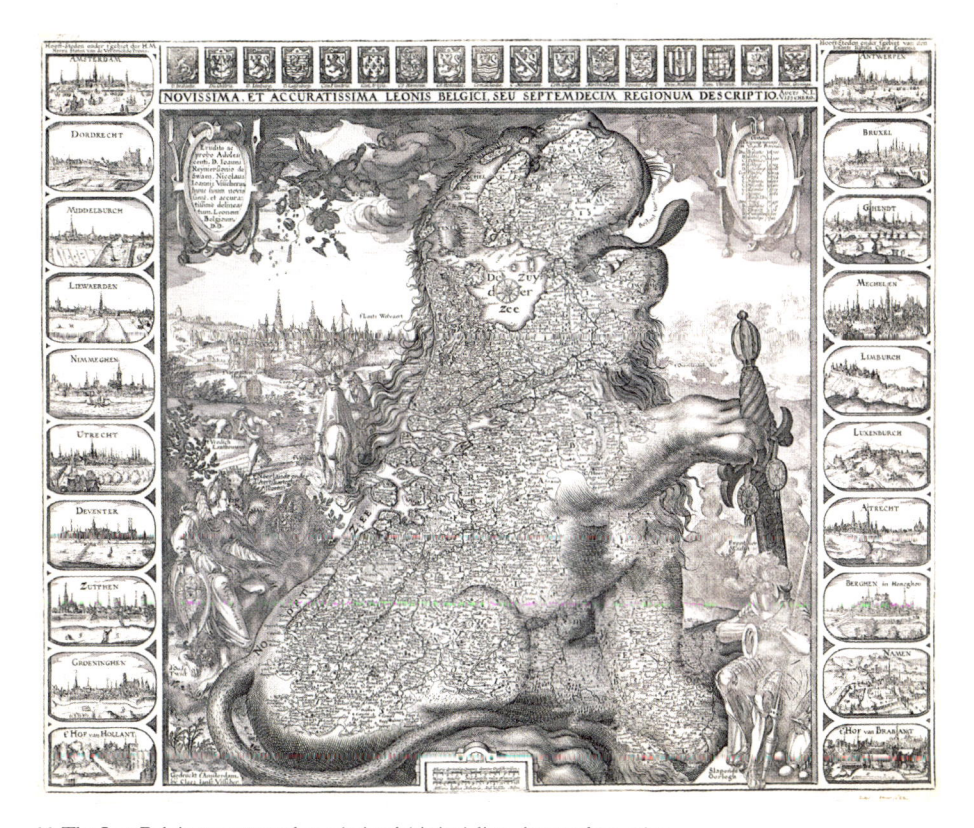

66 The Leo Belgicus portrayed as a 'sejant' (sitting) lion. Amsterdam, 1622.

population, who usually fell victim to both parties.[25] The Truce at least put a stop to all this misery for twelve years.

Under the Truce, the Iberian kingdoms were once again open to trading ships from Holland, and the Hollanders duly resumed their role as the cargo carriers of Europe. Their cheap ships were up to the task of carrying export goods, such as Spanish wool, to the north in bulk. They transported grain from the Baltic to Spain and Portugal and returned with gold and silver. Within a short time, they were once again indispensable in carrying semi-tropical fruits and salt from the Spanish coast to the Italian territories and back. Via the ports of Dunkirk and Ostend, trade once again flourished in Flanders and Brabant. It remained a bitter pill for Antwerp that, without direct access to the sea, it could not regain its leading position. In 1612 and 1613, the city sought dialogue with the province of Zeeland, arguing that a revival of Antwerp's trade would also be in the interest of the towns in the province. Flushing responded positively, but the powerful Middelburg obstructed all efforts at negotiation. Zeeland had received a pledge from Oldenbarnevelt and the other provinces that the Scheldt would remain closed in exchange for its support for the Truce.[26]

The response from industry was mixed. As a result of the increasing trade, many goods flows took a different route. Cheap textiles from the royalist Netherlands were a strong competitor for Spain's domestic producers and for those of the Republic. While economic activity expanded in the trade-dependent ports, it declined in inland industrial towns like Leiden, Delft, Haarlem and Utrecht. Agriculture and horticulture had almost come to a halt in the border areas affected by the war, but where that was not the case, they became a testing ground for countless new innovations. In both the Republic and the royalist Netherlands, the agricultural sector was characterized by crop diversity and high yields; there was even something of an agricultural revolution. High yields could have led to lower prices, but that did not happen as, throughout Europe, there was a great demand for grain, especially from the Baltic.[27] Because the Republic imported sufficient grain for its own use, it could focus on horticulture and cattle farming. That led to much land being reclaimed, especially the large inland seas in the province of Holland, to raise production. One of these lakes, the Beemster, drained in 1612, is now a UNESCO World Heritage site. But, in both north and south, it would take many years for a wide range of economic activities to return to their pre-Revolt level. One disadvantage was that, in both regions, the level of taxation remained high, partly as a result of the heavy burden of debt. And, because the war had only been temporarily suspended, military budgets remained substantial, despite being reduced by half.

Parallel with the recovery of prosperity, there was a restoration of pastoral care, among both Catholics and Protestants. For what is a man profited, if he shall gain the whole world, and lose his own soul? In both the north and the south, the widespread complaint was that the vineyard of the Lord may have been great, but that it had too few workers. In many places on both sides of the border, the work of the Lord had to be rebuilt from the ground up. When we imagine the Counter-Reformation in the south, we mainly think of the Church triumphant everywhere, of Rubens, of the Saint Carolus Borromeus church in Antwerp and of the pilgrimage site of Scherpenheuvel (Montaigu).[28] But that was only the end result of a long road that the Church still had to follow in the early years of the seventeenth century, and in the south, too, pastoral care had to be rebuilt from scratch. That was no better expressed than in the life of Matthias Hovius, archbishop of Mechelen from 1595 to 1620.[29] A greater contrast to Cardinal Granvelle, the Renaissance church leader who preferred foreign policy and staying at court to spending time in his diocese, is unthinkable. Hovius was concerned with saving souls. He was of simple origins, which was the reason why Philip II was initially reluctant to appoint him: he would rather have seen the position filled by someone of noble blood. But Hovius was the right man in the right place at the right time. With his tough resolve and patient persistence, he gave form and content to religious life in the royalist Netherlands. That included training new priests and supervising those in office and monastic orders; having baptized children registered and educating the young; providing an economic foundation for monasteries, convents and parish churches; ensuring the return to the Church of lapsed believers, lost either through indifference or the attraction of Protestantism; and binding believers not only by getting them to attend church and by organizing brotherhoods, but also by emphasizing important Catholic dogmas and the festivals associated with them, such as Corpus Christi.

While Hovius, as head of the ecclesiastical province of Mechelen, gave religious life structure and direction, Albert and Isabella did the same as leaders of the secular government. They attended many religious practices and personally led processions and pilgrimages. Old places of pilgrimage were reinstated and joined by other, newer ones. They donated religious works of art to churches, monasteries and convents and also took responsibility for the country's religious heritage.[30] Albert, for example, approved a proposal to transfer the remains of martyrs and saints kept in the Republic to the royalist Netherlands, where they would be given the respect they deserved. That included the martyrs of Gorinchem who had been buried just outside Brill after their deaths. In 1615, the bones of the monks were dug up in the deepest secrecy and transferred to Brussels, where they are displayed in a reliquary in the Church of St Nicholas.[31] Leading by example in this way, the archdukes contributed to the recovery of the Catholic Church – and thus to feelings of solidarity – within the royalist Netherlands.

At the time of the Twelve Years Truce, a third of the population of the Republic was Catholic, as were the vast majority of people in the Generality Lands. For Catholics, the Truce meant that they were free to cross the border and visit places of pilgrimage in the royalist Netherlands or in the Holy Roman Empire. The sacrament of confirmation could only be administered by a bishop, and many children in the Republic who had never been able to receive it could now travel to the south to do so. The Revolt and the Reformation had ended the hierarchy of the bishops in the Republic. Pastoral care was now organized by the Holland Mission, which provided the towns and villages with clergy. In parts of the Republic where public practice of the Catholic faith remained forbidden, Catholic believers would look for opportunities to attend Mass in barns or private houses. These clandestine churches did not, of course, go unnoticed, but were tolerated, though often in return for payment of bribes. In Holland in particular, many priests' libraries have been preserved: collections of books from the sixteenth to the eighteenth centuries passed on from priest to priest to educate themselves in theology and for their private piety.[32] Catholic women in the Republic who wanted to devote themselves to their religious community could no longer choose to enter a convent. However, where the community was large enough, they formed communes under the leadership of a house-mother, where they could practise their belief together and support social care for the less fortunate, the sick and the elderly.[33]

Division in the Reformed Church

During the Twelve Years Truce, a third of the population of the Republic was Reformed, the same proportion as were Catholic. In the Reformed church, however, a distinction was gradually made between members and 'devotees'. Those who considered themselves Reformed were usually baptized in the church. The number of people who also underwent confirmation once they reached the age of discretion was already declining. Full members – those who had undergone confirmation – took part in the Lord's Supper if they were found to be sufficiently pious in the faith and in their deeds. Devotees came to church only to attend services and did not wish to subject themselves to the obligations that official membership entailed, including the discipline of the Church. It is perhaps comparable to political parties today, where some people are members while others only vote for them in elections. There were, of course, disagreements among the members. It was, after all, a young church still in the process of formation. A large number of the rules about what the Church's teachings exactly were, what the Church could do and its relationship with the state had not as yet been put down on paper. That all still had to take shape – and was not achieved without conflict.

One significant dispute occurred during the period of the Truce. It started as a difference of opinion on one of the most controversial issues of the time: what exactly happens after death, and do we, as people, have any influence on that?[34] The dispute was mainly between two professors of theology at Leiden University. Franciscus Gomarus took the strict view that God's power was so great that mere humans could have no influence at all on whether we are chosen or not.[35] The Almighty decided from the very beginning who was to be elected and who not. Jacobus Arminius did not wish to call God's omnipotence into doubt, but believed that as humans we could decide voluntarily to reject God's grace.[36] Gomarus felt that Arminius was calling God's omnipotence into question and accused him of moving towards Catholicism. Catholics believe that they can secure their salvation by doing good works. Arminius insisted that he did not want to go that far, only to acknowledge the possibility that man could influence his own destiny. In 1604, they held a religious debate lasting ten days, which of course turned into a full-scale and long-lasting dispute. It demanded far too much of Arminius's nerves and constitution and, already suffering from tuberculosis, he died in 1609. But the affair had made its way to the pulpit: those who followed Gomarus in adopting a strict interpretation of the scriptures were in the majority, while the moderates – far fewer in number – supported Arminius. It would be anachronistic to ask what they got so worked up about. The States of Holland called the dispute nothing more than 'the scrapings of a fingernail'. But was that in itself not proof of their lack of understanding? According to the Gomarists, it was decidedly not the state's authority to determine the doctrine of the Church.

We also have to see this difference of opinion against the background of the fight against Spain, in which those who followed the teachings of Calvin considered their faith to be the only true religion and rejected Catholicism as 'Papist superstition'. As we stated in the introduction (p. 14), for most believers in the pre-modern era, alternative 'absolute truths' could not coexist. If the Reformed faith is the only true religion, there can be no division within it. And the conflict on land, at sea and in the media had made many people within the Reformed church ripe for a strict application of the doctrine. Allowing an alternative interpretation to fester was like admitting a disease into the body. Letting it run its course would testify to a lack of love for one's fellow man.

In any discussion about war or peace with the Papist Spaniards, about war or a truce, it is very tempting to conclude that prominent

Gomarists were in favour of continuing the war, and that the Arminians tended more towards peace or a truce. The simple, God-fearing folk – the baker, the cobbler, the blacksmith – chose the most direct line and were Gomarists, and they were in the majority across the country. The doctrine that left more room for nuance had more followers among the educated – and they are always in the minority. Who was to determine who was right and who was wrong? There was no Reformed pope. A decision could only be made by a church gathering of and for all those involved, in other words, a national synod. But who would convene it? The churchgoers themselves, or was that a job for the state?

The Dispute Tears the State in Two

During the talks preceding the Truce, Oldenbarnevelt and Maurice had rejected the Spanish king's call for freedom of religion for Catholics. Both insisted that the organization of the Church should remain subordinate to that of the state.[37] In the municipal authorities – which were, in the last instance, in control in the Republic – the Arminians were in the majority in Holland and Utrecht but far in the minority in the other provinces. Consequently, they were increasingly exposed to the criticisms, insults and heckling of the Gomarists. Rowdy rabble-rousers – by no means a rarity in Holland – allegedly ripped up cobble stones from the street and pelted their opponents with them to impress upon them the Word of the Lord.[38] The Arminians felt so persecuted that, in 1610, they submitted a petition to the States of Holland, asking for protection. The petition was referred to as a Remonstrance, and the Arminians were subsequently known as 'Remonstrants'. The following year, the Gomarists responded with a Counter-Remonstrance, and were given the name 'Counter-Remonstrants'.[39] In 1614, the States of Holland tried to ban religious issues from being discussed from the pulpit, but that did not stop a number of fanatical ministers who continued

67 *Johan van Oldenbarnevelt*, at 70 years of age. Anonymous copy of a portrait by Michiel Jansz. van Mierevelt (1566–1641).

68 *Prince Maurice.* Anonymous copy of a portrait by Michiel van Mierevelt dating from around 1621.

to fulminate in favour of the hardline standpoint. As the opposing sides became more deeply entrenched, the hardliners practised their beliefs in clandestine underground churches.

A divided Church and a divided state could of course present a serious danger in any resumption of the war against Spain. It would be unacceptable if Holland and Utrecht were to hold a different opinion to the other five provinces – and even have their own troops. That was something that Prince Maurice, as a man of the Union, could not tolerate. His standpoint was determined by political and military considerations.[40] After the Counter-Remonstrants had broken into the Kloosterkerk in The Hague – a former church in use as a cannon foundry – Maurice demonstratively attended a service there on Sunday 23 July 1617 with his entourage. Frederick Henry and his mother, Louise de Coligny, continued to worship at services led by Remonstrant preacher Johannes Uyttenbogaert. Oldenbarnevelt adhered to his interpretation of the Union of Utrecht that every province was sovereign on issues of religion. On 4 August 1617, he had the States of Holland draw up and adopt what was known as the 'Sharp Resolution'.[41] Under the resolution, the municipal authorities in towns that were suffering from Counter-Remonstrant aggression were permitted to set up armed militia to maintain public order. These mercenaries (known as *waardgelders*) had to swear allegiance to the States of Holland and not to the Union. At the end of the document, the States assured Prince Maurice of their loyalty to the House of Orange, but they were playing a dangerous game.

The conflict within the Reformed church of the Republic caused great amazement in the surrounding countries, including the royalist Netherlands. The Republic had fought for freedom of state and Church for forty years and now the Church itself was divided. Maurice, who liked to play chess, went to work systematically on the political chessboard. First, the States General decided, by four votes to three, to convene a national synod.[42] Maurice then travelled through the country to dismiss Remonstrant magistrates from municipal and provincial authorities. The States General discharged the mercenaries in Holland and Utrecht, with Maurice going to Utrecht in July 1618 to supervise the discharge in person. The Remonstrant dissidents – Oldenbarnevelt and his supporters – were now so isolated that Maurice had them arrested on 29 August 1618 by special order of the States General.

If the Republic had had a Supreme Court, Oldenbarnevelt and his followers would have had a chance. But the absence of such a high legal authority was one of the shortcomings of the young Dutch state. A Supreme Court could have assessed the decisions that had been made in the preceding years in light of the Union of Utrecht: sovereignty for each province, but not on defence and foreign policy. And, if it had contained wise men like Count William Louis of Nassau, it could have weighed up Oldenbarnevelt's decisions against his services for his country. William Louis was a committed Counter-Remonstrant but, for him, the arrest of Oldenbarnevelt was the absolute limit. He wrote Maurice a letter, urging him to spare the life of the Land's Advocate.[43] Unfortunately, there were no such wise men in the special court set up to try Oldenbarnevelt. Many of the 24 judges were Oldenbarnevelt's personal enemies. In the past, his discharge request as Land's Advocate of Holland had repeatedly been denied. Now the hatred against him had reached unprecedented heights. There were demands for his head. Oldenbarnevelt considered himself innocent of all charges, and those who are innocent ask for no clemency. Neither he nor Maurice would back down, and Oldenbarnevelt was beheaded on the Lord's Day, Sunday 13 May 1619. Where his head and body now rest, we do not know.[44]

Some years later, when the war had been resumed, Maurice was once heard to complain: 'When the old scoundrel still lived, there was counsel and money. Now there is neither.'

8

The Long Road from Truce to Peace

The North Victorious, the South between Hammer and Anvil: 1621–1648

War Within and Beyond Europe

It looked like a fait accompli: in the second half of the Eighty Years War, Frederick Henry captured 's-Hertogenbosch, Maastricht and Breda with the greatest of ease, at the expense of a Spanish empire that was in the process of disintegrating. The triumphant north acquired the borders it now still has as the Kingdom of the Netherlands. It seems like a story quickly told, but it was not as simple as it sounds. On both sides, the war had demanded an extreme effort at a very high cost. Once again, there had been bitter fighting on land and at sea, in the Netherlands, in Europe and in the newly discovered parts of the world.

What are the similarities and differences between the first and the second halves of the Eighty Years War? The early Revolt was a period characterized by constant change, with a wide range of parties involved. After 1588, the conflict between the Republic and the royalist Netherlands started to look more like a 'normal' war. And that normal war resumed after the Twelve Years Truce expired in 1621, again with many sieges and only intermittent battles. Both countries had a large number of fortified towns and forts, which cost massive amounts of money to maintain and garrison. Unlike during the years of the Revolt, the armies were now more disciplined and the war was conducted in a more 'reasonable' manner. With a few exceptions, the people of the towns and countryside no longer suffered the privations they had earlier been exposed to. Both sides considered the other worthy opponents and were largely willing to respect the rules of warfare as prevailed at the time. War is, however, never clean and tidy. Much more than before the Truce, the war was now an economic conflict, with embargos and blockades on both sides. From 1598, when the Hollanders made a breakthrough in the East Indies, the struggle took on a more global character. The

69 The royalist Flemish fleet and the Dunkirk privateers were a thorn in the side of the Republic for this entire period, causing extensive damage. In this drawing of 1641, States ships have driven a privateer onto the coast of North Holland between Wijk aan Zee and Castricum. The crew seek safety on land.

influence of the war beyond Europe had a direct impact on political and military policy.

As in the first half of the Eighty Years War, developments elsewhere in Europe played a decisive role. The sending of the Armada and Philip's intervention in France's internal affairs had given the Republic the opportunity to consolidate its own position. The Thirty Years War (1618–48), a succession crisis in Mantua (1627–31), a new war between Spain and France (from 1635), the separation of Portugal from Spain (1640–44) and an uprising in Catalonia (1640–44) also helped to relieve Spain's military pressure on the Republic. There was one major difference to the earlier phase of the war, in the nature of the war at sea. During the Revolt, Alba and Requesens had complained of lacking a fleet. Brussels and Madrid had learned their lesson from that and during the Truce had started building warships and privateers in Dunkirk and Ostend. The warships formed the royal fleet, while the privateers were operated by private individuals, many of whom came from the north. Together, they would cause staggering damage to the Republic's ships.

Lastly, a difference in mentality had emerged between the two states of the Netherlands. In the north, there was an awareness of being a new nation – and one that was here to stay; in the south, that awareness was also present, but here it was of belonging to a state that was loyal to the Catholic Church and the Spanish royal house.

A Futile Attempt to Extend the Truce

When the Twelve Years Truce came to an end, both sides began to ask themselves what should happen. Should the Truce be extended for a number of years and, preferably, be transformed into a peace agreement? Or should the war be resumed? There were internal divisions in both camps: extending the Truce had its benefits, as did resuming the war. In any case, talks between Brussels and The Hague started before the Truce expired. The advantage of the situation now was that the conditions – or rather the lack of them – in the agreement of 1609 could be taken as a starting point. Throughout the whole period between 1609 and 1648, there were many rounds of talks between Brussels (with Madrid in the background) and The Hague – not only in the final year of the Truce and in the run-up to the Peace of Münster. Whenever a crisis occurred, or when one side seemed to have achieved a decisive advantage over the other, it was seen as a reason to initiate a dialogue. And, of course, each side tried to negotiate from a position of strength, rather than weakness. Spain no longer had any illusions about conquering the Republic. There was great irritation that the Truce had brought the Republic considerable prosperity and so many new domains in Asia, while Spain itself had suffered only loss of face and inertia. It made a great difference that, in 1618, the Thirty Years War had broken out in the Holy Roman Empire, a conflict between the Catholic Emperor and his allies and the Protestant Prince-Electors and their foreign allies. Could the two branches of the House of Habsburg not join forces and take the Republic down a peg or two?

King Philip III asked Archduke Albert for advice on whether to extend the Truce or resume the war. It was most probably a pro forma request; Madrid would generally have been more likely to impose a diktat. Albert recalled the earlier demands of the Spanish crown: freedom for Catholics to practise their religion in the Republic and the Republic's withdrawal from non-European territories, and added another: reopening of the Scheldt.[1] The king made it clear to Albert that he was not to propose negotiations on his own initiative but, if he was invited to talks, he could agree to extend the Truce, as long as the Republic agreed to these three demands. For his part, Maurice maintained the pretence that the Republic wanted the Truce to be prolonged. He had shown himself to be a strong opponent of the Truce in 1609, but now his position as leader of the Republic was unassailable. Furthermore, the situation in the empire was so perilous because of the Thirty Years War that a strong army continued to be a necessity in the Republic. Holland and Zeeland were in favour of resuming the war, for economic reasons, while the inland provinces wanted peace. Maurice was nevertheless prepared to throw his weight in the scales to extend the Truce, on the basis of the agreements of 1609. But he felt that the initiative should come from the other side. Brussels, however, would not allow itself to be lured into suggesting extension of the Truce first, and did not come forward with the proposals that the Republic expected.

When the Truce expired on 9 April 1621, the talks on its extension were still in full swing, so the military conflict was not resumed directly. The economic battle, however, started immediately and was fought with great conviction by both sides. The Spanish king ordered the immediate closure of the ports on the Iberian peninsula to ships sailing under the Dutch flag, to ships built in the Republic and to goods from the Republic, even when they were being carried on ships from neutral countries. The new regulations were monitored so closely that very few goods found their way through the fine mesh of the surveillance net. This was of course of great benefit to shipping companies from England, the Hanseatic towns and elsewhere, who were always quick to report possible Dutch smugglers to the port authorities. For its part, the Republic blockaded ports in Flanders by placing a fleet offshore every year from 1 March to the end of October. The Republic also introduced levies on trade with hostile territories and obstructed the import of goods from Flanders and Brabant so as to stimulate its own industry. And it successfully prevented the enemy army from receiving supplies by cleverly regulating trade along the rivers.[2]

The death of Archduke Albert on 21 July 1621 was a sensitive loss for the royalist Low Countries. He had done everything within his power to guarantee the country's well-being. With the resources at his disposal, he had always shown himself to be a supporter of peace. After his death, Isabella acted as governor-general on behalf of the Spanish king and pursued the line that Albert had set out.

The war at sea resumed in August 1621, when Don Fadrique de Toledo defeated a Dutch convoy in the Straits of Gibraltar. In the same month, the two armies met on the battlefield, but these encounters were

AMBROSIVS SPINOLA marquis van   Sesti ende venafri hertog van Sansauerin, Ridder vant gulde Vlies, gouverneur generael van Syne catholique maiesteyt in nederlant..

70 Ambrogio Spinola, the mainstay of the archdukes. Spinola is erroneously referred to in the engraving as 'governor-general of the king', a position he never held.

little more than skirmishes. Spinola did lay siege to the small town of Julich, but this had little effect on the Republic. In 1622, he had his army surround Bergen op Zoom, but failed to do so completely and reinforcements from Breda and Zeeland immediately entered the town, enabling it to withstand a long siege. Spinola's troops were subjected to heavy bombardments and suffered heavy casualties. Like Parma in 1586, Spinola failed to capture the town and he lost half of his 18,000 men through either death or desertion. Furthermore, the siege had completely exhausted the war budget for the whole year. Consequently, the decision was taken in Madrid to conduct a defensive land war in the royalist Netherlands, alongside the active war at sea.[3]

Two Miraculous Years for Spain

Spinola's defeat may have been a setback for the royalist Netherlands, but for Spain itself 1622 was an *annus mirabilis*. In that year, four Spaniards were canonized by the pope, a clear illustration of the importance of Catholicism to the mental outlook of the Republic's Spanish opponents. The new saints were Ignatius of Loyola, founder of the Jesuit order; Franciscus Xaverius, the Jesuit who had taken the first steps to bring Christianity to China; Isidore, the patron of Madrid; and, lastly, Teresa of Ávila, a mystic who had enjoyed the special protection of the house of Alba.[4] A year earlier, the monarchy had also acquired a new king, Philip IV, who was only sixteen years old. Actual policy was determined by his chief minister, the Count-Duke of Olivares. As head of Philip's court before he had become king, Olivares had successfully manoeuvred himself to the centre of power and would wield the sceptre for thirty years. Both held on firmly to the idea of Spain as a leading world power and protector of the global Church. But Philip IV was a refined and art-loving ruler who lacked the rigidity of Philip II. He supported an uprising of Huguenots in the south of France. And he banned the application of the 'purity of blood' laws which discriminated against Jews who had converted to Catholicism. He even negotiated with Jewish bankers from Oran and allowed Portuguese-Jewish merchants to take part in the trade with the Indies.[5] The king and his chief minister shared views on the structural problems in the Spanish empire and drew up a regeneration plan, together with all the accompanying propaganda. It was their joint ambition to wipe out the shame of the peace policies of their predecessors, Philip III and the Duke of Lerma.[6]

When, during a subsequent round of talks, the Spanish felt that they were in a strong position, they even demanded that at least one Catholic church be founded in every town in the Republic.[7] The arms of the Habsburgs would in any case be blessed in those years. On 6 August 1623, the troops of the Holy Roman Empire, under the command of

71 'The familiarity with sacred things' – Rubens dared to portray everything. Here, Jesus listens to St Teresa of Ávila, who begs him to save Bernardino de Mendoza, a Spanish diplomat and historian, from purgatory.

Johan Tserclaes, Count of Tilly, defeated the army of Christian of Brunswick at the Battle of Stadtlohn, just a stone's throw across the border from Gelderland. The people of Gelderland and Overijssel held their breath, but the fighting remained on the eastern side of the border. That year, Spinola undertook no major projects, adhering to the order to conduct a defensive war, leading critics to accuse him of not daring to take the offensive.[8]

Spinola proved the critics wrong a year later on 28 August 1624 when, against the advice of his counsellors, he laid siege to Breda.[9] The town was solidly defended with fortifications and a large garrison. There

72 Justin of Nassau presents the keys of Breda to Spinola, 1625. This painting of 1634–5 by Diego Velázquez was intended for one of the Spanish king's palaces. Frederick Henry recaptured the city in 1637.

were heavy bombardments on both sides. From outside, the army of the Republic cut off the supply of food to Spinola's troops as far as possible. The response in Madrid was as negative as it had been to Spinola's operation against Bergen op Zoom: even if he took the town it would make no difference, as Breda offered no access to the heart of the Republic. There was widespread expectation that Spinola would again lose half his troops and goods – and that is exactly what happened. The siege lasted the whole winter. On 23 April 1625, Prince Maurice, who had been unable to relieve the town, died. His younger half-brother Frederick Henry succeeded him and on 27 May went to take stock of the situation around Breda with his own eyes. The town was past saving, and its commander, Justin of Nassau, surrendered under honourable conditions. The besieged people of the town proved, however, to be in far better health than the besieging troops, who were suffering shortages of practically everything. Many of the inhabitants of Breda, including Catholics, left the city after

73 The capture of Bahía from the Hollanders by Admiral Fadrique de Toledo in 1625. A clever printer, probably in the royalist Netherlands, published the account in Dutch and French. Not having a map of the real Bahía, he 'modified' one of the capture of Sluis in 1604.

the surrender and settled in nearby Geertruidenberg.[10] Isabella had herself invested as governor-general in Breda and a splendid book was of course published praising the town and its capture, which was translated into English, Spanish and French.[11] Spain celebrated the conquest as one of the greatest of the seventeenth century. The year 1625 was a second *annus mirabilis* for Philip IV, who from then on was known as *Felipe el*

Grande. In 1634–5, court artist Diego Velázquez painted a completely fabricated portrayal of the surrender of Breda for the Spanish king's Buen Retiro Palace.[12]

The Republic had no long-term maritime strategy and had to restrict themselves to escorting fishing and trading vessels. The most important of these were the hundreds of herring busses from Zeeland and Holland.[13] After them came the merchant ships in the Mediterranean and the Baltic, to Archangel and the Indies. Although the royalist ships in Ostend and Dunkirk were prevented from leaving port from early March to the end of October, the blockade was never watertight. As early as 1622, ships from Dunkirk had sunk dozens of herring busses and imprisoned their crews in the Flemish hinterland, from where their fellow townsfolk could buy their freedom.

In Asia, however, the East India Company was slowly but surely expanding its area of operations. It was so effective in the region that Philip's Council of Portugal, which advised him on Portuguese affairs, recommended that he conclude an agreement with the Republic as the war was becoming more impossible by the day.[14] In far-off Brazil, the Hollanders initially seemed to have achieved success with the capture of Salvador de Bahía in 1624. Because of the great distances, the news of the surprise victory reached Spain before the Republic. Consequently, Spanish ships sent to recapture the city under the command of Don Fadrique de Toledo arrived before the Dutch support fleet. The garrison, blockaded on the landward side by the Portuguese, quickly saw the futility of resistance and surrendered. The Spanish recovered – and kept – Salvador. This victory, too was commemorated on a tapestry for a new royal palace, the Buen Retiro, in Madrid.[15]

Victories for the Republic

For some time, Breda remained the last Spanish victory in the north. Important as possession of the Netherlands was for Spain, its domination in Italy weighed more heavily. That came under threat in Mantua as of 1627 because of the succession crisis. Spinola was put in command of the Italian campaign in Italy, a sensitive loss for the royal army in the Netherlands, as there was no replacement who could match his ability to lead the varied international tercios of which it consisted. Whole regiments from the army in the Low Countries were sent to Italy, so that Brussels had to limit itself to a defensive policy. After the fall of 's-Hertogenbosch in 1629 (see below), Philip IV and Isabella exerted great pressure on Spinola to return to the Netherlands. But he would not be persuaded by either orders or flattery, having lost all confidence that the war would receive sufficient financial support and no longer prepared to pay for it from his own pocket. He died in Montferrat on 25 September 1630.[16]

The new stadtholder of the Republic could therefore now prove himself. Like Maurice, Frederick Henry was an army man who, in close cooperation with his nephews, the stadtholders of Friesland and Groningen, chose to conduct an offensive war. Unlike in the south, the States General determined the Republic's objectives and the stadtholders pursued them. Frederick Henry was much more active politically than Maurice and tried, through loyal supporters, to influence decision-making in towns, the Provincial States and the States General. In 1625, he not only succeeded Maurice, but also married the German Countess Amalia of Solms. The following year, their first son, William – later to become stadtholder William II – was born. He was followed by four daughters, all of whom were to marry princes of equal (or higher) social standing. Consequently, as in the times of the Prince of Orange, there was once again a dynasty in Holland. Frederick Henry also played a leading role in foreign policy. In negotiations with Spain, he had an aversion to intervention by England and France, though he remained on friendly terms with both. It was a success for both his dynastic ambitions and his desire to increase the prestige of the House of Orange in Europe when, at the age of fifteen, his son William married Mary Henrietta, daughter of the English king, Charles I. That was certainly above his station. He needed a good relationship with France because of the war with Spain and, in 1627, spared neither himself nor the Republic by helping France isolate and capture the Protestant port of La Rochelle. In exchange, France gave the Republic significant annual war subsidies and the prince the splendid title of *Son Altesse*, His Highness.

In his own land, in the east, Oldenzaal was a thorn in the side in Overijssel, as was Groenlo in the border region of Gelderland. Oldenzaal fell into the hands of the Republic in 1626, after being besieged by Ernst Casimir, stadtholder of Friesland and Groningen. The following year it was the turn of Groenlo. That was not without risk, as Groenlo was quite a distance from the major rivers, making the supply lines of arms and food vulnerable. Frederick Henry laid siege to the town on 20 July. According to the prevailing rules of warfare, he had the army seal off access to the town and set up a line of attack facing inwards. Two and a

74 This print, glorifying Frederick Henry, was published in 1628, before he had obtained his greatest victories. The freedom he brought allowed trade and industry, agriculture and livestock breeding, and the arts and sciences to flourish.

half kilometres further away, he set up a defensive line facing outwards, to repel any attempts to relieve the town. Groenlo endured an intimidating and devastating bombardment, and on 20 August, with the trenches close enough to breach the defensive walls, the townspeople did what was customary in such circumstances – they surrendered. Groenlo did not fall into Spanish hands again.[17]

In the same year, Piet Hein, who commanded a squadron of privateer ships in the service of the West India Company, launched an attack on Salvador de Bahía, where he made off with 2,500 crates of sugar. But silver was much more attractive loot than sugar, and on 8 and 9 September 1628, Hein overpowered the Spanish silver fleet in the Bay of Matanzas on Cuba. The fleet was carrying the yield from the Spanish silver mines in Central and South America to Sevilla. The silver, brought back to Spain twice a year, was the main source of income for the Spanish government. And now it had fallen into the hands of the *rebeldes*. The fleet consisted of only three ships, but the market value of the silver was eleven million guilders, the equivalent of two-thirds of the annual budget for the army. The greatest part went to the state, and a considerable share of that to the stadtholder. Piet Hein was fobbed off with 7,000 guilders, causing him to resign immediately from the Company. The regular seamen came off even worse.[18]

There was of course considerable discussion in the States General about what this gigantic windfall should be spent on: reducing government debts, a military campaign or a maritime expedition. Zeeland in particular would have been pleased with financial support for the ailing West India Company, which could then launch a new attack on Brazil. On land, the choice fell on 's-Hertogenbosch, a powerful city, with strong fortifications.[19] The siege was, once again, extensive and therefore expensive, but Frederick Henry's army attracted a large number of foreign officers who were pleased to come and learn their trade at their own expense. The prince's troops were so well entrenched that the enemy resorted to attacks elsewhere. Southern nobleman Hendrik van den Bergh mounted an invasion of the Veluwe, in Gelderland, but did not capture any land of lasting value. Much more dangerous was the invasion by a combined Spanish-Imperial army from the Holy Roman Empire. It was the only time that the Thirty Years War had any direct impact on the Eighty Years War. Under their commander Raimondo Montecuccoli, the enemy crossed the River IJssel and on 13 August 1629 captured Amersfoort. Panic spread throughout the Republic, but Frederick Henry kept his head and did not allow himself to be lured away from 's-Hertogenbosch. Fortunately, he was joined by a group of stout men who told him that repairs were being carried out on the defensive works in Wesel, the centre of the supply lines for the Spanish-Imperial army, and that he could take advantage of the weak spot to take over the town. He gave them sufficient men and they captured Wesel, putting a stop to the imperial intervention in the Republic. Seeing that further resistance was futile, 's-Hertogenbosch surrendered. Now it was the turn of the siege of 's-Hertogenbosch to be immortalized in a book. These events were poignantly summarized by one of Holland's greatest poets:

De Prins belegerde Den Bosch and vloog in Wezel
Dat was een brave sprong, van de os op de ezel.[20]

The prince laid siege to 's-Hertogenbosch and surprised Wesel
That was a mighty jump by the fox on the weasel.

The loss of 's-Hertogenbosch caused great dismay in the royalist Netherlands. High-ranking nobles and clergymen met secretly and petitioned Isabella to reduce the influence of the Spanish in the national government and the army, and appoint more people from the Low Countries.[21]

In this perilous situation, Isabella acquired the assistance of a new adviser, the Catalan Marquis of Aytona. Aytona had proved his diplomatic talents in Spain and as Spanish ambassador in Vienna. He urged the king to respect the wishes of the high nobles in the Netherlands for self-determination and participation in decision-making. On his advice, Isabella appointed the bishop of Ghent, Antoon Triest, and the archbishop of Mechelen, Jacob Boonen, to the Council of State.[22] The Council, which was rarely convened, regained some of its influence. Both bishops, who had important voices in the States of Flanders and Brabant respectively, thus acted as a bridge between the States and the central government.[23] Antwerp jurist Pieter Roose, also appointed to the Council, was a fervent proponent of centralized royal government and no builder of bridges. Within a short time, he was sent to Madrid to advise the king.

The year 1631 was much less successful for the Republic. With the war of the Mantuan succession coming to an end, the Spanish troops left Italy and marched back to the Low Countries at the double, arriving just in time to stop Frederick Henry laying siege to Bruges. The house at number 28 in the city's Wollestraat has three reliefs on its gable depicting the approach and retreat of Frederick Henry.[24] The corner of the house is buttressed by the barrel of a cannon bearing the inscription *Auriacus Brugam venit, vidit, abiit* (Orange came to Bruges, saw and left).[25] The royal troops did not pursue those of the prince, so as not to give the impression that they had driven the prince away. The papal nuncio wrote that, had the prince landed a month earlier, the suffering would have been incalculable.[26] However, an attempt by the royal side to enter the inland waters of Zeeland with a large fleet ended up as a fiasco. Aware of the plans, the States stationed a fleet under the leadership of Marinus Hollaer at Bergen op Zoom, ready to engage the invaders in battle. Under the leadership of Johan of Nassau-Siegen, a noble from the house of Nassau who had remained loyal to king and Church, the royal ships were soundly defeated on 10 September at the Battle of the Slaak, to the west of Tholen. The commanders escaped, but 4,000 regular seamen and troops on board were captured. The financial loss for Brussels was estimated at four million guilders.[27]

The following year, 1632, was another high point in the Republic's military struggle. In June, Frederick Henry initiated a risky campaign along the River Maas, which was successful largely due to the dissatisfaction of a number of high-ranking southern nobles, of whom Hendrik van den Bergh was the most prominent. During the campaign, the Republic captured Venlo and Roermond, and the biggest prize of all, Maastricht. An appeal by Hendrik van den Bergh to his countrymen to throw off the Spanish yoke fell on deaf ears.[28] As during the invasion by Prince Maurice in 1600, the people of the southern Netherlands remained loyal to their government, governor-general Isabella and King Philip IV. But indignation and dissatisfaction were rife, and Isabella called the States General together again for the first time since 1600. She had the support of her new adviser: Aytona simply informed the king that the States General had been convened, without asking permission. In this respect, both Isabella and Aytona showed some fortitude in standing up to the king. Philip, of course, refused to give his permission, but that was kept from the States General. Eleven provinces met in Brussels in October 1632. The king's chief minister Olivares thought it worth reminding Isabella of 'the strictness of the times of Philip II'.[29] Aytona responded by writing to the king that they had to convene the States General, otherwise the latter would no longer provide money for the war. The provinces, he said, were not against the war as such, as long as they were listened to. The Walloon provinces wanted only higher positions for the officers, which usually went to Spaniards and Italians.[30] At the next round of peace negotiations, the Republic increased its demands. It now wanted tolerance for Protestants in the royalist Netherlands, and the same rights for Jews from the Low Countries in Spain and Portugal as for other Netherlands' citizens. The demands, of course, fell on deaf ears.

Just as the governor-general acquired Aytona to advise her after the crisis of 1629, Olivares sent Pieter Roose back to Brussels after the crisis of 1632. Roose had the full confidence of the chief minister and Philip IV. He ate out of Philip's hand and was more royalist than the king himself. Olivares gave Roose permission to play the parties in the royalist Netherlands off against each other. He even suggested he conclude a treaty with the Republic behind the governor-general's back.[31] This is yet another example of Spanish disloyalty to its own people. Isabella died on 1 December 1633. Amsterdam poet Joost van den Vondel, who had converted to Catholicism, praised her in an elegy as the mother of the fatherland.[32]

The Final Spanish Offensive

After Isabella's death, the royalist Netherlands once again acquired a prince of royal blood as governor-general. Ferdinand of Austria was a brother of Philip IV and, as is often the case with the brothers of kings, it was no simple task finding him a suitable position. The restless young man had no desire to take up an ecclesiastical career, but after receiving what were known as 'minor holy orders', he was appointed archbishop of Toledo, which yielded the Spanish crown 400,000 escudos a year. He was then promptly promoted to cardinal and bore the title Cardinal-Infante (*Infante* pertaining to his status as a royal prince). Isabella had warned the king that 'they do not take too kindly to cardinals here in the Netherlands', by which she was of course referring to Granvelle.[33] Detached to the imperial army in the Thirty Years War, Ferdinand had succeeded (or was he just lucky?) in defeating the Swedish at the Battle of Nördlingen on 6 September 1634. His fame as a war hero quickly preceded him, and in December 1634 he took office as governor-general. He brought 11,000 troops with him, which, added to the 30,000 men in Aytona's land army, constituted a formidable force. That was sorely needed as in the same year the Republic had concluded an offensive and defensive alliance with France. In 1635, France declared war on Spain.

In the years from 1634 to 1640, Olivares succeeded in mounting a large-scale military offensive by land and sea, financed by increasing taxes. He was now better organized than in the previous campaigns. After many decades of war, Madrid finally understood how the war in the Low Countries should be fought, but unfortunately still without asking themselves whether and how the war was compatible with the interests of the people of the Netherlands themselves. Successful transports of thousands of men by sea and investments in the Flemish fleet now gave Spain a much stronger starting position. The first operation by the Cardinal-Infante, laying siege to the citadel of Philippine in Zeeland, was a failure. Ferdinand blamed his commanding officers; according to the papal nuncio, however, it was because he had been out hunting while the people in all the towns were praying for the siege to come to a good end.[34]

The lowest point in the history of the royalist Netherlands was the joint invasion of Brabant by France and the Republic in June 1635. The small town of Tienen, to the east of Brussels, was captured on 10 June and French and States soldiers went on the rampage, looting, raping and killing. Such atrocities had not been seen for many years and there was a widespread public outcry, including in political pamphlets.[35] After the invading army had taken Diest and Aarschot, it laid siege to Leuven, against the advice of Frederick Henry. Leuven was surrounded by fortified towns and would not be held for long. The garrison, citizens and students bravely resisted, saving the city. As the French and States

75 Tienen burns after being sacked by French and States troops. The group at the front are the delegates of the States General from the Republic. In the middle, with the 'F' on his tunic, is Frederick Henry.

76 Gerrit van Santen, *The Siege of Schenkenschans by Prince Frederik Hendrik*, c. 1636–84. This fort, strategically located at a fork in the River Rhine, is now the peaceful German village of Schenkenschanz, across the river (and the border) from the Dutch town of Lobith.

armies retreated, French soldiers were lynched by enraged farmers and townspeople. They cut off their ears in retaliation for the ears of a statue of the Virgin Mary being cut off during the capture of Tienen, and sent them to Aytona in a basket.[36]

Spain and the royalist Netherlands were delighted with the capture of the Schenkenschans, an important fort at the strategic point where the Rhine and Waal rivers divide. On 26 July 1635, royal troops from Geldern had taken the fort by surprise. It is difficult to imagine the euphoria in Madrid when they heard that this fort had been taken. Did the years of frustration go so deep that this single victory had to be blown up and presented as a great historical event? Yes, Ferdinand and an army of 40,000 men lay to the east of this pimple on the landscape; but Frederick Henry lay to the north and west with just as many. Olivares considered the capture of Schenkenschans as important as taking Paris or The Hague. Philip IV believed that, from there, he could bring the war to the heart of Holland. Other court strategists claimed that the fort was as important as Antwerp and Brazil together. Ferdinand himself soon had serious doubts about whether the fort could be held; on 30 April 1636, the occupying army surrendered and the Republic's defensive line was once again closed. Olivares's delight at taking this one – albeit important – fort may have been excessive and misplaced, but it was matched on both counts by his despair at its loss.[37]

In 1637, the French proposed taking Dunkirk jointly with the Republic. Frederick Henry was in favour of the plan but, after being held up for three weeks at Rammekens by unfavourable winds, he called the attack off. Had he perhaps learned from the similar plans in 1600,

77 Peter Paul Rubens's design for the triumphal car of Kallo, *c.* 1638.

which foundered in Nieuwpoort? He redirected all his troops to nearby Breda and had surrounded the city before Ferdinand could get to him from the French border. Unable to prevent the siege, the Cardinal-Infante moved on eastwards, where Venlo and Roermond as good as fell into his lap. Much to Olivares's annoyance, he then focused his attention once more on France rather than the Republic. Breda surrendered to the Republican troops on 7 October 1637 after more than half of the garrison had perished. This was a bitter pill for Madrid to swallow, with the paint hardly dry on Velázquez's majestic painting of the surrender of Breda to the royalist troops in 1625.

In 1638, the Republic set its sights on capturing Antwerp – against the wishes of Frederick Henry, who thought the plan unfeasible. Amsterdam, too, was opposed to bringing the city within the Republic's borders, as it could once again become a formidable trade rival. But it was for this very reason that other towns in Holland and the other provinces considered Antwerp an important acquisition, to counterbalance Amsterdam's trading power.[38] Extensive preparations were made in Zeeland. Under the leadership of William of Nassau-Siegen, a distant relative of the stadtholder, 6,000 men landed on the left bank of the Scheldt with the intention of capturing the forts that defended the city from there. In the best Castilian tradition, the energetic commander of Antwerp immediately launched a counterattack. Surprisingly enough, the Republican troops had not expected such a direct and forceful response, and during what became known as the Battle of Kallo (after one of the forts), they suffered a heavy defeat. Several hundred men were killed and 2,500 were taken prisoner. All their weapons also fell into the hands of the royal troops. It was a complete fiasco for the Republic and a great boost for the city of Antwerp and the south.[39] Rubens designed a triumphal car for a procession through Antwerp to celebrate this decisive victory, which of course he immortalized on canvas. When Ferdinand then defeated the French at St Omer and threatened to take Paris, and a French invasion of Spain itself (at Fuentarebbía) was repelled, it looked as though the Spanish could look to the future with confidence.

The Closing Stages of the War

Spain initially invested all that confidence in a second Armada. The enormous fleet was intended to defeat the Republic's naval power, commanded by upcoming talent Maarten Harpertszoon Tromp. Olivares was so certain of victory that he gave orders to attack the Dutch ships even if they sought safe haven in an English port.[40] But his plan literally backfired: Tromp took the offensive against the Armada in the English Channel, lining his ships up one behind the other, so that they could fire broadsides against the enemy with all their cannons. They then put about and did the same from the other side. And so it was the Spanish ships that sought refuge in the

Downs, a sheltered area of sea just off the English coast. Tromp was given permission to ignore the English and attacked the Spanish fleet again. The Armada was decimated. Dozens of Spanish ships were lost, together with 9,000–10,000 of those on board. The victory was not quite total, as more than 5,000 of the original 8,500 infantrymen destined for the royalist Netherlands made it to the safety of the shore. English ships later took them across to Flanders. Three million escudos in silver to replenish the war coffers also made it to Flanders safe and sound.[41] The defeat, however, did put a stop to all further Spanish ambitions in the Low Countries.

78 Maarten Harpertsz. Tromp with, at the bottom, a depiction of the Battle of the Downs.

The magnificence of the victory of the Republican fleet over the second Armada in 1639 was tempered by the disappointing progress of the fight against the Dunkirk privateers. It was as though the Dutch lion were being pestered by a swarm of hornets. Despite the Republic's continued attempts to defeat the privateers, it suffered staggering losses in the decade from 1630 to 1640. Not only was the Flemish fleet two to three times larger, but its cannon power had also increased enormously.[42]

The conflict showed the same variegated picture in the strip of land ruled by the Republic in Brazil. The regime there received a boost when Count John Maurice of Nassau-Siegen was appointed governor. As an experienced general, he soon took charge of expanding and consolidating the Republic's territory. His government acquired almost legendary allure after he announced religious freedom, also for Catholics and Jews, raised sugar production so that the economy thrived, and appointed artists to portray the natural environment. But his rule had a darker side: he imported large numbers of black slaves from Africa to work in the sugar plantations, for the enrichment of the colony and of himself.[43]

A new naval attack on Salvador de Bahía under John Maurice's leadership ended in failure. Furthermore, governing the colony cost much more than the profits made by the West India Company – and for the

Company, of course, profitability was the main priority. That placed the Republic's financial resources under excessive pressure. After Portugal regained its independence from Spain in December 1640, to a significant extent made possible – irony of ironies – by the Republic, it set its sights on regaining its lost colonies. After weighing up the pros and cons of its relationship with Portugal, the Company threw in the towel.

The events of 1640 made Spain ready for peace. First, it lost Artois in the war with France. Then it was faced with uprisings within its own borders, when the Catalans rebelled against the king. The Portuguese revolt in December caused great consternation in Madrid. Portugal chose its own king from an old Portuguese noble family, the House of Bragança, and declared independence. The Republic recognized Portugal's independence immediately and was more than pleased to start supplying the country with all the food and military equipment it needed. It even sent troops to reinforce the Portuguese army. However, a squadron commanded by admiral Artus Gijsels, sent by the States to support a revolt in Andalusia, got no further than Cape St Vincent, the southernmost point of Portugal. There it ran into the Spanish fleet, which was waiting there for the silver fleet to arrive. A fierce battle ensued, from which neither side emerged victorious, but the Dutch fleet was forced to return home. The years 1640 and 1641 were disastrous for Olivares, who, with Castile depopulated and impoverished, found himself between two hotspots: Portugal and Catalonia.[44] But he held his ground.

In the Netherlands, Cardinal-Infante Ferdinand lost all stomach for the fight, while his 2,300 cavalrymen had to make do without horses. Victories on both sides were restricted to smaller prizes. In the summer of 1641, for example, Frederick Henry captured the Limburg town of Gennep, south of Nijmegen on the River Maas. In the south, the army commanders spent most of their time squabbling with each other. In the words of René Vermeir, the expert on this period, 'no one could get on with anyone else.'[45] Vermeir also comes to the astonishing conclusion that the Spanish commanders had no knowledge of the basics of warfare, such as ballistics.[46] On 9 November 1641, the Cardinal-Infante died at the age of 32. His successor as governor-general, Portuguese nobleman Don Francisco de Melo, was resolute in his actions, which brought him much sympathy and cooperation among the royalist population. But, on 19 May 1642, he suffered a crushing defeat against the French army at Rocroi, in the French Ardennes.[47] As after the fall of 's-Hertogenbosch and Maastricht, this led to widespread public unrest. Philip IV tried once

The Long Road from Truce to Peace

again to appoint one of his bastard sons as governor-general, but that was no longer an option for the Catholic south.

In 1644, the royalist Netherlands lost the towns of Sas van Gent to the Republic and Gravelines to France.[48] In the same year, de Melo made way for Manuel de Moura Corte-Real, Marquis of Castel Rodrigo, who took over as temporary governor general. With few financial resources, Castel Rodrigo determined policy in consultation with the two bishops, Triest and Boonen. From sheer necessity, Philip IV finally agreed that the States themselves could take responsibility for paying the troops. That had become the rule in Holland nearly eighty years earlier![49]

The year 1645 was to become yet another disastrous one for the royalist Netherlands, with the army leadership yet again divided by internal squabbling. The French achieved a series of victories in the border zone with the Royalist Netherlands. Frederick Henry captured Hulst, as a result of which large parts of Flanders were forced

79 Monstrance, *c.* 1640. When Frederick Henry captured Hulst in 1645, the Catholics took this monstrance with them to their bishopric, Ghent. In 1780, it was returned to the Catholics in Hulst.

to pay tribute to avoid being looted. Moreover, the fighting around the now peaceful towns of Sas van Gent and Hulst became increasingly fierce, with heavy bombardments and consequent damage.[50] In crisis, the States of the royalist Netherlands called for immediate talks with the Republic. The Republic made it clear that it was prepared to talk, but only as part of the wider peace negotiations in Münster.[51]

In 1646, despite these developments, the armies of the Republic and France once again initiated military campaigns. The French moved northwards along the coast, encountering as little resistance as Frederick Henry's campaign along the Maas in 1632. The absolute high point of this campaign was the capture of Dunkirk. The French ambassador to the Republic recounted that, on hearing this news, the skin of mayor of Amsterdam Cornelis Bicker turned 'whiter than his collar'.[52] At the same time, Frederick Henry laid siege to Venlo, but the town

199

garrison had just been reinforced and it put up a strong resistance. The prince abandoned the siege, possibly because he knew how far the peace negotiations in Münster had progressed.

A Complicated Peace

Of course, the Republic saw the peace treaty as a victory. But the Republic was a country made up of seven provinces, each with its own leaders and people, and the road to peace became a quasi-endless discussion between and within them. The general public followed the discussions closely and critically. In regularly recurring heated public debates, hundreds of pamphlets were published, for and against peace. Once again, we will distil the main thread of developments from all these confusing discussions and complicating details.

Unlike during the negotiations on the Truce, the Republic could now act independently, without the need for coordination and guidance by England or France. In fact, although France was officially an ally of the Republic, it did everything it could to sabotage the talks. The great powers had agreed in December 1641 to come together in Münster and Osnabrück for parallel peace talks, which had started in July 1643. The Republic could not even agree who was to attend and what their instructions would be. It took until 14 July 1645 for the provinces to decide to send delegates to Münster, by six votes to one. Zeeland – and a number of other interest groups – remained intransigent. The delegation did not arrive until January 1646. In the meantime, Brussels regularly sent representatives to Frederick Henry to conclude a separate peace agreement with the Republic. They tried to convince him that the unstoppable rise of France could not possibly be to the Republic's advantage. Frederick Henry assured them that he was committed to peace and that, no, he did not wish to be appointed Duke of Gelderland, as such gifts from Spain would not be appreciated in the Republic.

A key figure in the peace talks in Münster was the leader of the Spanish delegation, Gaspar de Bracamonte, Count of Peñaranda. He found a settlement with the Republic more important than one with France, writing, 'I find the Hollanders more conscientious and trustworthy in keeping their promises and honouring the peace agreement than the French and we can thus rely with greater certainty on what we agree with them.'[53] He added that the Hollanders did not speak of the Spaniards with hatred, as the French did. An excellent illustration of his prophetic vision was his insistence that it was best to keep the Republic strong, with all its Huguenots from France, so that it could form a coalition with Sweden and other Protestant countries if France needed reining in.

The first talks started on 16 January 1646, but the Republic broke them off immediately on a matter of procedure. Peñaranda then leaked the information that the French had proposed a marriage between Crown Prince Louis (later to become King Louis XIV) and a Spanish princess, who would receive the southern Netherlands as her dowry. That was enough to bring the Republic back to the negotiating table in May. The goal was to reach a truce for twelve or twenty years. The Republic had a list of no less than 71 conditions, but with the exception of a few contentious items, agreement was reached on most of them. When that became known, in the summer of 1646, a heated public discussion broke out. Opponents of peace were once again up in arms but, unlike in earlier clashes, those in favour were now conspicuously in the majority. The man in the street continued to believe that his life was at stake and that the rich merchants had undoubtedly been bribed by the Spanish.[54]

In September, Holland proposed in the States General no longer to negotiate a new truce but to aim for a real peace treaty, and on 27 October the proposal was adopted, with one vote against – Zeeland again standing alone and screaming blue murder that the proposal violated the Union of Utrecht. In December, the Dutch delegates were in Münster again to discuss the final obstacles. Peñaranda had found out about their secret instructions and knew that none of the obstacles should be allowed to stand in the way of an agreement. Under his watchful eye, the agreements were finalized and signed on 8 January 1647. That unleashed a new wave of discussions, in every town and every region. The opponents of peace were still not convinced and still too strong to be ignored. The French ambassador continued to stoke unrest where he could. The delegates did not return to Münster until 17 September. The Spanish were by now extremely irritated by all the endless deliberations. After yet another round of talks, the agreements were finally signed on 30 January 1648. But, as though it would never end, supporters and opponents of peace took advantage of the ratification process to initiate another pamphlet war, which lasted from February to May. Both sides simply continued to repeat their standpoints. A delegation from the States General went to Middelburg on 28 April to bring Zeeland to its senses, but with no success, largely due to the Zeelanders refusing to give up privateering. Finally, on 15 May 1648, the ceremonial signing of the Peace of Münster by the representatives of the Spanish king and of the Republic – as immortalized by artist Gerard Terborch – took place in Münster. Zeeland had sent no representative, but the Peace was presented in the province on 30 May. The Zeelanders acquiesced with the decision of the States General to 'preserve the unity and harmony of the United Netherlands', as it was so poetically described. An official day of celebration was held in the Republic on 5 June, with thanks given to God and public displays of merriment. It was the day on which, exactly eighty years earlier, the counts of Egmont and Horn had been beheaded.

Epilogue: By Way of Conclusion

It was unavoidable: the story of the Revolt in the Low Countries had to be one of a clash between many different interests and widely varying political and religious perspectives. These conflicts caused a protracted succession of coincidental and unpredictable events, of political, economic and military chain reactions. There are countless moments during the Revolt when it is possible to say that, if events had taken a different turn, the whole Revolt could have followed a completely different course.

In history, questions that start with 'what if' are generally of little use. Here, however, they have a significant role to play. Every turn of events reminds us of the old lesson that things could have turned out differently. And what should we learn from that old lesson? That, in history, we should not look for determining factors, whether they be political, economic or religious. The borders of the present-day Kingdom of the Netherlands were the consequence of military events and are therefore completely artificial. No divine predetermination called on Dutch Protestants to form their own state. No economic principle guaranteed the success of the northern trading republic of rich merchants and the defeat of the southern state ruled by king, cleric and nobleman.

Since 1433, Brabant, Flanders and Holland had been the core provinces of the Low Countries under Philip the Good, Duke of Burgundy. The Burgundian and Habsburg princes had extended their domains to embrace the traditional seventeen principalities. These principalities gradually formed a whole, referred to as the Netherlands, Le Pays-Bas or *Belgium nostrum*. The main differences within that whole lay not between Groningen and Friesland in the north and Artois and Hainaut in the south, but between the urbanized coastal principalities of Brabant, Flanders and Holland, with their trade and industry, and the predominantly agrarian

80 The Seventeen Provinces. On the left, the ten virgins symbolizing the royalist Netherlands. To the right, the seven virgins representing the seven provinces of the Republic. All can be identified by their coats of arms. Draft design by Hendrick de Clerck for a painting that adorned one of the triumphal arches during the Joyous Entry of Albert and Isabella in Brussels, probably in 1599.

periphery inland. After 150 years of shared history, the three core provinces revolted jointly against the regime of their sovereign lord. The conflict was most intense in these three regions because power over the other provinces depended on who controlled the wealthy cities. By holding power in Flanders and Brabant, where the Revolt had once raged most fiercely, Parma assured the Spanish crown of control of all the other provinces in the south of the Netherlands.

King Philip II did not want to admit Protestants to his patrimonial domains at any price. He therefore resisted every form of settlement or peace agreement. For their part, the Calvinists were also to blame for the impossibility of finding a solution: they wanted religious freedom for themselves but did not wish – once they had gained power – to permit Catholics the same freedom. This was, in essence, the cause of the split in the country; the rest is only consequence. The numerical weakness of the Protestants in the Republic made it relatively simple for the regents to get tolerance accepted both in theory and in practice. They also had little other choice.

With its great economic potential, Holland would play the dominant role in the Dutch Republic for two centuries. It absorbed the many tens of thousands of Protestants and followers of other faiths who fled the Catholic south. With their knowledge, capital and trade contacts, these southern immigrants made an enormous contribution to the growth of the Republic's prosperity. At the same time, from their refuge in the north, the most fervent Calvinist immigrants hoped to continue the fight to free the south and that one day they would be able to return to Bruges, Ghent or Antwerp. Stadtholder Frederick Hendrik may have captured Breda, 's-Hertogenbosch and Maastricht, but attempts to take the other three major cities failed. The country was only clearly divided between Protestant and Catholic when it became two separate states.

What is astounding about the war in the Netherlands, the focus of this book, is that – at the same time – both the Republic and the royalist Netherlands experienced a period of spiritual and cultural growth: scientifically and intellectually through their universities and inventors, and culturally with their writers and poets, artists and composers. Economically, too, despite their darker periods, they also had many glittering

81 Stylized portrayal of the Compromise of Nobles. The name of the Lord in Hebrew letters gives the moment a religious character. Illustration from the *Nederlandtsche Gedenck-clanck* by Adriaen Valerius, published in 1626. The arms on the beggar's bag are those of the Prince of Orange.

successes. These developments would require a separate study to do them justice.

When the Count of Egmont asked in desperation how he could best serve the king, he was told: 'by obeying him'. But the people of the Low Countries were no great lovers of Spanish *obediencia*. English secretary of state Francis Walsingham once received a letter from an unknown adviser who wrote the following about the search of the United Provinces for a head of state: 'Those towns want to have a lord to obey them, and not to obey him.' There is a lot of truth in that. When Matthias of Austria accepted the position as sovereign lord of all the provinces of the Netherlands, he did so under such restrictive conditions that it had all the features of a constitutional monarchy. The conditions were little different to those proposed to the Prince of Orange for his investiture as Count of Holland. Orange, who had grown up as a high-ranking noble in the south of the Low Countries, did not consider himself too high and mighty to be the leader of nobles, burghers and peasants, indeed of Hans Cheesemonger and Hans Miller. It is then very tempting to conclude that he would have been a sovereign who was indeed prepared to obey his subjects and serve the community. And that is the basis on which the twin monarchies of modern-day Belgium and the Netherlands are still founded.

Chronology of Main Events

1555	25 October: Charles v abdicates as sovereign of the Netherlands
1557	Spanish state declared bankrupt
1559	3 April: Peace of Cateau-Cambrésis between Spain and France
	12 May: the pope makes the Netherlands an independent ecclesiastical province
	25 August: Philip II leaves for Spain
1561–2	High-ranking nobles dissatisfied about their lack of influence on the government of the country
1563	Orange, Egmont and Horn in opposition against Granvelle
1564	March: Granvelle departs
1565	January–April: Egmont visits the king as representative of the opposition
	October: letters from the woods of Segovia; Philip insists on stricter prosecution of heretics
1566	5 April: the Compromise of Nobles presents the Request. They call themselves 'beggars'; the governor-general promises moderation, and Protestants return
	10 August: start of the iconoclastic fury in Flanders
	23 August: Margaret of Parma permits Protestant preaching and the Compromise of Nobles is disbanded
	29 November: Philip II appoints the Duke of Alba to restore order in the Netherlands
1567	January: Tournai captured by government troops
	13 March: beggars' army defeated at Oosterweel
	14 March: Van Straelen quells unrest in Antwerp
	24 March: Valenciennes recaptured by government troops
	April: Orange leaves for Dillenburg

	August: arrival of Alba
	9 September: Egmont and Horn arrested
1568	23 May: Louis of Nassau defeats a Spanish army at Heiligerlee
	5 June: Egmont and Horn beheaded in Brussels
	21 July: Louis of Nassau defeated at Jemmingen
	October: unsuccessful invasion by Orange
1569	Alba wants to introduce the Tenth Penny tax, resulting in fierce resistance
1572	1 April: Water beggars capture Brill
	24 May: Louis of Nassau captures Mons, in Hainaut
	June and July: the Revolt spreads, mainly in Holland
	9 July: martyrs of Gorinchem hanged in Brill
	23–24 August: St Bartholomew's Day massacre in France ends hope of assistance from the Huguenots
	August–September: second unsuccessful invasion by Orange
	Punitive expedition by Don Fadrique against Mechelen, Zutphen and Naarden
	December: Don Fadrique lays siege to Haarlem
1573	12 July: Don Fadrique captures Haarlem and has the garrison executed
	8 October: victory begins at Alkmaar; Alba succeeded by Requesens
	11 October: the beggars' fleet achieves a victory on the Zuiderzee
1574	27 January: the beggars' fleet defeats the royal fleet at Reimerswaal
	9 February: Mondragón surrenders Middelburg to the prince
	14 April: Louis and Henri of Nassau die at the Battle of Mookerheyde
	3 October: relief of Leiden
1575	March: peace talks in Breda fail
	11 July: States of Holland confer Orange with the Supreme Authority
	8 August: Spanish atrocities in Oudewater
	1 September: Spanish state declared bankrupt for the second time
1576	5 March: death of Requesens
	29 June: Zierikzee surrenders to the Spanish
	Summer: Spanish troops mutiny after not being paid for several years
	States of Brabant convene the States General
	8 November: Pacification of Ghent: all provinces join forces to get the Spanish troops out of the country

Chronology of Main Events and Maps

1577	9 January: First Union of Brussels – a closer Catholic union within the Pacification
	12 February: with the Perpetual Edict, new governor-general Don John endorses the Pacification of Ghent and sends the foreign troops out of the country
	23 September: Orange makes triumphant entry into Brussels; the nobles have asked Archduke Matthias of Austria to become governor-general
	10 December: Second Union of Brussels, now more tolerant
1578	31 January: State troops defeated by royal army at Gembloux
	February: radical Calvinists from Ghent start an offensive in Flanders
	Orange proposes a religious peace: allowing Protestants and Catholics to practise their religion freely where more than 100 families request it
	1 October: Don John dies; he is succeeded by Alexander Farnese, Prince of Parma
1579	6 January: Artois and Hainaut unite in the Catholic Union of Arras
	23 January: Union of Utrecht
	May: peace talks start in Cologne, but are unsuccessful
	29 June: Parma captures Maastricht
1580	15 March: ban of outlawry on Orange
	29 September: treaty between the States General and Anjou, who is to be 'Defender of the Liberties of the Netherlands'
	Philip's conquest of Portugal forces Parma into inaction
1581	26 July: the States of the rebellious provinces renounce Philip as sovereign lord
	Practising the Catholic faith forbidden in Antwerp and Brussels
1582	19 February: Anjou invested in Brabant
	18 March: attempt to assassinate Orange fails
	August: Anjou invested in Flanders
	Autumn: French army in the Netherlands
1583	18 January: French fury in Antwerp – Orange's French policy discredited
	Parma continues his advance
1584	10 July: Orange murdered in Delft
	Parma captures the main towns of Flanders
1585	Parma captures Brussels and Antwerp
	20 August: Elizabeth I of England supports the rebellious provinces
	13 November: Maurice becomes stadtholder of Holland and Zeeland

1586	January: Leicester becomes governor-general in the rebellious provinces; his regime fails
	16 March: Oldenbarnevelt becomes Land's Advocate of Holland
1587	Leicester departs; the Republic becomes de facto independent
1588	Summer: Spain's 'invincible Armada' suffers heavy losses in battles with the English and in storms
1590	King Philip II deploys Parma in the field against the French
	4 March: Peat-barge of Breda; Maurice and William Louis start a successful offensive
1592	3 December: death of Parma
1594	Reduction of Groningen
1596	21 June–5 July: English-Holland fleet commits atrocities in Cádiz
	Archduke Albert captures Calais and Hulst
1597	24 January: Victory for the Republic in the cavalry battle at Turnhout
1598	Philip II gives the Netherlands to his daughter Isabella as a dowry
	Philip II dies; he is succeeded by his son Philip III
1599	Archduke Albert and Archduchess Isabella accept power in Brussels
1600	Battle of Nieuwpoort
1601–4	Siege of Ostend, which is captured for the archdukes
1602	Dutch East India Company founded
1605–6	Spinola captures Oldenzaal and Groenlo in the east of the Republic
1609–21	Twelve Years Truce
1618	Coup against the Remonstrants by Maurice
1619	13 May: Oldenbarnevelt beheaded in the Binnenhof in The Hague
1620	31 May: Death of William Louis
1621	9 April: Truce expires and economic warfare starts
	3 June: the States General issue patent to West India Company
	21 July: death of Archduke Albert; Isabella continues as governor-general
	Death of Philip III; he is succeeded by Philip IV
	From now, the Republic suffers heavy losses caused by Dunkirk privateers
1622	Spinola unsuccessfully lays siege to Bergen op Zoom
1625	23 April: death of Maurice; he is succeeded by Frederick Henry
	31 May: Spinola captures Breda
1627	20 August: Frederick Henry captures Groenlo; all territory north of the rivers now restored to the Republic

1628	Piet Hein captures the silver fleet
1629	Frederick Henry captures Den Bosch; a dangerous enemy invasion across the River IJssel is defeated by capturing Wesel
1631	10 September: Battle of the Slaak – South Netherlands fleet under the command of Johan van Nassau-Siegen soundly defeated
1632	Frederick Henry launches campaign along the River Maas: Venlo, Roermond and Maastricht are captured
	The States General meet in the royalist Netherlands for the first time since 1600
1633	1 December: death of Archduchess Isabella
1634	Ferdinand of Austria appointed governor-general of the royalist Netherlands
	The Republic concludes an offensive and defensive alliance with France
1635	10 June: Tienen captured by Frederick Henry and the French; troops commit atrocities
	26 July: royal troops capture Fort Schenkenschans; euphoria in the Spanish camp
1636	30 April: William of Nassau-Siegen recaptures Schenkenschans
1637	10 October: Frederick Henry captures Breda
1638	June: Humiliating defeat for the States army at Kallo
1639	Maarten Harpertsz. Tromp defeats a second Spanish Armada at the Downs
1640	Spain under pressure because of revolts in Catalonia and Portugal
1641	27 July: Frederick Henry captures Gennep
	6 November: death of Ferdinand of Austria
1644	29 July: French troops capture Gravelines
	5 September: Frederick Henry captures Sas van Gent
1645	4 November: Frederick Henry captures Hulst
1646	The French capture Dunkirk; Frederick Henry gives up siege of Venlo
1647	14 March: death of Frederick Henry. He is succeeded by his son William II
1648	15 May: Peace of Münster signed

Maps

Map 1 (page 215)
Under Charles v, the Netherlands had a population of approximately three million, three-quarters of whom lived in Brabant, Flanders, Holland and Zeeland (Zeaeland, shown on the map in yellow). These provinces formed the core of the Burgundian-Habsburg state and generated the lion's share of tax revenues. The Prince-Bishopric of Liège (shown in grey) was neutral territory. For the sake of clarity, small independent lordships are not given.

Map 2 (page 216)
The Netherlands at the time of the Unions of Arras and Utrecht.
Purple: provinces that did not take part in the Revolt
Dark red: Union of Arras
Green: Union of Utrecht

Map 3 (page 217)
The Netherlands during the advance of Parma.
Purple: provinces that did not take part in the Revolt
Dark red: Union of Arras
Red: captured by Parma 1579–84
Light red: captured by Parma 1584–90

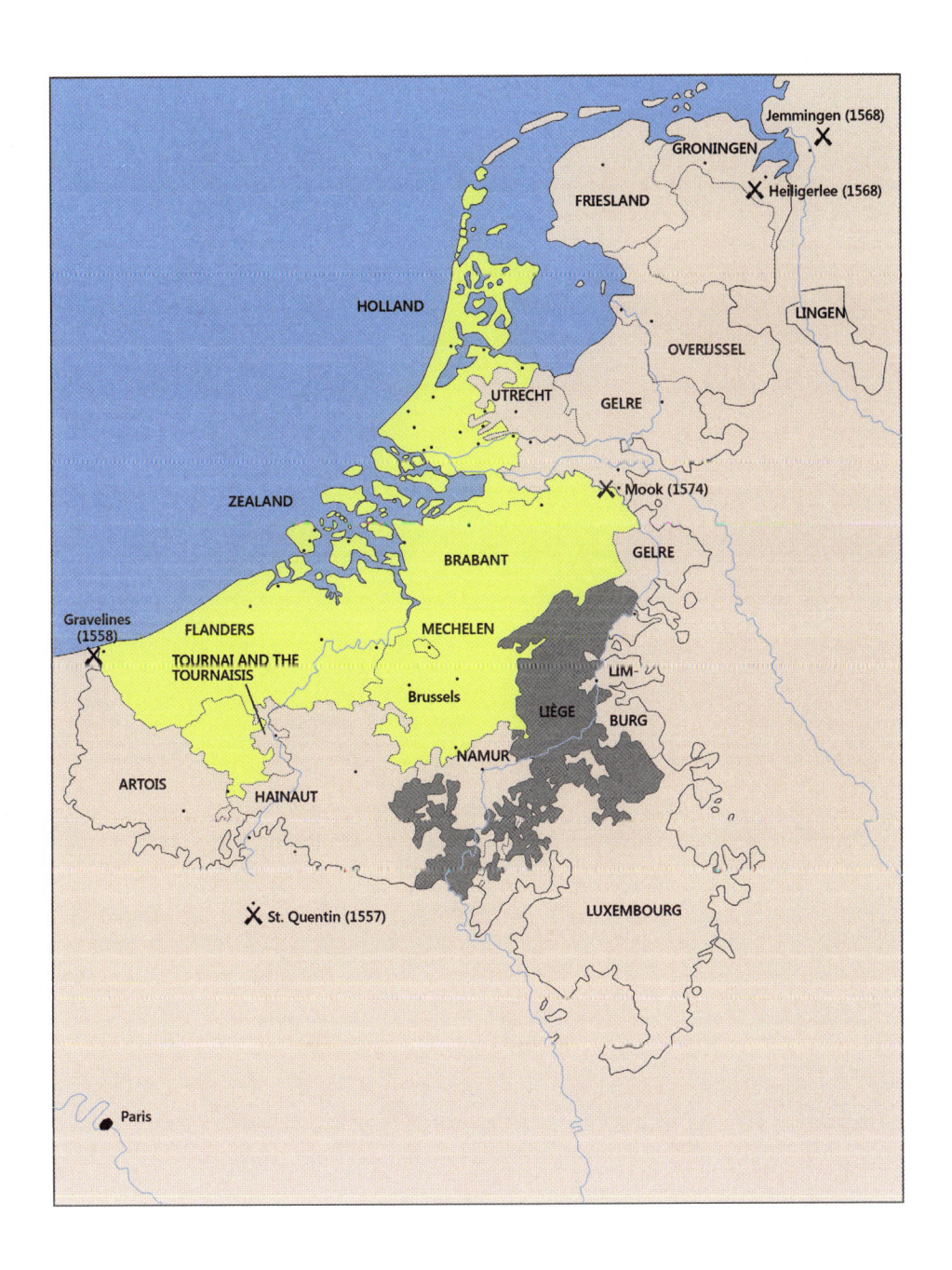

Maps

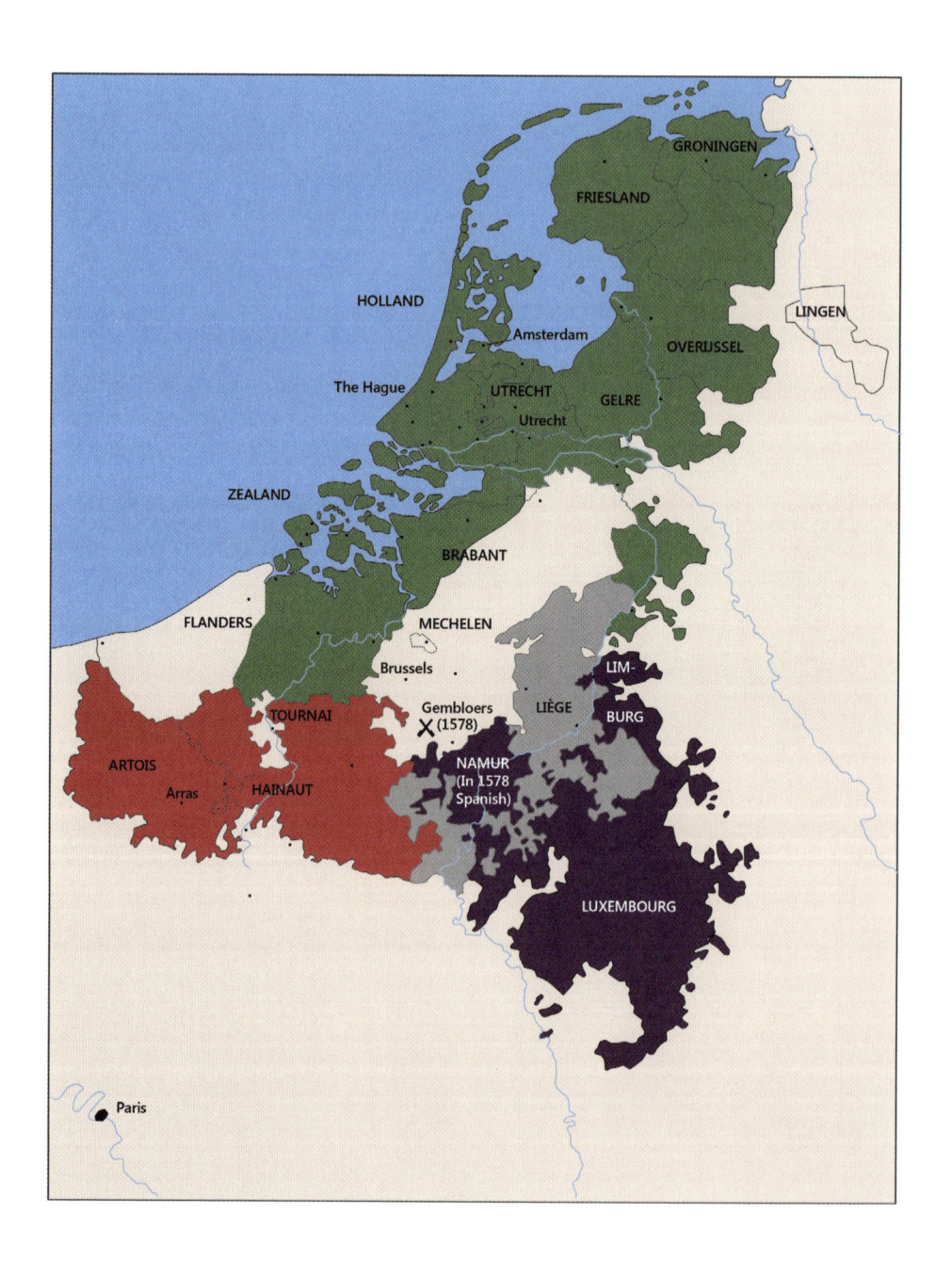

REVOLT in the NETHERLANDS

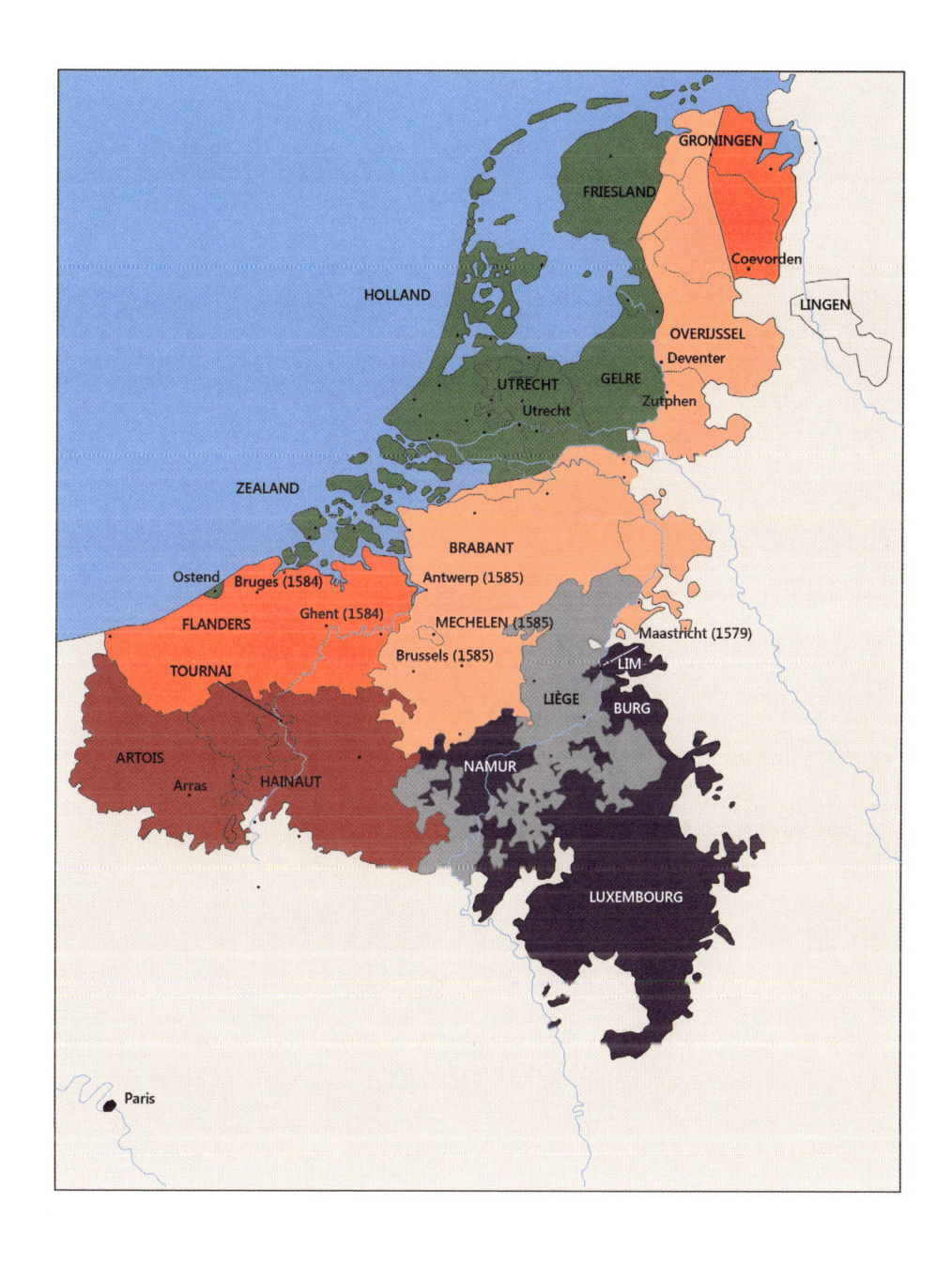

Maps

References

In the References, there are regular references to *De Bello Belgico*, the Leiden University website on the subject of the Revolt (http://dutchrevolt.leiden.edu). The site provides access to some 1,500 items in Dutch and a limited number of others in different languages. Rather than giving links, the notes refer directly to sections on the site where more information can be found. See, for example, note 10: http://dutchrevolt.leiden.edu > *Geografie* > *Antwerpen*.

1 The 'Lands Over Here'

1 Friedrich Schiller, *Geschichte des Abfalls der vereinigten Niederlande von der Spanischen Regierung* (Leipzig, 1788), p. 26: 'ein neuer Staat in Europa, dem nichts als der Name fehlte'; J. Huizinga, 'Uit de voorgeschiedenis van ons nationaal besef', in Huizinga, *Verzamelde Werken*, 9 vols (Haarlem, 1948–53), vol. II, p. 125; Alastair Duke, *Dissident Identities in the Early Modern Low Countries*, ed. Judith Pollmann and Andrew Spicer (Farnham, 2009), especially Chapter One: 'Elusive Netherlands'.
2 The stadtholder (*stadhouder* in Dutch) represents the king in one or more provinces, with the associated rights. It is a difficult term to translate. The French use *gouverneur*.
3 The use of the word 'province' requires some explanation. We use the term because there is no general term to designate the terms duchy, county and lordship. It was, however, not used under the Dukes of Burgundy. It only came into regular use during the reign of Charles V. In my opinion, historians devote insufficient attention to this sensitive distinction and tend to speak of provinces for the sake of convenience before they existed in a formal sense.
4 *De blijde inkomst van de hertogen van Brabant Johanna en Wenceslas*, ed. Ria van Bragt (Leuven, 1956).
5 J. H. Elliott, 'A Europe of Composite Monarchies', *Past and Present*, CXXXVII (1992).
6 Dagmar Eichberger, *Dames met klasse: Margareta van York, Margareta van Oostenrijk* (Leuven, 2005); Jacqueline Kerkhoff, *Maria van Hongarije en haar hof: 1505–1558* ([Amsterdam], 2005).

7 Anton van der Lem, 'Menno Simons in de Nederlandse geschiedschrijving', *Doopsgezinde Bijdragen*, 22 (1996), pp. 10–19; S. Zijlstra, *Om de ware gemeente en de oude gronden: Geschiedenis van de dopersen in de Nederlanden 1531–1675* (Hilversum and Leeuwarden, 2000).
8 These sensitive issues, and the different ways they have been interpreted by German, Belgian and Dutch historians are discussed in Monique Weis, *Les Pays-Bas espagnols et les états du Saint Empire (1559–1579): Priorités et enjeux de la diplomatie en temps de troubles* (Brussels, 2003), Chapter Two.
9 M. J. Rodríguez-Salgado, *The Changing Face of Empire: Charles V, Philip II and Habsburg Authority, 1551–1559* (Cambridge, 1988, repr. 2008), p. 7: *sosiego*, Spanish for calmness and composure.
10 Calvete de Estrella, *El felicíssimo viaje del muy alto y muy poderoso príncipe don Phelippe* (Madrid, [2001]). The three editions, all in Leiden University Library, are mentioned at http://dutchrevolt.leiden.edu > Geografie > Antwerpen.

2 The Troubles

1 M. J. Rodríguez-Salgado, *The Changing Face of Empire: Charles V, Philip II and Habsburg Authority, 1551–1559* (Cambridge, 1988, repr. 2008), p. 126: 'Contemporaries were aghast'.
2 Louis-Prosper Gachard, *Retraite et mort de Charles-Quint au monastère de Yuste* (Brussels, 1854), p. 78.
3 Manuel Fernández Alvarez, *Charles V: Elected Emperor and Hereditary Ruler* (London, 1975), pp. 167–9.
4 Harry Kelsey, *Philip of Spain King of England: The Forgotten Sovereign* (London, 2012), pp. 79 (marriage), 101–2 (Catholicism restored), 103 (summoned to Brussels) and 111 (phantom pregnancy).
5 Olaf Mörke, *Wilhelm von Oranien, 1533–1584: Fürst und 'Vater' der Republik* (Stuttgart, 2007), pp. 57–8.
6 Prudencio de Sandoval, *Historia de la vida y hechos del emperador Carlos V*, 2 vols (Pamplona, 1618–19), vol. II, pp. 806–7.
7 M. van Durme, *Antoon Perrenot, bisschop van Atrecht, kardinaal van Granvelle, minister van Karel V en van Filips II (1517–1586)* (Brussels, 1953), p. 150.
8 Rodríguez-Salgado, *The Changing Face of Empire*, p. 129.
9 Ibid., p. 132. She disagrees with Gachard's opinion that Charles really had influence.
10 Rodríguez-Salgado, *The Changing Face of Empire*, pp. 235–6; Van Durme, *Antoon Perrenot*, p. 157.
11 Rodríguez-Salgado, *The Changing Face of Empire*, p. 236.
12 James B. Tracy, *Holland under Habsburg Rule, 1506–1566: The Formation of a Body Politic* (Berkeley, CA, 1990), pp. 123–4, 132.
13 Ibid., pp. 183, 186.
14 Ibid., pp. 140, 181.
15 P. D. Lagomarsino, 'Court Factions and the Formulation of Spanish Policy towards the Netherlands, 1559–1567', PhD thesis, University of Cambridge, 1973, p. 324.

16 Marjolein C. 't Hart, *The Dutch Wars of Independence: Warfare and Commerce in the Netherlands, 1570–1680* (Abingdon, 2014), pp. 150–51.
17 Tracy, *Holland under Habsburg Rule*, p. 176.
18 Rodríguez-Salgado, *The Changing Face of Empire*, p. 192.
19 Ibid., p. 128.
20 Ibid., p. 160.
21 Geoffrey Parker, *The Grand Strategy of Philip II* (New Haven, CT, 1998), p. 89.
22 Kelsey, *Philip of Spain*, p. 131.
23 Rodríguez-Salgado, *The Changing Face of Empire*, p. 179.
24 Kelsey, *Philip of Spain*, p. 149.
25 The names of towns and cities in the Netherlands and France are cited according to recognized international usage (e.g. Antwerp, Brussels, Dunkirk, Ypres, The Hague). Otherwise, towns in the Dutch-speaking Low Countries are cited using their Dutch name and those in the French-speaking regions by their French names.
26 Braudel, Fernand, *La Méditerranée et le monde méditerranéen à l'époque de Philippe II*, 2 vols (Paris, 1966); English translation: *The Mediterranean and the Mediterranean World in the Age of Philip II*, 2 vols (New York and London, 1972–3).
27 Rodríguez-Salgado, *The Changing Face of Empire*, pp. 329–30; William of Orange, *The Apologie of William of Orange against the Proclamation of the King of Spaine*, edited after the English edition of 1581 by H. Wansink (Leiden, 1969), p. 61.
28 Rodríguez-Salgado, *The Changing Face of Empire*, Chapter Seven: 'Rebellion in the Spanish Realms'.
29 Rodríguez-Salgado, *The Changing Face of Empire*, p. 173; Kelsey, *Philip of Spain*.
30 Peter Arnade, *Beggars, Iconoclasts, and Civic Patriots: The Political Culture of the Dutch Revolt* (Ithaca, NY, 2008), p. 60. For Margaret: Charlie R. Steen, *Margaret of Parma: A Life* (Leiden, 2013).
31 Refuting this is the main argument in Michel Baelde, *De Collaterale Raden onder Karel V en Filips II (1531–1578): Bijdrage tot de geschiedenis van de centrale instellingen in de zestiende eeuw* (Brussels, 1965). For Baelde himself, see http://dutchrevolt.leidenuniv.edu/dutch: *Geschiedschrijvers > Baelde*. See also Tracy, *Holland under Habsburg Rule*, p. 177: 'rumors, not now credited by historians'.
32 Henri Pirenne, *Histoire de Belgique*, 7 vols (Brussels, 1923–32), vol. IV, p. 54.
33 Parker, *The Grand Strategy*, p. 117.
34 A. C. Duke, *Reformation and Revolt in the Low Countries* (London, 1990), p. 71.
35 William Monter, 'Heresy Executions in Reformation Europe, 1520–1565', in Ole Peter Grell and Bob Scribner, *Tolerance and Intolerance in the European Reformation* (Cambridge, 1996), p. 49.
36 Hugo de Groot, *Kroniek van de Nederlandse Oorlog: De Opstand 1559–1588*, trans. and epilogue Jan Waszink (Nijmegen, 2014), vol. I, par. 30.
37 J. J. Woltjer, *Friesland in Hervormingstijd* (Leiden, 1962), pp. 90–104.
38 See http://dutchrevolt.leiden.edu > *Bronnen (1559)* > *Super universas: de paus maakt de Nederlanden tot een zelfstandige kerkprovincie*.

39 The decree forbidding people from the Netherlands from studying abroad dated from 3 March 1570. In practice, of course, it was impossible to enforce.
40 Postma, 'Nieuw licht op een oude zaak: De oprichting van de nieuwe bisdommen in 1559', *Tijdschrift voor Geschiedenis*, 103 (1990), p. 22.
41 Geoffrey Parker, *The Dutch Revolt* (London, 1977), p. 283, n. 24; Gustaaf Janssens, *Brabant in het verweer: Loyale oppositie tegen Spanje's bewind in de Nederlanden van Alva tot Farnese 1567–1578* (Kortrijk and Heule, 1988), p. 110.
42 K. W. Swart, 'The Black Legend During the Eighty Years' War', in *Britain and the Netherlands*, vol. v, ed. J. S. Bromley and E. H. Kossmann (The Hague, 1975).
43 Werner Thomas, *La represión del protestantismo en España 1517–1648* and *Los protestantes y la Inquisición en España en tiempos de Reforma y Contrarreforma* (Leuven, 2001).
44 Rodríguez-Salgado, *The Changing Face of Empire*, p. 219.
45 Lagomarsino, 'Court Factions', pp. 42, 76–7.
46 Gerard van der Kooi, *De Wynberch des heren: Godsdienstige veranderingen op Texel 1514–1572* (Hilversum, 2005), pp. 278–9, 175.
47 Liesbeth Geevers, *Gevallen vazallen: De integratie van Oranje, Egmont en Horn in de Spaans-Habsburgse monarchie (1559–1567)* (Amsterdam, 2008), p. 94: Orange actually wrote the letter, but Egmont did not send it for a month because there was no courier available! It was eventually sent to the court by emergency courier on 25 August, with an accompanying note from Egmont. Geevers emphasized that it was important that the letter reached the king through Francisco de Eraso, representative of the moderate party, who could then explain it to the king in person.
48 Ibid., pp. 104ff. Egmont sent this letter with a private courier, not to Eraso but to Charles de Tisnacq, adviser to the king on matters relating to the Netherlands. De Tisnacq delivered the letter without explanation.
49 Arnade, *Beggars, Iconoclasts and Civic Patriots*, p. 63; H.F.K. van Nierop, 'A Beggar's Banquet: The Compromise of the Nobility and the Politics of Inversion', *European History Quarterly*, XXI (1991), p. 433.
50 Lagomarsino, 'Court Factions', pp. 60, 75.
51 He said this, of course, in French. Florentius van der Haer, *De initiis tumultuum Belgicorum* (Douai, 1587), pp. 186–7; Lagomarsino, 'Court Factions', p. 91: 'spoke frankly of liberty of conscience'. For an overview, see http://dutchrevolt.leiden.edu > *Bronnen* > *1564* > *Willem van Oranje spreekt de Raad van State toe*.
52 In a letter to Philip II dated 6 October 1562. Thanks to Gustaaf Janssens, who saw the original. Gachard summarized it as follows: 'Jusqu'ici la conduite personnelle du prince d'Orange en matière de religion est irrépréhensible' (Louis-Prosper Gachard, ed., *Correspondance de Philippe II sur les affaires des Pays-Bas* (Brussels, 1848–79), vol. I, p. 218).
53 Lagomarsino, 'Court Factions', p. 99.
54 Ibid., p. 119.
55 Ibid., pp. 173–81.

56 Ibid., pp. 186–200.
57 In the Netherlands he is usually referred to as Parma, and in Belgium as Farnese. We will use Parma here. The title 'prince' indicates not the sovereign of a princedom, but the son of a monarch.
58 Enno van Gelder, *Van beeldenstorm tot pacificatie: Acht opstellen over de Nederlandse revolutie der zestiende eeuw* (Amsterdam, 1964); H.F.K. van Nierop, *Van ridders tot regenten: De Hollandse adel in de zestiende en de eerste helft van de zeventiende eeuw*, 2nd edn (Amsterdam, 1990).
59 Arlette Jouanna, *Le Devoir de révolte: La noblesse française et la gestation de l'État moderne, 1559–1661* (Paris, 1989), p. 178.
60 Pirenne, *Histoire de Belgique*, vol. III, p. 420.
61 Ibid., p. 245.
62 Parker, *The Dutch Revolt*, p. 76.
63 Ibid., pp. 76–8.
64 Pirenne, *Histoire de Belgique*, vol. III, p. 468.
65 Otto J. de Jong, *Beeldenstormen in de Nederlanden* (Groningen, 1964), p. 6; Hans Cools, 'De Beeldenstorm in de Nederlanden', http://dutchrevolt.leiden.edu > *Begrippen* > *Beeldenstorm*.
66 Jurjen Vis, 'Tot meerdere eer en glorie van God. Kunst en muziek in en om de kerk', in *Geschiedenis van Alkmaar*, ed. Diederik Aten et al. (Zwolle, 2007), pp. 178–9.
67 For an overview of the various theories, see Judith Pollmann, 'Countering the Reformation in France and the Netherlands: Clerical Leadership and Catholic Violence, 1560–1585', *Past and Present: A Journal of Scientific History*, CXC (2006), pp. 84, 89, and *Catholic Identity and the Revolt of the Netherlands, 1520–1635* (Oxford, 2011).
68 Pollmann, *Catholic Identity*, p. 72. There is a printed copy of the petition in the University Library in Amsterdam.
69 Christin, 'France et Pays-Bas: Le second iconoclasme', in *Iconoclasme: Vie et mort de l'image médiévale*, ed. Cécile Dupeux et al. (Zurich, 2001), p. 57.
70 Lagomarsino, 'Court Factions', p. 244: 'Philip shocked into insensibility'.
71 See also C. Rooze-Stouthamer, *De opmaat tot de Opstand: Zeeland en het centraal gezag (1566–1572)* (Hilversum, 2009), pp. 46ff. John Marnix and his troops returned from a failed attempt to capture the fort at Rammekens, on Walcheren.

3 Loyalty Tested

1 Geoffrey Parker, *The Dutch Revolt* (London, 1977), p. 86.
2 P. D. Lagomarsino, 'Court Factions and the Formulation of Spanish Policy towards the Netherlands, 1559–1567', PhD thesis, University of Cambridge, 1973, p. 245; W. S. Maltby, *Alba: A Biography of Fernando Alvarez de Toledo, Third Duke of Alba, 1507–1582* (Berkeley and Los Angeles, CA, 1983), p. 131.
3 All of the Spaniards referred to in the following chapters can be found at http://dutchrevolt.leiden.edu > *Personen*.
4 Maltby, *Alba*, p. 124. Lagomarsino, 'Court Factions', p. 27, sees Alba's faction as promoting war and diplomacy, and that of Eboli as concerning itself with the finances. Henry Kamen, *The Duke of Alba*

(New Haven, CT, 2004), pp. 38 and 56, claims that there are no ideological differences between the factions.
5 Kamen, *Duke of Alba*, p. 72.
6 Maltby, *Alba*, pp. 138–9.
7 Geoffrey Parker, *The Army of Flanders and the Spanish Road, 1567–1659*, 2nd edn (Cambridge, 2004).
8 Friedrich Schiller, *Geschichte des Abfalls der vereinigten Niederlande von der Spanischen Regierung* (Leipzig, 1788), p. 263.
9 Fruin, 'Willem de Zwijger', in Fruin, *Verspreide Geschriften*, 10 vols (The Hague, 1900–1905), vol. VIII, p. 407, from Anonymous, *Pandorae sive Veniae Hispanicae Belgicis exulibus* (n.p., 1574), vol. VI: 'Si (inquit) astutus Guilielmus evasit, non erunt solida gaudia.' The expression was later erroneously attributed to Granvelle.
10 See also http://dutchrevolt.leiden.edu > *Spreuken* > *Zwijger*.
11 Andrew Pettegree, *Emden and the Dutch Revolt: Exile and the Development of Reformed Protestantism* (Oxford, 1992). For the diaspora in general, see Johannes Martin Müller, *Exile Memories and the Dutch Revolt: The Narrated Diaspora, 1550–1750* (Leiden, 2014).
12 Karel Bostoen, 'Waar kwam de Historie van B. Cornelis (1569) van de pers? Het spoor terug naar plaats van uitgave, boekverkoper en boekdrukker', *Handelingen van het Genootschap voor Geschiedenis te Brugge*, CLI (2014), pp. 65–111. Theme issue *Dutch Crossing*.
13 Louis Paul Boon, *Het Geuzenboek* (Amsterdam, 1979); M. Backhouse, *Beeldenstorm en bosgeuzen in het westkwartier (1566–1568): Bijdrage tot de geschiedenis van de godsdiensttroebelen der Zuidelijke Nederlanden in de XVIe eeuw* (Kortrijk, 1971).
14 Maltby, *Alba*, pp. 148–9. The most prominent of these officials were, on the one side, Alba's secretary Juan de Albornoz and his close friend, corrupt paymaster Francisco de Lixalde; on the other side were quartermaster-general Francisco de Ibarra and Gerónimo de Curiel, Philip II's financier in Antwerp. The later was stabbed one evening in the dark after leaving Alba's residence in Brussels.
15 Maltby, *Alba*, pp. 147–8.
16 Julie Versele, *Louis del Río (1537–1578): Reflets d'une période troublée* (Brussels, 2004).
17 Gustaaf Janssens, *Brabant in het verweer: Loyale oppositie tegen Spanje's bewind in de Nederlanden van Alva tot Farnese 1567–1578* (Kortrijk and Heule, 1988), p. 146.
18 Gustaaf Janssens, 'The Duke of Alba: Governor of the Netherlands in Times of War', in *Alba*, ed. Maurits A. Ebben et al. (Rotterdam, 2013), p. 98.
19 Monique Weis, *Les Pays-Bas espagnols et les états du Saint Empire (1559–1579): Priorités et enjeux de la diplomatie en temps de troubles* (Brussels, 2003).
20 Johan Brouwer, *Philips Willem, de Spaansche prins van Oranje* (Zutphen, 1940).
21 A. Th. van Deursen, *Mensen van klein vermogen: Het kopergeld van de Gouden Eeuw* (Amsterdam, 1991), p. 193.
22 Marijke van de Vrugt, *De Criminele ordonnantiën van 1570: Enkele beschouwingen over de eerste strafrechtcodificatie in de Nederlanden* (Zutphen, 1978).

References

23 Paul Scholten, 'Christelijke vrijheid en Nederlanderschap', in H. B. Wiardi Beckman, B. M. Telders and Paul Scholten, *Den Vaderlant ghetrouwe* (Haarlem, 1940), p. 45: 'liberteyt van religie en conscientie'; Kamen, *Duke of Alba*, p. 87.

24 W. Bergsma, *Tussen Gideonsbende en publieke kerk: Een studie over het gereformeerd protestantisme in Friesland, 1580–1650* (Hilversum, 1999), p. 260.

25 Maltby, *Alba*, pp. 161–2. Early in 2014 there was some commotion in the media about the discovery of a 'lost' battle, at Dahlem (now Dahlheim, in Germany to the east of Roermond). This defeat for Orange's army was of course already known; see J. Presser et al., *De Tachtigjarige Oorlog* (Amsterdam, 1941), p. 46: 'we have not yet even spoken of the insignificant attempts [at military action] by de Villers and Coqueville [Orange's generals]'; I. L. Uijterschout, *Beknopt overzicht van de belangrijkste gebeurtenissen uit de Nederlandsche krijgsgeschiedenis van 1568 tot heden* (Kampen, [1935]), pp. 18–19, does not mention the defeat, because he specifically wants the war to start with a victory.

26 Maltby, *Alba*, pp. 162–3.

27 Jasper van der Steen, *Memory Wars in the Low Countries, 1566–1700* (Leiden, 2014), Chapter One.

28 Anton van der Lem, 'Echos de la Révolte: Montaigne et les Pays-Bas du XVIe siècle', in *Montaigne and the Low Countries (1580–1700)*, ed. Paul J. Smith and Karel A. E. Enenkel (Leiden, 2007), pp. 47–62.

29 Van Deursen, *Mensen van klein vermogen*, p. 236.

30 Erik Swart, *Krijgsvolk: Militaire professionalisering en het ontstaan van het Staatse leger, 1568–1590* (Amsterdam, 2006), p. 130.

31 Maltby, *Alba*, p. 178. See also René Quatrefages, 'Alba Cunctator', in *Alba*, ed. Ebben et al.

32 P. J. Blok, *Willem de Eerste, prins van Oranje*, 2 vols (Amsterdam, 1919–20), vol. I, p. 192.

33 H. Klink, *Opstand, politiek en religie bij Willem van Oranje 1559–1568: Een thematische biografie* (Heerenveen, 1997), attempts to interpret Orange's fight in terms of the theory of Calvinist resistance, but it is clear why the author stops at Liège: the siege of this city, which had nothing to do with the conflict, belies his argument, which is otherwise underpinned by extensive knowledge of the subject matter. Orange did not attend the Lord's Supper until 1573, and then not ostentatiously. At the end of the 1570s, while in Brussels, he resumed his practice of attending Catholic Mass.

34 Ad den Besten, *Wilhelmus van Nassouwe: Het gedicht en zijn dichter* (Leiden, 1983). English edition: *The Beehive of the Romish Church*, translated from Dutch to English by George Gilpin the Elder (London, 1598).

35 Eberhard Nehlsen, *Wilhelmus von Nassauen: Studien zur Rezeption eines niederländischen Liedes im deutschsprachigen Raum vom 16. bis 20. Jahrhundert* (Münster, 1993); Abraham Maljaars, *Het Wilhelmus: Auteurschap, datering en strekking: een kritische toetsing en nieuwe interpretatie* (Kampen, 1996).

36 Maltby, *Alba*, p. 181.
37 Nicolas le Roux, *Les Guerres de religion 1559–1629* (Paris, 2009), p. 125; Hugues Daussy, 'Louis de Nassau et le parti huguenot', in *Entre Calvinistes et Catholiques: Les relations religieuses entre la France et les Pays-Bas du Nord (XVIe–XVIIIe siècle)*, ed. Yves Krumenacker and Olivier Christin (Rennes, 2010), pp. 31–43.
38 Violet Soen, *Geen pardon zonder Paus!: Studie over de complementariteit van het koninklijk en pauselijk generaal pardon (1570–1574) en over inquisiteur-generaal Michael Baius (1560–1576)* (Brussels, 2007); *Vredehandel: Adellijke en Habsburgse verzoeningspogingen tijdens de Nederlandse Opstand (1564–1581)* (Amsterdam, 2012).
39 Ferdinand H. M. Grapperhaus, *Alva en de Tiende Penning* (Zutphen, 1982).
40 Map of the raids by the sea beggars in Petra Groen et al., eds, *De Tachtigjarige Oorlog: Van opstand naar geregelde oorlog 1568–1648* (Amsterdam, 2013), pp. 50–51.
41 Parker, *The Dutch Revolt*, p. 133.
42 Maltby, *Alba*, p. 229, refers to Morillon, who wrote to Granvelle that Alba always said this when faced with a setback.
43 Morillon, in Charles Piot, ed., *Correspondance du cardinal de Granvelle, 1565–1583* (Brussels, 1877–96), vol. IV, p. 174, mentioned eighty dead.
44 Anton van der Lem, 'Den Briel: Sint-Catharinakerk; Watergeuzen veroveren Brielle, 1 april 1572', in *Plaatsen van herinnering: Nederland in de zeventiende en achttiende eeuw*, ed. Maarten Prak (Amsterdam, 2006); B. Hartmann, *De martelaren van Gorcum: Volgens het getuigenis van Guilielmus Estius geschreven in 1572*, trans., introduction and commentary B. Hartmann (Oegstgeest, 2009); Roy Tepe, *Oog in oog met de Martelaren van Gorcum. Catalogus bij de tentoonstelling in het Gorcums Museum – 2012* (Gorinchem, 2012), gives the most details.
45 J. J. Woltjer, *Tussen vrijheidsstrijd en burgeroorlog* (Amsterdam, 1994), p. 59.
46 Johanna K. Oudendijk, 'Den coninck van hispaengien heb ick altijt gheeert', in *Dancwerc: Opstellen aangeboden aan Prof. Dr. D. Th. Enklaar ter gelegenheid van zijn 65ste verjaardag* (Groningen, 1959), p. 272.
47 B. Hartmann, *De martelaren van Roermond in het kader van de politieke en kerkelijke situatie van hun tijd* (Oegstgeest, 2009).
48 Maltby, *Alba*, p. 237; Raymond Fagel, *Kapitein Julián: De Spaanse held van de Nederlandse Opstand* (Hilversum, 2011), p. 47.
49 *Declaration des jvstes causes du saccaigement de la ville de Mailine* (dated 4 October 1572) (n.p., [1572]); Pieter Chr. Bor, *Oorsprongk, begin en vervolgh der Nederlandsche oorlogen, beroerten, en borgerlyke oneenigheden etc.*, 4 vols (Amsterdam, 1679–84), vol. I, pp. 409–10; Kamen, *Duke of Alba*, p. 110.
50 A.C.J. de Vrankrijker, *De historie van de vesting Naarden*, 3rd edn (Haarlem and Naarden, 1978), pp. 45–53. See also Marianne Eekhout, *Material Memories of the Dutch Revolt: The Urban Memory Landscape in the Low Countries, 1566–1700* (Leiden, 2014).
51 Kamen, *Duke of Alba*, p. 116.
52 Maltby, *Alba*, p. 250.
53 Ibid., p. 259; Kamen, *Duke of Alba*, p. 117.

54 Maltby, *Alba*, p. 259.
55 Theodorus Velius, *Kroniek van Hoorn*, 2 vols (Hoorn, 2007), vol. II, p. 532. This present-day Dutch translation of Velius is recommended reading for a good understanding of the period. The same applies to the translation of *Hadrianus Junius, Holland is een eiland*.
56 H.F.K. van Nierop, *Het foute Amsterdam* (Amsterdam, 2000).
57 See Els Kloek, *Kenau en Magdalena: Vrouwen in de Tachtigjarige Oorlog* (Nijmegen, 2014), pp. 228–9, for the true facts.
58 Eekhout, *Material Memories*.
59 Maltby, *Alba*, p. 124.

4 The Netherlands, or *Belgium Nostrum*

1 Geoffrey Parker, *The Dutch Revolt* (London, 1977), devotes subsequent chapters to the first, second and third revolts; Ferdinand H. M. Grapperhaus, *Alva en de Tiende Penning* (Zutphen, 1982), p. 280.
2 Marjolein C. 't Hart, *The Dutch Wars of Independence: Warfare and Commerce in the Netherlands, 1570–1680* (Abingdon, 2014), p. 2; this whole section is based on Erik Swart, *Krijgsvolk: Militaire professionalisering en het ontstaan van het Staatse leger, 1568–1590* (Amsterdam, 2006).
3 P. Noordeloos, *Cornelis Musius (Mr Cornelius Muys): Pater van Sint Agatha te Delft: humanist, priester, martelaar* (Utrecht, 1955); Ton Oosterhuis, *Lumey, de vossestaart: Admiraal van de Geuzen* (Amsterdam, 1996).
4 't Hart, *The Dutch Wars of Independence*, p. 42.
5 Ibid., p. 88. This was a weekly advance on the soldiers' pay. Every few months, the balance would be calculated and they would receive the rest. In practice, however, they often had to wait for the final settlement. Thanks to Erik Swart for the additional information.
6 Marie-Ange Delen, *Het hof van Willem van Oranje* (Amsterdam, 2004).
7 They were, in Northern Holland: Alkmaar, Hoorn, Enkhuizen, Medemblik, Edam, Monnickendam and Purmerend; and in southern Holland: Brill, Vlaardingen, Rotterdam, Gorinchem and Schoonhoven.
8 K. W. Swart, *William of Orange and the Revolt of the Netherlands, 1572–84*, with introductory chapters by Alastair Duke and Jonathan I. Israel; ed. R. P. Fagel, M.E.H.N. Mout and H.F.K. van Nierop (Aldershot, 2003), pp. 39–40.
9 *Catonis disticha moralia* (1, 27), proverbs attributed to Roman statesman Cato the Elder; Dousa used an edition by Erasmus.
10 Karel Bostoen, *Hart voor Leiden: Jan van Hout (1542–1609), stadssecretaris, dichter en vernieuwer* (Hilversum, 2009), pp. 48–54.
11 Th.F. Wijsenbeek-Olthuis, *Honger* (Leiden, 2006).
12 't Hart, *The Dutch Wars of Independence*, pp. 103, 106.
13 Swart, *William of Orange*, p. 63.
14 Nettie Stoppelenburg, *De Oudewaterse moord* (Oudewater, 2005).
15 Swart, *William of Orange*, pp. 89–90.
16 Johan Brouwer, *Kronieken van Spaansche soldaten uit het begin van den Tachtigjarigen Oorlog* (Zutphen, 1933, 1980), p. 240.

17 Swart, *William of Orange*, p. 92.
18 N. M. Sutherland, 'The Foreign Policy of Queen Elizabeth, the Sea Beggars and the Capture of Brill, 1572', in Sutherland, *Princes, Politics and Religion, 1547–1589* (London, 1984), pp. 183–206. For the general attitude to the Revolt in England, see Hugh Dunthorne, *Britain and the Dutch Revolt, 1560–1700* (Cambridge, 2013).
19 Swart, *William of Orange*, p. 101.
20 Nicolas le Roux, *Les Guerres de religion 1559–1629* (Paris, 2009), p. 203.
21 Swart, *William of Orange*, p. 109.
22 J. van Roey, *De val van Antwerpen 17 augustus 1585 – voor en na* (Antwerp, 1985), p. 30.
23 Parker, *The Dutch Revolt*, p. 178 cites the traditional figure of 8,000. Modern counts come to 2,500.
24 Hugo de Schepper, *'Belgium Nostrum' 1500–1650: Over integratie en desintegratie van het Nederland* (Antwerp, 1987), pp. 5–6; De Schepper, *'Belgium dat is Nederlandt': Identiteiten en identiteitenbesef in de Lage Landen, 1200–1800: epiloog: Koninkrijk der Nederlanden, 1815–1830* (Breda, 2014).
25 Swart, *William of Orange*, p. 123.
26 Parker, *The Dutch Revolt*, p. 303, n. 16.
27 Guido Marnef, 'Het protestantisme te Brussel', pp. 293–40.

5 The Netherlands Divided

1 P.J.H. Ubachs, 'De Nederlandse religievrede van 1578', *Nederlands Archief voor Kerkgeschiedenis*, LXXVII (1997), pp. 41–61. The 27 towns were Aalst, Antwerp, Bolsward, Breda, Bruges, Brussels, Deventer, Franeker, Ghent, Groningen, Haarlem, Harlingen, 's-Hertogenbosch, Kampen, Kortrijk, Leeuwarden, Mechelen, Montfoort, Nijmegen, Oudenaarde, Rhenen, Sneek, Utrecht, Venlo, Wijk bij Duurstede, Ypres and Zwolle.
2 Henri Pirenne, *Histoire de Belgique*, 7 vols (Brussels, 1923–32), vol. IV, p. 61.
3 Ibid., p. 73.
4 Pieter Chr. Bor, *Oorsprongk, begin en vervolgh der Nederlandsche oorlogen, beroerten, en borgerlyke oneenigheden etc.*, 4 vols (Amsterdam, 1679–84), vol. I, pp. 893–6.
5 Guido Marnef, 'Het protestantisme te Brussel', pp. 250–51.
6 J. Decavele, *Het einde van een rebelse droom: Opstellen over het calvinistisch bewind te Gent (1577–1584) en de terugkeer van de stad onder de gehoorzaamheid van de koning van Spanje* [17 September 1584] (Ghent, 1984), p. 40.
7 Pirenne, *Histoire de Belgique*, vol. IV, p. 109.
8 Ferdinand H. M. Grapperhaus, *Convoyen en licenten* (Zutphen, Deventer, 1986).
9 J. H. Kernkamp, *De handel op den vijand*, 2 vols (Utrecht, 1931–[35]).
10 K. W. Swart, *William of Orange and the Revolt of the Netherlands, 1572–84*, with introductory chapters by Alastair Duke and Jonathan I. Israel; ed. R. P. Fagel, M.E.H.N. Mout and H.F.K. van Nierop (Aldershot, 2003), p. 158.

11 Decavele, *Het einde van een rebelse droom*, p. 50.
12 Pirenne, *Histoire de Belgique*, vol. IV, pp. 140–41.
13 Ibid., vol. IV, p. 147.
14 Hugo de Schepper, *'Belgium Nostrum' 1500–1650: Over integratie en desintegratie van het Nederland* (Antwerp, 1987), p. 18.
15 Geoffrey Parker, *The Dutch Revolt* (London, 1977), p. 202.
16 De Schepper, *Belgium nostrum*, p. 19.
17 Parker, *The Dutch Revolt*, p. 195.
18 Francisco Verdugo, *Voor God en mijn koning: Het verslag van kolonel Francisco Verdugo over zijn jaren als legerleider en gouverneur namens Filips II in Stad en Lande van Groningen, Drenthe, Friesland, Overijssel en Lingen (1581–1595)*, introduction, translation and explanatory notes by Jan van den Broek (Assen, 2009).
19 Guido Marnef, *Het calvinistisch Bewind te Mechelen (1580–1585)* (Kortrijk and Heule, 1988), p. 117.
20 Swart, *William of Orange*, p. 197.
21 Parker, *The Dutch Revolt*, p. 208.
22 Marnef, *Het calvinistisch bewind te Mechelen*, pp. 189, 298.
23 Swart, *William of Orange*, p. 227.
24 Ibid., p. 201.
25 Ibid., p. 250.
26 J.P.A. Coopmans, 'De huldigingsvoorwaarden voor Willem van Oranje van 1583: Een nieuw type gezagsovereenkomst', in *Beleid en bestuur in de oude Nederlanden: Liber amicorum prof. dr. M. Baelde*, ed. Hugo Soly and René Vermeir (Ghent, 1993), p. 58.
27 Swart, *William of Orange*, p. 247.
28 Ibid.
29 Ibid., p. 255.
30 For more information see http://dutchrevolt.leiden.edu > *Spreuken* > *Mon Dieu, mon Dieu*.
31 Swart, *William of Orange*, p. 124.

6 An Offensive War

1 Henri Pirenne, *Histoire de Belgique*, 7 vols (Brussels, 1923–32), vol. IV, p. 189.
2 Thanks to Erik Swart. Léon van der Essen, *Alexandre Farnèse, prince de Parme*, 5 vols (Brussels, 1933–7), vol. II, 152.
3 Werner Thomas and Luc Duerloo, *Albert & Isabella, 1598–1621: Essays* ([Turnhout], 1998), p. 9.
4 See http://dutchrevolt.leiden.edu > *Personen* > *Florianus*.
5 See also J. Presser et al., *De Tachtigjarige Oorlog* (Amsterdam, 1941), p. 68: 'De bakermat van onze Opstand!'
6 Geoffrey Parker, *The Dutch Revolt* (London, 1977), p. 218.
7 F. G. Oosterhoff, *Leicester and the Netherlands, 1586–1587* (Utrecht, 1988).
8 Pieter Chr. Bor, *Oorsprongk, begin en vervolgh der Nederlandsche oorlogen, beroerten, en borgerlyke oneenigheden etc.*, 4 vols (Amsterdam, 1679–84), vol. I, p. 205. Translated by Alastair Duke in A. C. Duke, *Reformation and Revolt in the Low Countries* (London, 1990)

9 A.Th. van Deursen, *Maurits van Nassau: De winnaar die faalde* (Amsterdam, 2000), p. 42.
10 Parker, *The Dutch Revolt*, p. 226.
11 Magdalena Pi Corrales, *España y las potencias nordicas: 'La otra invencible' 1574* (Madrid, 1983).
12 Garrett Mattingly, *The Armada* (Boston, MA, 1959); Robert Hutchinson, *The Spanish Armada* (London, 2014).
13 Geoffrey Parker, 'Was Parma Ready? The Army of Flanders and the Spanish Armada in 1588', in *Beleid en bestuur in de oude Nederlanden: Liber amicorum prof. dr. M. Baelde*, ed. Hugo Soly and René Vermeir (Ghent, 1993), pp. 279–97; see also Fernando Riaño Lozano, *Los medios navales de Alejandro Farnese (1587–1588)* (Madrid, 1999).
14 Petra Groen et al., eds, *De Tachtigjarige Oorlog: Van opstand naar geregelde oorlog 1568–1648* (Amsterdam, 2013), p. 222.
15 Arlette Jouanna, *Le Devoir de révolte: La noblesse française et la gestation de l'État moderne, 1559–1661* (Paris, 1989), p. 191.
16 Geoffrey Parker, *The Grand Strategy of Philip II* (New Haven, CT, 1998); Patrick Williams, *Philip II* (Basingstoke, 2001).
17 Anton van der Lem, '"Het groote pleit beslecht". Anderhalve eeuw Tien Jaren van Robert Fruin', in *Aangeraakt: Boeken in contact met hun lezers. Een bundel opstellen voor Wim Gerretsen en Paul Hoftijzer*, ed. Kasper van Ommen, Arnoud Vrolijk, Geert Warnar (Leiden, 2007), pp. 231–8.
18 Ubbo Emmius, *Willem Lodewijk, graaf van Nassau (1560–1620), stadhouder van Friesland, Groningen en Drenthe* (Hilversum, 1994), p. 105.
19 See Groen et al., *De Tachtigjarige Oorlog* and Ronald de Graaf, *Oorlog, mijn arme schapen: Een andere kijk op de Tachtigjarige Oorlog 1565–1648* (Franeker, 2004) for excellent overviews.
20 Marjolein C. 't Hart, *The Dutch Wars of Independence: Warfare and Commerce in the Netherlands, 1570–1680* (Abingdon, 2014), p. 34.
21 Herbert Boland, *De list met het turfschip van Breda* (Breda, 2011), p. 15.
22 P. Louwerse and J. J. Moerman, *Geïllustreerde vaderlandse geschiedenis: Voor jong en oud Nederland*, (Amsterdam, 1961), chapter 'Twee jonge veldheren'.
23 Van Deursen, *Maurits*, pp. 125, 128.
24 Groen et al., *De Tachtigjarige Oorlog*, p. 106.
25 't Hart, *The Dutch Wars of Independence*, p. 22; Christi M. Klinkert, *Nassau in het nieuws: Nieuwsprenten van Maurits van Nassaus militaire ondernemingen uit de periode 1590–1600* (Zutphen, 2005), Chapter Eleven.
26 Van Deursen, *Maurits*, p. 45.
27 Robert Fruin, *Tien jaren uit den Tachtigjarigen oorlog* (Leiden, 1857), pp. 191–2; De Graaf, *Oorlog, mijn arme schapen*, p. 302; Arthur Lens, *Lier: Ontstaan en evolutie van een kleine stad* (Lier, 1993), p. 37.
28 Van Deursen, *Maurits*, p. 157; De Graaf, *Oorlog, mijn arme schapen*, pp. 28–329; Klinkert, *Nassau in het nieuws*, Chapter Fourteen; D.B.J. Trim, 'Sir Francis Vere (1560/1–1621), Army Officer and Diplomat', *Oxford Dictionary of National Biography*, www.oxforddnb.com.
29 Van Deursen, *Maurits*, p. 158.

30 For more on Mansfeld, see the biography by Hugo de Schepper at http://dutchrevolt.leiden.edu > *Personen* > *Mansfeld*. See also Mousset, *Un prince de la Renaissance*.
31 Thomas and Duerloo, *Albert & Isabella*; Dries Raeymaekers, *One Foot in the Palace: The Habsburg Court of Brussels and the Politics of Access in the Reign of Albert and Isabella, 1598–1621* (Leuven, 2013); Luc Duerloo, *Dynasty and Piety: Archduke Albert (1598–1621) and Habsburg Political Culture in an Age of Religious Wars* (Farnham, 2012).
32 Van Deursen, *Maurits*, p. 154.
33 There were rumours that Philip knew that his daughter was barren or would be unable to bear children. If that were true, it would make the transfer of power in the Netherlands a cynical joke. Paul C. Allen, *Philip III and the Pax Hispanica, 1598–1621: The Failure of Grand Strategy* (New Haven, CT, 2000), p. 18, n. 29, referring to Cabrera de Córdoba, *Felipe Segundo*, vol. IV, p. 285.
34 Joseph Lefèvre, *Correspondance de Philippe II sur les affaires des Pays-Bas*, 2 vols (Brussels, 1940–60), part II, vol. II, no. 1399, pp. 465–6, summary in French.
35 Margit Thøfner, *A Common Art: Urban Ceremonial in Antwerp and Brussels During and After the Dutch Revolt* (Zwolle, 2007).
36 Van Deursen, *Maurits*, p. 146.
37 B. Cox, *Vanden Tocht in Vlaenderen: De logistiek van Nieuwpoort 1600* (Zutphen, 1986); Anthonis Duyck, *De slag bij Nieuwpoort: Journaal van de tocht naar Vlaanderen in 1600*, trans. Vibeke Roeper, introduction and annotation Wilfried Uitterhoeve (Nijmegen, 2000).
38 Klinkert, *Nassau in het nieuws*, Chapter Sixteen.
39 I. L. Uijterschout, *Beknopt overzicht van de belangrijkste gebeurtenissen uit de Nederlandsche krijgsgeschiedenis van 1568 tot heden* (Kampen, [1935]), p. 64; 't Hart, *The Dutch Wars of Independence*, pp. 24, 69; Allen, *Philip III*, p. 127.
40 Van Deursen, *Maurits*, p. 194; Allen, *Philip III*, pp. 85, 89.
41 Allen, *Philip III*, p. 88.
42 Anton van der Lem, 'De strijd om de Vlaamse havens tijdens de Tachtigjarige Oorlog', in Dirk de Vries, *Oostende verloren, Sluis gewonnen, 1604: een kroniek in kaarten. Catalogus bij een tentoonstelling in de Leidse universiteitsbibliotheek van 12 augustus – 12 september 2004* (Leiden, 2004), pp. 9–26.
43 Werner Thomas, *De val van het nieuwe Troje: Het beleg van Oostende, 1601–1604* (Leuven, 2001); Allen, *Philip III*, p. 138. The siege had lasted three years and 77 days.
44 Allen, *Philip III*, p. 146.
45 Ibid., p. 145. In Spanish documents, this part of the Republic was consistently referred to as *Frisia*.
46 Allen, *Philip III*, p. 151.
47 J. E. van der Pluijm, *De vestingstad Grol: Geschiedenis van de vestingwerken van Groenlo* (Groenlo, 1999).
48 Groen et al., *De Tachtigjarige Oorlog*, pp. 187–8.
49 Ibid., pp. 213 and 216.
50 Ibid., p. 217.

51 Ibid., p. 233.
52 Ibid., p. 236; Maurits A. Ebben, 'El ataque de Pieter van der Does a Canarias y la expansión neerlandesa a finales del siglo XVI y comienzos del siglo XVII', in *Coloquio internacional Canarias y el Atlántico, 1580–1648: IV centenario del ataque de Van der Does a las Palmas de Gran Canaria, 1999*, ed. Massieu Antonio de Béthencourt (Las Palmas de Gran Canaria 2001), pp. 147–68.
53 Groen et al, *De Tachtigjarige Oorlog*, p. 252.
54 Ibid., pp. 254–55; 't Hart, *The Dutch Wars of Independence*, p. 25.

7 The Twelve Years Truce

1 W.J.M. van Eysinga, *De wording van het Twaalfjarig Bestand van 9 april 1609* (Amsterdam, 1959); J. I. Israel, *The Dutch Republic and the Hispanic World, 1606–1661* (Oxford, 1986); Paul C. Allen, *Philip III and the Pax Hispanica, 1598–1621: The Failure of Grand Strategy* (New Haven, CT, 2000); Simon Groenveld, *Het Twaalfjarig Bestand 1609–1621: De jongelingsjaren van de Republiek der Verenigde Nederlanden* (Hilversum, 2009).
2 Illustrating this is the central argument in Allen, *Philip III*.
3 Groenveld, *Het Twaalfjarig Bestand*, p. 50.
4 Allen, *Philip III*, p. 15.
5 Yolanda Rodríguez Pérez, *De Tachtigjarige Oorlog in Spaanse ogen: De Nederlanden in Spaanse historische en literaire teksten (circa 1548–1673)* (Nijmegen, 2003); S. A. Vosters, *De Nederlanden in de Spaanse literatuur (van 1200 tot 1700)* (Breda, 2014), passim.
6 Allen, *Philip III*, p. 12.
7 Ibid., p. 52.
8 See also the maxim 'France as a friend, but not as a neighbour' > http://dutchrevolt.leiden.edu > *Spreuken* > *Gallia amica, non vicina*.
9 Groenveld, *Het Twaalfjarig Bestand*, p. 36.
10 Israel, *The Dutch Republic and the Hispanic World*, p. 5.
11 Allen, *Philip III*, p. 161.
12 In the Treaty of Tordesillas, 7 June 1494.
13 Allen, *Philip III*, p. 192, makes a good distinction between freedom of conscience and freedom of worship for Catholics, but in almost all other cases he uses the first where it should have been the second (pp. 186, 205, 208, 225, 226 etc.).
14 Allen, *Philip III*, p. 183.
15 Ibid., p. 216.
16 Groenveld, *Het Twaalfjarig Bestand*, p. 49: 'comme avec Etats libres, sur lesquels le roi d'Espagne et les archiducs ne prétendent rien.'
17 Allen, *Philip III*, p. 229.
18 Groenveld, *Het Twaalfjarig Bestand*, p. 52: 'Hauts et Puissants Seigneurs'.
19 Ibid., pp. 54–5; the full text can be found in Groenveld, *Unie – Bestand – Vrede: Drie fundamentele wetten van de Republiek der Verenigde Nederlanden* (Hilversum, 2009), pp. 115–27.
20 'De voor-seyde Heeren Eertzhertoghen verclaeren, soo wel in hunnen naem, als in den neem des voorseyden Heeren Conings, dat sy te vreden zijn te handelen met de voor-seyde Heeren Staeten Generael

References

van de Vereenighdde Provintien in qualiteyt ende als de selve houdende voor vrye Landen, Provincien ende Staten, op de welcke sy niet en pretenderen'.

21 Henk den Heijer, *De geschiedenis van de WIC* (Zutphen, 2002).
22 Israel, *The Dutch Republic and the Hispanic World*, p. 22.
23 This expression was used after Dutch intervention in the Øresund in 1644 during the Dano-Swedish war.
24 Israel, *The Dutch Republic and the Hispanic World*, p. 23.
25 Tim Piceu, *Over vrybuters en quaetdoenders: Terreur op het Vlaamse platteland (eind 16de eeuw)* (Leuven, 2008); Han Verschure, *Overleven buiten de Hollandse tuin Raamsdonk, Waspik, 's Gravenmoer, Capelle, Sprang en Besoijen tijdens de Tachtigjarige Oorlog* (n.p., 2004); Leo Adriaenssen, *Staatsvormend geweld: Overleven aan de frontlinies in de meierij van Den Bosch, 1572–1629* (Tilburg, 2007); Jos Wassink and Wil Nouwen, *Boerenschansen: verscholen voor Staatsen en Spanjaarden* (Weert, 2008); 't Hart, *The Dutch Wars of Independence*, Chapter Five.
26 Israel, *The Dutch Republic and the Hispanic World*, pp. 15, 49.
27 Ibid., p. 49.
28 Luc Duerloo and Marc Wingens, *Scherpenheuvel: Het Jeruzalem van de Lage Landen* (Leuven, 2002).
29 Craig Harline and Eddy Put, *A Bishop's Tale: Matthias Hovius among his Flock in Seventeenth-century Flanders* (New Haven, CT, 2000).
30 Judith Pollmann, *Catholic Identity and the Revolt of the Netherlands, 1520–1635* (Oxford, 2011), Chapter Six.
31 Roy Tepe, *Oog in oog met de Martelaren van Gorcum. Catalogus bij de tentoonstelling in het Gorcums Museum – 2012* (Gorinchem, 2012), p. 21.
32 Willem Heijting and Willem Frijhoff, *Hollandse priesterbibliotheken uit de tijd van de Republiek* (Amstelveen, 2005). Those of Aarlanderveen, Assendelft, Buitenveldert, Voorburg and Zevenhoven are kept in the Library of the Free University of Amsterdam; those of Edam, Kethel, Langeraar, Nieuwkoop and Noordwijk are kept at the University Library in Leiden.
33 Joke Spaans, *De levens der maechden: Het verhaal van een religieuze vrouwengemeenschap in de eerste helft van de zeventiende eeuw* (Hilversum, 2012), offers a fascinating glimpse into the lives of these devout Catholic women, known as *kloppen* in Haarlem.
34 A. Th. van Deursen, *Bavianen en slijkgeuzen: Kerk en kerkvolk ten tijde van Maurits en Oldenbarnevelt*, 4th, revised and illustrated edn (Franeker, 2010); A. Th. van Deursen, *Maurits van Nassau: De winnaar die faalde* (Amsterdam, 2000); Geert H. Janssen, *Het stokje van Oldenbarnevelt* (Hilversum, 2001); Ben Knapen, *De man en zijn staat: Johan van Oldenbarnevelt (1547–1619)* (Amsterdam, 2005); Groenveld, *Het Twaalfjarig Bestand*.
35 Franciscus Gomarus (1563, Bruges–1641, Groningen), professor at Leiden 1594–1611. See also *Reformatorica: Teksten uit de geschiedenis van het Nederlandse protestantisme*, ed. C. Augustijn et al. (Zoetermeer, 1996), pp. 118–19.
36 Jacobus Arminius (1560, Oudewater–1609, Leiden), professor at Leiden 1603–9. See also *Reformatorica*, pp. 116–17. For a clearer and more

comprehensive examination of Arminius, see the web presentation *Arminius, Arminianisme en Europa* at www.library.leidenuniv.nl. See also Judith Pollmann, *Religious Choice in the Dutch Republic: The Reformation of Arnoldus Buchelius (1565–1641)* (Manchester, 1999), pp. 105–6.

37 Joris van Eijnatten and Fred van Lieburg, *Nederlandse religiegeschiedenis*, 2nd edn (Hilversum, 2006), p. 175.
38 Van Deursen, *Bavianen en slijkgeuzen*, p. 366.
39 Both in *Reformatorica*, no. 60, pp. 120–22, and no. 61, 122–24.
40 The claim that Maurice said that he did not know whether predestination 'was green or blue' was expertly debunked by Van Deursen. Van Deursen, *Maurits*, p. 233.
41 Knapen, *De man en zijn staat*, p. 299; the full text can be found at http://dutchrevolt.leiden.edu > Bronnen > 1619 > De Scherpe Resolutie.
42 The National Synod acted as expected and expelled the Remonstrants from the church, resulting in the dismissal of some 200 preachers. *Reformatorica*, no. 63, pp. 125–7; W. van 't Spijker et al., *De Synode van Dordrecht in 1618 en 1619*, 2nd edn (Houten, 1994).
43 http://dutchrevolt.leiden.edu > Brieven > 10 april 1619.
44 Knapen, *De man en zijn staat*, pp. 335–6.

8 The Long Road from Truce to Peace

1 J. I. Israel, *The Dutch Republic and the Hispanic World, 1606–1661* (Oxford, 1986), p. 69.
2 Ibid., p. 86.
3 Ibid., pp. 100–103. For the actual siege, see Yolande Kortlever, 'Ambrogio Spinola, militair grootmeester (1569–1630)', in *Ambrogio Spinola 1622*, ed. Frans van Dongen and Han Verbeem (Bergen op Zoom, 2008), pp. 9–39.
4 Alain Hugon, *Philippe IV: Le siècle de Vélasquez* (Paris, 2014), p. 122; Werner Thomas, 'Alba and Religion', in *Alba*, ed. Maurits A. Ebben et al. (Rotterdam, 2013), pp. 120–22.
5 R. A. Stradling, *Philip IV and the Government of Spain, 1621–1665* (Cambridge, 1988); Maurits A. Ebben, *Zilver, brood en kogels voor de koning: Kredietverlening door Portugese bankiers aan de Spaanse kroon, 1621–1665* (Leiden, 1996), pp. 112–13. See also Maurits Ebben's biographical sketch of Philip IV in http://dutchrevolt.leiden.edu > Personen > Filips IV van Spanje.
6 J. H. Elliott, *Imperial Spain 1469–1716* (London, 1963) still provides an insightful overview; Elliott, *The Count-Duke of Olivares: The Statesman in an Age of Decline* (New Haven, CT, and London, 1986) may deter some readers because of its size. A good introduction is Jonathan Brown and J. H. Elliott, *A Palace for a King: The Buen Retiro and the Court of Philip IV* (New Haven, CT, 1993).
7 Israel, *The Dutch Republic and the Hispanic World*, p. 226.
8 Ibid., p. 106.
9 S. A. Vosters, *Het beleg en de overgave van Breda*, 3 vols (Breda, 1993).
10 Israel, *The Dutch Republic and the Hispanic World*, p. 108.

References

11 Hermann Hugo, *Obsidio Bredana armis Philippi IIII: auspiciis Isabellæ ductu Ambr. Spinolæ perfecta* (Antwerp, 1626).

12 Brown and Elliott, *A Palace for a King*, pp. 178–84; Andrés Úbeda de los Cobos, *Paintings for the Planet King: Philip IV and the Buen Retiro Palace* (Madrid, 2005), pp. 132–3.

13 A. P. van Vliet, *Vissers in oorlogstijd: De Zeeuwse zeevisserij in de jaren 1568–1648* (Middelburg, 2003).

14 Israel, *The Dutch Republic and the Hispanic World*, p. 122.

15 Brown and Elliott, *A Palace for a King*, pp. 184–92; Úbeda de los Cobos, *Paintings for the Planet King*, pp. 122–5.

16 Joseph Lefèvre, *Spinola et la Belgique (1601–1627)* (Brussels, 1947), pp. 100–103.

17 J. E. van der Pluijm, *De vestingstad Grol: Geschiedenis van de vestingwerken van Groenlo* (Groenlo, 1999).

18 Israel, *The Dutch Republic and the Hispanic World*, pp. 196–7.

19 Peter de Cauwer, *Tranen van bloed: Het beleg van 's-Hertogenbosch en de oorlog in de Nederlanden, 1629* (Amsterdam, 2008).

20 Daniel Heinsius, *Rerum ad Sylvam-Ducis atque alibi in Belgio aut a Belgis anno MDCXXIX gestarum historia* (Leiden, 1631), translation: Heinsius, *Het beleg van 's-Hertogenbosch in 1629 en andere gebeurtenissen uit die tijd*, trans. and introduction Jan van Boxtel (Den Bosch, 2013); Constantijn Huygens, *Gedichten*, vol. IV (4 February 1645), p. 136.

21 Israel, *The Dutch Republic and the Hispanic World*, p. 237; René Vermeir, *In staat van oorlog: Filips IV en de Zuidelijke Nederlanden, 1629–1648* (Maastricht, 2001), p. 17.

22 Vermeir, *In staat van oorlog*, p. 27.

23 Ibid., p. 41.

24 Petra Groen et al., eds, *De Tachtigjarige Oorlog: Van opstand naar geregelde oorlog 1568–1648* (Amsterdam, 2013), p. 273, shows the splendid reliefs depicting the withdrawal of Frederick Henry on the same house, Wollestraat 28.

25 Groen et al., *De Tachtigjarige Oorlog*, p. 272.

26 Vermeir, *In staat van oorlog*, pp. 45–6.

27 Groen et al., *De Tachtigjarige Oorlog*, p. 273.

28 Vermeir, *In staat van oorlog*, pp. 58–9.

29 Ibid., pp. 66–8.

30 Israel, *The Dutch Republic and the Hispanic World*, p. 239.

31 Ibid., pp. 243–7.

32 Joost van den Vondel, *Werken*, ed. J.F.M. Sterck et al., 10 vols (Amsterdam, 1927–37), vol. III, pp. 403–4.

33 Vermeir, *In staat van oorlog*, p. 104.

34 Israel, *The Dutch Republic and the Hispanic World*, p. 252. That the Cardinal-Infante did not only hunt game was well known.

35 *Tienen 1635: Geschiedenis van een Brabantse stad in de zeventiende eeuw* (Tienen, 1985).

36 Ibid.; Vermeir, *In staat van oorlog*, pp. 117–19.

37 Israel, *The Dutch Republic and the Hispanic World*, pp. 253–5; Vermeir, *In staat van oorlog*, pp. 120–26.

38 Israel, *The Dutch Republic and the Hispanic World*, pp. 259–60.

39 Vermeir, *In staat van oorlog*, p. 146.
40 Israel, *The Dutch Republic and the Hispanic World*, p. 269.
41 Vermeir, *In staat van oorlog*, pp. 150–52.
42 Israel, *The Dutch Republic and the Hispanic World*, pp. 270–71.
43 The University Library at Leiden has a number of exceptional handwritten documents pertaining to this earliest recorded history of Brazil. Michiel van Groesen, *Amsterdam's Atlantic: Print Culture and the Making of Dutch Brazil* (Philadelphia, PA, 2017).
44 Israel, *The Dutch Republic and the Hispanic World*, pp. 313–14.
45 Vermeir, *In staat van oorlog*, pp. 172, 184.
46 Ibid., p. 177.
47 Israel, *The Dutch Republic and the Hispanic World*, p. 317; Vermeir, *In staat van oorlog*, p. 253.
48 Vermeir, *In staat van oorlog*, pp. 261, 282.
49 Ibid., pp. 261, 283.
50 Israel, *The Dutch Republic and the Hispanic World*, pp. 320–21.
51 Vermeir, *In staat van oorlog*, pp. 288–9.
52 Ibid., p. 290.
53 Israel, *The Dutch Republic and the Hispanic World*, p. 359: 'tengo a los holandeses por mas religiosos y seguros en observar la promesa y juramento de la Paz que a los franceses, y asi se pudiera quedar con mas seguridad en lo que con los holandeses se asentase'.
54 Ibid., pp. 360–65.

Bibliography

Adriaenssen, Leo, *Staatsvormend geweld: Overleven aan de frontlinies in de meierij van Den Bosch, 1572–1629* (Tilburg, 2007)

Allen, Paul C., *Philip III and the Pax Hispanica, 1598–1621: The Failure of Grand Strategy* (New Haven, CT, 2000)

Andriessen, J., *De jezuïeten en het samenhorigheidsbesef der Nederlanden 1585–1648* (Antwerp, 1957)

Arnade, Peter, *Beggars, Iconoclasts, and Civic Patriots: The Political Culture of the Dutch Revolt* (Ithaca, NY, 2008)

Arndt, Johannes, *Das Heilige Römische Reich und die Niederlande 1566 bis 1648: Politisch-konfessionelle Verflechtung und Publizistik im Achtzigjährigen Krieg* (Cologne, 1998)

Asaert, G., *1585: De val van Antwerpen en de uittocht van Vlamingen en Brabanders* (Tielt, 2004; 2nd edn 2010)

Atlas van historische verdedigingswerken in Nederland: Groningen, Friesland, Drenthe (Utrecht, 2013)

Augustijn, C., 'Anabaptisme in de Nederlanden', *Doopsgezinde Bijdragen*, 12–13 (1987), pp. 13–29

Backhouse, M., *Beeldenstorm en bosgeuzen in het westkwartier (1566–1568): Bijdrage tot de geschiedenis van de godsdiensttroebelen der Zuidelijke Nederlanden in de XVIe eeuw* (Kortrijk, 1971)

Baelde, Michel, *De Collaterale Raden onder Karel V en Filips II (1531–1578): Bijdrage tot de geschiedenis van de centrale instellingen in de zestiende eeuw* (Brussels, 1965)

Bergsma, W., *De wereld volgens Abel Eppens: Een Ommelander boer uit de zestiende eeuw* (Groningen/Leeuwarden, 1988)

—, *Tussen Gideonsbende en publieke kerk: Een studie over het gereformeerd protestantisme in Friesland, 1580–1650* (Hilversum, 1999)

Berkelbach van der Sprenkel, J.W., *Oranje en de vestiging van de Nederlandse staat* (Amsterdam, 1946)

Besten, Ad den, *Wilhelmus van Nassouwe: Het gedicht en zijn dichter* (Leiden, 1983)

Blockmans, Wim, *Keizer Karel V, 1500–1558: De utopie van het keizerschap* (Leuven/Amsterdam, 2000)

Blok, P. J., *Willem de Eerste, prins van Oranje*, 2 vols (Amsterdam, 1919–20)
Blokker, Jan, 'De tachtigjarige oorlog: Een gat in de markt', supplement to *Vrij Nederland* (27 September 1986), pp. 4–29
Boland, Herbert, *De list met het turfschip van Breda* (Breda, 2011)
Boogman, J. C., 'De overgang van Gouda, Dordrecht, Leiden en Delft in de zomer van het jaar 1572', *Tijdschrift voor Geschiedenis*, 57 (1942), pp. 81–112
Boon, Louis Paul, *Het Geuzenboek* (Amsterdam, 1979)
Bor, Pieter Chr., *Oorsprongk, begin en vervolgh der Nederlandsche oorlogen, beroerten, en borgerlyke oneenigheden etc.*, 4 vols (Amsterdam, 1679–84)
Bostoen, Karel, 'Reformation, Counter-Reformation and Literary Propaganda in the Low Countries in the Sixteenth Century: The Case of Brother Cornelis', in *The Education of a Christian Society: Humanism and the Reformation in Britain and the Netherlands*, ed. N. Scott Amos, Andrew Pettegree and Henk van Nierop (Aldershot, 1999), pp. 164–89
——, *Hart voor Leiden: Jan van Hout (1542–1609), stadssecretaris, dichter en vernieuwer* (Hilversum, 2009)
——, 'Waar kwam de Historie van B. Cornelis (1569) van de pers? Het spoor terug naar plaats van uitgave, boekverkoper en boekdrukker', *Handelingen van het Genootschap voor Geschiedenis te Brugge*, 151 (2014), pp. 65–111
Braekman, E. M., *Les Médailles des Gueux et leurs résurgences modernes* (Brussels, 1972)
Braudel, Fernand, *La Méditerranée et le monde méditerranéen à l'époque de Philippe II*, 2 vols (Paris, 1966)
——, *The Mediterranean and the Mediterranean World in the Age of Philip II*, 2 vols (New York and London, 1972–3)
Brouwer, Johan, *Philips Willem, de Spaansche prins van Oranje* (Zutphen, 1940)
——, *Kronieken van Spaansche soldaten uit het begin van den Tachtigjarigen Oorlog* [1933] (Zutphen, 1980)
Brown, Jonathan, and J. H. Elliott, *A Palace for a King: The Buen Retiro and the Court of Philip IV* (New Haven, CT, 1993)
Bruin, G. de, 'De geschiedschrijving over de Nederlandse Opstand', in *Kantelend geschiedbeeld: Nederlandse historiografie sinds 1945*, ed. W. W. Mijnhardt (Utrecht/Antwerp, 1984), pp. 48–82
——, 'De Nederlandse Opstand (1555–1588)', *Spiegel Historiael*, XXIX (1994), pp. 441–52
Busken Huet, Conrad, *Het Land van Rembrand*, ed. Olf Praamstra (Amsterdam, 1987)
Cabrera de Córdoba, Luís, *Filipe Segundo, rey de España*, 4 vols (Madrid, 1876–7)
Caldecott-Baird, Duncan, *The Expedition in Holland, 1572–1574. From the manuscript of Walter Morgan* (London, 1976)
Calvete de Estrella, *El felicíssimo viaje del muy alto y muy poderoso príncipe don Phelippe* (Madrid, [2001])
Cauwer, Peter de, *Tranen van bloed: Het beleg van 's-Hertogenbosch en de oorlog in de Nederlanden, 1629* (Amsterdam, 2008)

Christin, Olivier, 'France et Pays-Bas: Le second iconoclasme', in *Iconoclasme: Vie et mort de l'image médiévale*, ed. Cécile Dupeux et al. (Zurich, 2001), pp. 57–66

Cools, Hans, 'De Beeldenstorm in de Nederlanden', http://dutchrevolt. leiden.edu > *Begrippen* > *Beeldenstorm*

Coopmans, J.P.A., 'De huldigingsvoorwaarden voor Willem van Oranje van 1583: Een nieuw type gezagsovereenkomst', in *Beleid en bestuur in de oude Nederlanden: Liber amicorum prof. dr. M. Baelde*, ed. Hugo Soly and René Vermeir (Ghent, 1993)

Cox, B., *Vanden Tocht in Vlaenderen: De logistiek van Nieuwpoort 1600* (Zutphen, 1986)

Daussy, Hugues, 'Louis de Nassau et le parti huguenot', in *Entre Calvinistes et Catholiques: Les relations religieuses entre la France et les Pays-Bas du Nord (XVIe–XVIIIe siècle)*, ed. Yves Krumenacker and Olivier Christin (Rennes, 2010), pp. 31–43

Decavele, J., *De dageraad van de Reformatie in Vlaanderen (1520–1565)*, 2 vols (Brussels, 1975)

——, 'De aanloop tot de Reformatie in Frans-Vlaanderen', *De Franse Nederlanden: jaarboek = Les Pays-Bas français: annuaire* (1977), pp. 121–35

——, *Het einde van een rebelse droom: Opstellen over het calvinistisch bewind te Gent (1577–1584) en de terugkeer van de stad onder de gehoorzaamheid van de koning van Spanje* [17 September 1584] (Ghent, 1984)

——, *Vlaanderen tussen Spanje en Oranje: Willem de Zwijger en de Lage Landen in de zestiende eeuw* (Ghent, 1984)

——, 'Het calvinisme en de Opstand', *Spiegel Historiael*, XXIX (1994), pp. 453–9

——, 'Ketters en Papisten in het Kortrijkse stadsbestuur 1561–1580', *Handelingen van de Maatschappij voor Geschiedenis en Oudheidkunde*, Ghent, XLIX (1995), pp. 221–50

——, *De eerste protestanten in de Lage Landen: Geloof en heldenmoed* (Leuven and Zwolle, 2004)

Delen, Marie-Ange, *Het hof van Willem van Oranje* (Amsterdam, 2004)

Deursen, A.Th. van, *Mensen van klein vermogen: Het kopergeld van de Gouden Eeuw* (Amsterdam, 1991)

——, *Maurits van Nassau: De winnaar die faalde* (Amsterdam, 2000)

——, *Bavianen en slijkgeuzen: Kerk en kerkvolk ten tijde van Maurits en Oldenbarnevelt*, 4th revd and illustrated edn (Franeker, 2010)

——, and H. de Schepper, *Willem van Oranje: Een strijd voor vrijheid en verdraagzaamheid* (Weesp/Tielt, 1984)

Deyon, Solange, and Alain Lottin, *Les casseurs de l'été 1566: L'iconoclasme dans le Nord* (Lille, 1986)

Dierickx, M. J., *De oprichting der nieuwe bisdommen in de Nederlanden onder Filips II 1559–1570* (Antwerp/Utrecht, 1950)

Dorren, Gabrielle, 'Lorenzo de Villavicencio en Alonso del Canto: Twee Spaanse informanten over de Nederlandse elite (1564–1566)', *Tijdschrift voor Geschiedenis*, III (1998), pp. 352–76

Duerloo, Luc, *Dynasty and Piety: Archduke Albert (1598–1621) and Habsburg Political Culture in an Age of Religious Wars* (Farnham, 2012)

——, and Marc Wingens, *Scherpenheuvel: Het Jeruzalem van de Lage Landen* (Leuven, 2002)
Duke, A. C., *Reformation and Revolt in the Low Countries* (London, 1990)
——, *Dissident Identities in the Early Modern Low Countries*, ed. Judith Pollmann and Andrew Spicer (Farnham, 2009)
Dunthorne, Hugh, *Britain and the Dutch Revolt, 1560–1700* (Cambridge, 2013)
Dupeux, Cécile, ed., *Iconoclasme: Vie et mort de l'image médiévale* (Berne, Strasbourg and Zurich, 2001)
Duquenne, Frédéric, *L'entreprise du duc d'Anjou aux Pays-Bas de 1580 à 1584: Les responsabilités d'un échec à partager* (Villeneuve d'Asq, 1998)
Durme, M. van, *Antoon Perrenot, bisschop van Atrecht, kardinaal van Granvelle, minister van Karel V en van Philip II (1517–1586)* (Brussels, 1953)
Duyck, Anthonis, *De slag bij Nieuwpoort: Journaal van de tocht naar Vlaanderen in 1600*, trans. Vibeke Roeper, introduction and annotation Wilfried Uitterhoeve (Nijmegen, 1600)
Ebben, Maurits A., *Zilver, brood en kogels voor de koning: Kredietverlening door Portugese bankiers aan de Spaanse kroon, 1621–1665* (Leiden, 1996)
——, 'El ataque de Pieter van der Does a Canarias y la expansión neerlandesa a finales del siglo XVI y comienzos del siglo XVII', in *Coloquio internacional Canarias y el Atlántico, 1580–1648: IV centenario del ataque de Van der Does a las Palmas de Gran Canaria, 1999*, ed. Massieu Antonio de Béthencourt (Las Palmas, 2001), pp. 147–68
——, Margriet Lacy-Bruijn and Rolof van Hövell tot Westerflier, eds, *Alba: General and Servant to the Crown* (Rotterdam, 2013)
Eekhout, Marianne, *Material Memories of the Dutch Revolt: The Urban Memory Landscape in the Low Countries, 1566–1700* (Leiden, 2014)
Eichberger, Dagmar, *Dames met klasse: Margareta van York, Margareta van Oostenrijk* (Leuven, 2005)
Eijnatten, Joris van, and Fred van Lieburg, *Nederlandse religiegeschiedenis*, 2nd edn (Hilversum, 2006)
Elliott, J. H., *Imperial Spain, 1469–1716* (London, 1963)
——, *The Count-Duke of Olivares: The Statesman in an Age of Decline* (New Haven, CT, and London, 1986)
——, 'A Europe of Composite Monarchies', *Past and Present*, 137 (1992), pp. 48–71
Emmius, Ubbo, *Willem Lodewijk, graaf van Nassau (1560–1620), stadhouder van Friesland, Groningen en Drenthe* (Hilversum, 1994)
Essen, Léon van der, *Alexandre Farnèse, prince de Parme*, 5 vols (Brussels, 1933–7)
——, 'Kritisch onderzoek betreffende de oorlogsvoering van het Spaans leger in de Nederlanden in de zestiende eeuw, nl. de bestraffing van de opstandige steden tijdens het bewind van Alva', *Mededelingen van de Koninklijke Vlaamse Academie voor wetenschappen, letteren en schone kunsten van België*, XII (1950), pp. 3–36
Esteban Estringana, Alicia, *Guerra y finanzas en los Países Bajos católicos: De Farnesio a Spínola (1592–1630)* (Madrid, 2002)
Eysinga, W.J.M. van, *De wording van het Twaalfjarig Bestand van 9 april 1609* (Amsterdam, 1959)

Fagel, Raymond, *Leids beleg en ontzet door Spaanse ogen* (The Hague, 1997)
——, *Kapitein Julián: De Spaanse held van de Nederlandse Opstand* (Hilversum, 2011)
Fernández Alvarez, Manuel, *Charles v: Elected Emperor and Hereditary Ruler* (London, 1975)
Final de la Guerra de Flandes (1621–1648): 350 aniversario de la paz de Münster (Madrid, 1998)
Frijhoff, Willem, 'Hoe Noord en Zuid van godsdienst verwisselden: Katholiek en protestant', in *Het geheugen van de Lage Landen*, ed. Jo Tollebeek and Henk te Velde (Rekkem, 2009), pp. 120–28
Fritschy, W., 'Holland en de financiering van de Opstand (1568–1648): Deel I en II', *Economisch Statistische Berichten*, LXXXIX/4437 (2004), pp. 328–30, and LXXXIX/4438 (2004), pp. 353–5
——, 'Willem van Oranje en de overheidsfinanciën', in W. Fritschy, *William of Orange Lecture* (Delft, 2006), pp. 7–29
Fruin, Robert, *Tien jaren uit den Tachtigjarigen oorlog* (Leiden, 1857) (multiple reprints)
——, 'Willem de Zwijger', in Fruin, *Verspreide Geschriften*, 10 vols (The Hague, 1900–1905), vol. VIII, pp. 404–9
Gachard, Louis-Prosper, ed., *Correspondance de Philippe II sur les affaires des Pays-Bas* (Brussels, 1848–79)
——, *Retraite et mort de Charles-Quint au monastère de Yuste*, 2 vols (Brussels, 1854)
——, 'Sur l'origine du nom de gueux, donné aux révolutionnaires des Pays-Bas dans le XVIe siècle', in Fruin, *Études et notices historiques concernant l'histoire des Pays-Bas*, 3 vols (Brussels, 1890), vol. I, pp. 130–41
García García, Bernardo J., *Tiempo de paces: La Pax Hispanica y la Tregua de los Doce Años* (Madrid, 2009)
Geevers, Liesbeth, *Gevallen vazallen: De integratie van Oranje, Egmont en Horn in de Spaans-Habsburgse monarchie (1559–1567)* (Amsterdam, 2008)
Gelder, H. A. Enno van, 'Een historiese vergelijking: De Nederlandse Opstand en de Franse godsdienstoorlogen', *Verslag van de algemeene vergadering der leden van het Historisch Genootschap* (Utrecht, 1930), pp. 21–42
——, *Van beeldenstorm tot pacificatie: Acht opstellen over de Nederlandse revolutie der zestiende eeuw* (Amsterdam, 1964)
Gelderblom, Oscar, *Zuid-Nederlandse kooplieden en de opkomst van de Amsterdamse stapelmarkt (1578–1630)* (Hilversum, 2000)
Gelderen, M. van, *Op zoek naar de Republiek: Politiek denken tijdens de Nederlandse Opstand (1555–1590)* (Hilversum, 1991)
——, *The Political Thought of the Dutch Revolt, 1555–1590* (Cambridge, 1992)
——, 'Van vrijheden naar vrijheid: De legitimatie van de Nederlandse Opstand', *Spiegel Historiael*, XXIX (1994), pp. 494–500
Geurts, P.A.M, *De Nederlandse Opstand in de pamfletten 1566–1584* (Nijmegen, 1956; Utrecht, 1983, 3rd edn)
Goosens, Aline, *Les inquisitions modernes dans les Pays-Bas méridionaux, 1520–1633*, 2 vols (Brussels, 1997–8)
Gosses, I. H., 'Friesland in den eersten tijd van den Tachtigjarigen Oorlog', in Gosses, *Verspreide Geschriften* (Groningen/Batavia, 1946), pp. 451–70

Graaf, Ronald de, *Oorlog, mijn arme schapen: Een andere kijk op de Tachtigjarige Oorlog 1565–1648* (Franeker, 2004)
Grapperhaus, Ferdinand H. M., *Alva en de Tiende Penning* (Zutphen, 1982)
——, *Convoyen en licenten* (Zutphen, Deventer, 1986)
Groen, Petra, et al., eds, *De Tachtigjarige Oorlog: Van opstand naar geregelde oorlog 1568–1648* (Amsterdam, 2013)
Groenveld, S., 'Trouw en verraad tijdens de Nederlandse Opstand', *Zeeuws Tijdschrift*, XXXVII (1987), pp. 3–12
Groenveld, Simon, *T'is ghenoegh, oorloghsmannen: De Vrede van Munster: de afsluiting van de Tachtigjarige Oorlog* (The Hague, 1997)
——, 'Filips van Montmorency, Graaf van Horn (1524–1568): Een Habsburgs edelman tussen vorstenmacht en verzet', *Limburgs Geschied- en Oudheidkundig Genootschap, Publications de la Société Historique et Archéologique de Limbourg*, CXXXIX (2003), pp. 39–99
——, *Het Twaalfjarig Bestand 1609–1621: De jongelingsjaren van de Republiek der Verenigde Nederlanden* (Hilversum, 2009)
——, *Unie – Bestand – Vrede: Drie fundamentele wetten van de Republiek der Verenigde Nederlanden* (Hilversum, 2009)
——, and H.L.Ph. Leeuwenberg, eds, *De Unie van Utrecht: Wording en werking van een verbond en een verbondsacte* (The Hague, 1979)
——, M.E.H.N. Mout et al., *De kogel door de kerk?* and *De bruid in de schuit*, 2 vols (Zutphen, 2013)
Groesen, Michiel van, *Amsterdam's Atlantic: Print Culture and the Making of Dutch Brazil* (Philadelphia, PA, 2017)
Groot, Hugo de, *Kroniek van de Nederlandse Oorlog: De Opstand 1559–1588*, trans. and epilogue Jan Waszink (Nijmegen, 2014)
Grosfeld, J. F., W. Klinkert and J. P. Meeuwissen, *Het turfschip van Breda 1590–1990* (Breda, 1990)
Haer, Florentius van der, *De initiis tumultuum Belgicorum* (Douai, 1587)
Hageman, Maarten, *Het kwade exempel van Gelre: De stad Nijmegen, de Beeldenstorm en de Raad van Beroerten, 1566–1568* (Nijmegen, 2005)
Harline, Craig, and Eddy Put, *A Bishop's Tale: Matthias Hovius among his Flock in Seventeenth-century Flanders* (New Haven, CT, 2000)
Hart, Marjolein C. 't, *In Quest for Funds: Warfare and State Formation in the Netherlands, 1620–1650* (Leiden, 1989)
——, *The Making of a Bourgeois State: War, Politics and Finance during the Dutch Revolt* (Manchester and New York, 1993)
——, *The Dutch Wars of Independence: Warfare and Commerce in the Netherlands, 1570–1680* (Abingdon, 2014)
Hartmann, B., *De martelaren van Roermond in het kader van de politieke en kerkelijke situatie van hun tijd* (Oegstgeest, 2009)
——, *De martelaren van Gorcum: Volgens het getuigenis van Guilielmus Estius geschreven in 1572*, trans., introduction and commentary B. Hartmann (Oegstgeest, 2009)
Heijer, Henk den, *De geschiedenis van de WIC* (Zutphen, 2002)
Heinsius, Daniel, *Rerum ad Sylvam-Ducis atque alibi in Belgio aut a Belgis anno MDCXXIX gestarum historia* (Leiden, 1631)
——, *Het beleg van 's-Hertogenbosch in 1629 en andere gebeurtenissen uit die tijd*, trans. and introduction Jan van Boxtel (Den Bosch, 2013)

Bibliography

Heijting, Willem, and Willem Frijhoff, *Hollandse priesterbibliotheken uit de tijd van de Republiek* (Amstelveen, 2005)
Hoeven, Marco van der, ed., *Exercise of Arms: Warfare in the Netherlands, 1568–1648* (Leiden, 1997)
Hooft, P. C., *Nederlandsche historien*, 2 vols, 2nd edn (Amsterdam, 1677)
Horst, Daniel, *De Opstand in zwart-wit: Propagandaprenten uit de Nederlandse Opstand 1566–1584* (Zutphen, 2003)
Houwaert, J. B., *Declaratie van die triumphante incompst vanden prince van Oraignien, binnen die princelijcke stadt van Brusselse* (Antwerp, 1579)
Hugo, Hermann, *Obsidio Bredana armis Philippi IIII: auspiciis Isabellæ ductu Ambr. Spinolæ perfecta* (Antwerp, 1626)
Hugon, Alain, *Philippe IV: Le siècle de Vélasquez* (Paris, 2014)
Huizinga, J., 'Uit de voorgeschiedenis van ons nationaal besef', in Huizinga, *Verzamelde Werken*, 9 vols (Haarlem, 1948–53), vol. II, pp. 97–160, esp. sec. III, 'Namen en teekens voor de Bourgondische staatseenheid'
Hutchinson, Robert, *The Spanish Armada* (London, 2014)
Huygens, Constantijn, *Gedichten*, ed. J. A. Worp, 9 vols (Groningen, 1892–9)
IJzerman, A. W., *De 80-jarige oorlog* (Leiden, [1948])
Israel, J. I., 'The Holland Towns and the Dutch-Spanish Conflict, 1621–1648', *Bijdragen en Mededelingen betreffende de Geschiedenis der Nederlanden*, 94 (1979), pp. 41–69
——, *The Dutch Republic and the Hispanic World, 1606–1661* (Oxford, 1986)
——, *The Dutch Republic: Its Rise, Greatness, and Fall, 1477–1806* (Oxford, 1995)
Janssen, Geert H., *Het stokje van Oldenbarnevelt* (Hilversum, 2001)
——, *The Dutch Revolt and Catholic Exile in Reformation Europe* (Cambridge, 2014)
Janssens, Gustaaf, *'De eerste jaren van Filips II (1555–1566)'*, in *Algemene Geschiedenis der Nederlanden VI*, ed. M. Cloet et al. (Haarlem, 1979), pp. 186–201
——, *Brabant in het verweer: Loyale oppositie tegen Spanje's bewind in de Nederlanden van Alva tot Farnese 1567–1578* (Kortrijk and Heule, 1988)
——, 'The Duke of Alba: Governor of the Netherlands in Times of War', in *Alba*, ed. Ebben et al., pp. 90–115
Janssens, Paul, *België in de 17de eeuw: De Spaanse Nederlanden en het prinsbisdom Luik*, 2 vols (Ghent, 2006)
Jong, Michiel de, *'Staat van oorlog': Wapenbedrijf en militaire hervorming in de Republiek der Verenigde Nederlanden, 1585–1621* (Hilversum, 2005)
Jong, Otto J. de, *Beeldenstormen in de Nederlanden* (Groningen, 1964)
Jonge, Krista de, and Gustaaf Janssens, eds, *Les Granvelle et les Anciens Pays-Bas* (Leuven, 2000)
Jouanna, Arlette, *Le Devoir de révolte: La noblesse française et la gestation de l'État moderne, 1559–1661* (Paris, 1989)
Junius, Hadrianus, *Holland is een eiland: De Batavia van Hadrianus Junius* [1511–75], introduction, trans. and annotation Nico de Glas (Hilversum, 2011)
Kamen, Henry, *The Duke of Alba* (New Haven, CT, 2004)
Kaplan, Benjamin J., *Calvinists and Libertines: Confession and Community in Utrecht, 1578–1620* (Oxford, 1995)

Kaptein, Herman, *De beeldenstorm* (Hilversum, 2002)
Kelsey, Harry, *Philip of Spain, King of England: The Forgotten Sovereign* (London, 2012)
Kerkhoff, Jacqueline, *Maria van Hongarije en haar hof: 1505–1558* ([Amsterdam], 2005)
Kernkamp, J. H., *De handel op den vijand*, 2 vols (Utrecht, 1931–[35])
Kinds, Karel, *Kroniek van de Opstand in de Lage Landen 1555–1609: actuele oorlogsverslaggeving uit de zestiende eeuw met 228 gravures van Frans Hogenberg*, 2 vols (Wenum Wiesel, [2000])
Klink, H., *Opstand, politiek en religie bij Willem van Oranje 1559–1568: Een thematische biografie* (Heerenveen, 1997)
Klinkert, Christi M., *Nassau in het nieuws: Nieuwsprenten van Maurits van Nassaus militaire ondernemingen uit de periode 1590–1600* (Zutphen, 2005)
Kloek, Els, *Kenau en Magdalena: Vrouwen in de Tachtigjarige Oorlog* (Nijmegen, 2014)
Kluiver, J. H., ed., *De correspondentie tussen Willem van Oranje en Jan van Nassau (1578–1584)* (Amsterdam, 1984)
Knapen, Ben, *De man en zijn staat: Johan van Oldenbarnevelt (1547–1619)* (Amsterdam, 2005)
Knoops, W. A., and F. Ch. Meijer, *De Spaanse Armada: De tocht en ondergang van de Onoverwinnelijke Vloot in het jaar 1588* (Amsterdam, 1988)
Koenigsberger, H. G., 'Why did the States General of the Netherlands Become Revolutionary in the Sixteenth Century?', *Parliaments, Estates and Representation*, II (1982), pp. 103–11
——, 'Orange, Granvelle and Philip II', *Bijdragen en Mededelingen betreffende de Geschiedenis der Nederlanden*, XCIX (1984), pp. 573–95
Kohler, Alfred, *Karl V 1500–1558: eine Biographie* (Munich, 1999)
Kooi, Gerard van der, *De Wynberch des heren: Godsdienstige veranderingen op Texel 1514–1572* (Hilversum, 2005)
Koopmans, J. W., *De Staten van Holland en de Opstand: De ontwikkeling van hun functies en organisatie in de periode 1544–1588* (The Hague, 1990)
Kortlever, Yolande, 'Ambrogio Spinola, militair grootmeester (1569–1630)', in *Ambrogio Spinola 1622*, ed. Frans van Dongen and Han Verbeem (Bergen op Zoom, 2008), pp. 9–39
Kossmann, E. H., and A. F. Mellink, eds, *Texts Concerning the Revolt of the Netherlands* (Cambridge, 1975)
Kuipers, Jan J. B., *De Staats-Spaanse linies: Monumenten van conflict en cultuur* (Vlissingen, 2013)
Kuttner, Erich, *Het hongerjaar 1566*, 3rd edn (Amsterdam, 1974)
Lacarta, Manuel, *Felipe III* (Madrid, 2003)
Lacroix, A., *Apologie de Guillaume de Nassau [. . .] Justification du Taciturne* (Brussels and Leipzig, 1858)
Lademacher, Horst, *Die Stellung des Prinzen von Oranien als Statthalter in den Niederlanden* (Bonn, 1958)
Lagomarsino, P. D., 'Court Factions and the Formulation of Spanish Policy Towards the Netherlands, 1559–1567', PhD thesis, University of Cambridge, 1973
Leestmans, Charles-J.A., *Soldats de l'armée des Flandres 1621–1715* (Brussels, 2013)

Lefèvre, Joseph, *Spinola et la Belgique (1601–1627)* (Brussels, 1947)
——, ed., *Correspondance de Philippe II sur les affaires des Pays-Bas*, 2 vols (Brussels, 1940–1960)
Lem, Anton van der, 'Menno Simons in de Nederlandse geschiedschrijving', *Doopsgezinde Bijdragen*, XXII (1996), pp. 10–19
——, 'Van de prins geen kwaad: De moordplannen van en op prins Willem van Oranje', in *Koningsmoorden*, ed. Tom Verschaffel (Leuven, 2000), pp. 159–72, 285–7
——, 'De strijd om de Vlaamse havens tijdens de Tachtigjarige Oorlog', in Dirk de Vries, *Oostende verloren, Sluis gewonnen, 1604: een kroniek in kaarten. Catalogus bij een tentoonstelling in de Leidse universiteitsbibliotheek van 12 augustus – 12 september 2004* (Leiden, 2004), pp. 9–26
——, 'Epos voor de vrijheid: Boek Friedrich Schiller over Opstand na twee eeuwen vertaald', *Mare di Libri: Boekenbijlage van het Leids Universitair Weekblad Mare*, II/3 (17 March 2005), p. 5
——, 'Den Briel: Sint-Catharinakerk; Watergeuzen veroveren Brielle, 1 april 1572', in *Plaatsen van herinnering: Nederland in de zeventiende en achttiende eeuw*, ed. Maarten Prak (Amsterdam, 2006), pp. 24–35
——, 'Willem van Oranje verheerlijkt en verguisd', in *Bronnen van kennis. Wetenschap, kunst en cultuur in de collecties van de Leidse Universiteitsbibliotheek*, ed. Paul Hoftijzer et al. (Leiden, 2006), pp. 73–84
——, 'Kampf im Druck: Die Anfangsjahre des niederländischen Aufstandes in Pamphleten und Bildern', in Martina Fuchs, Alfred Kohler, Ralph Andraschek-Holzer (Hrsg.), *Geschichte in Bildern?, Wiener Zeitschrift zur Geschichte der Neuzeit*, 6 (2006), vol. II, pp. 69–86
——, *Verbeeldingen van vrijheid: Partijtekens en nationale symboliek in de eerste decennia van de Tachtigjarige Oorlog 1564–1584* (Utrecht, 2006)
——, '"Het groote pleit beslecht". Anderhalve eeuw Tien Jaren van Robert Fruin', in *Aangeraakt: Boeken in contact met hun lezers. Een bundel opstellen voor Wim Gerretsen en Paul Hoftijzer*, ed. Kasper van Ommen, Arnoud Vrolijk and Geert Warnar (Leiden, 2007), pp. 231–8
——, 'Echos de la Révolte: Montaigne et les Pays-Bas du XVIe siècle', in *Montaigne and the Low Countries (1580–1700)*, ed. Paul J. Smith and Karel A. E. Enenkel (Leiden, 2007), pp. 47–62
——, 'Willem van Oranje, een strateeg van formaat', *Protestants Nederland. Maandblad van de Vereniging Protestants Nederland*, LXXIV/4 (April 2008), pp. 5–9; LXXIV/5 (May 2008), pp. 13–17; LXXIV/6–7 (June/July 2008), pp. 14–20
——, 'Een voordelige vrede: het Twaalfjarig Bestand, 1609–1621', *Geschiedenis magazine*, XLIV/3 (April 2009), pp. 14–19
Lens, Arthur, *Lier: Ontstaan en evolutie van een kleine stad* (Lier, 1993)
Le Roux, Nicolas, *Les Guerres de religion 1559–1629* (Paris, 2009)
Lesaffer, Randall, *Defensor pacis Hispanicae: De kardinaal-infant, de Zuidelijke Nederlanden en de Europese politiek van Spanje: van Nördlingen tot Breda (1634–1637)* (Kortrijk and Heule, [1994])
Lottin, Alain, *La Révolte des Gueux en Flandre, Artois et Hainaut (politique, religion et société au XVIe siècle)* (Lillers, 2007)
Louwerse, P., and J. J. Moerman, *Geïllustreerde vaderlandse geschiedenis: Voor jong en oud Nederland*, 10th edn (Amsterdam, 1961)

Lovett, A.W., 'The Governorship of Don Luis de Requesens, 1573–1576: A Spanish View', *European Studies Review*, II (1972), pp. 187–99

Malengreau, G., *L'Esprit particulariste et la révolution des Pays-Bas au 16e siècle, 1578–1584* (Leuven, 1936)

Maljaars, Abraham, *Het Wilhelmus: Auteurschap, datering en strekking: een kritische toetsing en nieuwe interpretatie* (Kampen, 1996)

Maltby, W. S., *Alba: A Biography of Fernando Alvarez de Toledo, Third Duke of Alba, 1507–1582* (Berkeley and Los Angeles, CA, 1983)

Marañon, Gregorio, *El conde-duque de Olivares* (Madrid, 1953)

Marnef, Guido, 'Het protestantisme te Brussel onder de "Calvinistische Republiek", ca. 1577–1585', in *Staat en religie in de 15e en 16e eeuw*, ed. W. P. Blockmans and H. van Nuffel (Brussels, 1986), pp. 231–99

——, 'Brabants calvinisme in opmars: De weg naar de calvinistische republieken te Antwerpen, Brussel en Mechelen, 1577–1580', *Bijdragen tot de Geschiedenis*, LXX (1987), pp. 7–21

——, *Het calvinistisch Bewind te Mechelen (1580–1585)* (Kortrijk and Heule, 1988)

——, *Antwerpen in de tijd van de Reformatie: Ondergronds protestantisme in een handelsmetropool 1550–1577* (Amsterdam and Antwerp, 1996)

——, 'The Dynamics of Reformed Militancy in the Low Countries: The Wonderyear', in *The Education of a Christian Society: Humanism and the Reformation in Britain and the Netherlands*, ed. N. Scott Amos, Andrew Pettegree and Henk van Nierop (Aldershot, 1999), pp. 193–210

Mattingly, Garrett, *The Armada* (Boston, MA, 1959)

Meij, J.C.A. de, *De Watergeuzen en de Nederlanden 1568–1572* (Amsterdam and London, 1972)

——, 'De watergeuzen: Gangmakers van de Opstand', *Spiegel Historiael*, XXIX (1994), pp. 482–7

Men sagh Haerlem bestormen (Haarlem, 1973)

Mertens, Jozef, Franz Aumann, eds, *Krijg en kunst: Leopold Willem (1614–1662), Habsburger, landvoogd en kunstverzamelaar* (Bilzen, 2003)

Mesa Gallego, Eduardo de, *La pacificación de Flandes: Spínola y las campañas de Frisia (1604–1609)* (Madrid, 2009)

Meteren, Emanuel van, *Historien der Nederlanden, en haar naburen oorlogen tot het jaar 1612* (Amsterdam, 1652)

Monter, William, 'Heresy Executions in Reformation Europe, 1520–1565', in Ole Peter Grell and Bob Scribner, *Tolerance and Intolerance in the European Reformation* (Cambridge, 1996), pp. 48–64

Mörke, Olaf, *Wilhelm von Oranien, 1533–1584: Fürst und 'Vater' der Republik* (Stuttgart, 2007)

Mousset, Jean-Luc, *Un prince de la Renaissance: Pierre-Ernest de Mansfeld (1517–1604)* (Luxembourg, 2007)

Mout, M.E.H.N., *Plakkaat van Verlatinge 1581*, introduction, transcription and translation in modern-day Dutch (The Hague, 1979)

——, 'Van arm vaderland tot eendrachtige republiek: De rol van politieke theorieën in de Nederlandse Opstand', *Bijdragen en Mededelingen betreffende de Geschiedenis der Nederlanden*, CI (1986), pp. 345–65

Müller, Johannes Martin, *Exile Memories and the Dutch Revolt: The Narrated Diaspora, 1550–1750* (Leiden, 2014)

Nehlsen, Eberhard, *Wilhelmus von Nassauen: Studien zur Rezeption eines niederländischen Liedes im deutschsprachigen Raum vom 16. Bis 20. Jahrhundert* (Münster, 1993)

Nierop, H.F.K. van, *Van ridders tot regenten: De Hollandse adel in de zestiende en de eerste helft van de zeventiende eeuw*, 2nd edn (Amsterdam, 1990)

——, 'A Beggar's Banquet: The Compromise of the Nobility and the Politics of Inversion', *European History Quarterly*, XXI (1991), pp. 419–43

——, 'De adel en de Opstand', *Spiegel Historiael*, XXIX (1994), pp. 460–67

——, 'De troon van Alva: Over de interpretatie van de Nederlandse Opstand', *Bijdragen en Mededelingen betreffende de Geschiedenis der Nederlanden*, 110 (1995), pp. 205 23

——, *Het foute Amsterdam* (Amsterdam, 2000)

Nimwegen, Olaf van, *'Deser landen crijchsvolck': Het Staatse leger en de militaire revoluties (1588–1688)* (Amsterdam, 2006)

Noordeloos, P., *Cornelis Musius (Mr Cornelius Muys): Pater van Sint Agatha te Delft: humanist, priester, martelaar* (Utrecht, 1955)

Nuffel, Herman van, *Lamoraal van Egmont in de geschiedenis, literatuur, beeldende kunst en legende* (Leuven, 1968)

Oosterhoff, F.G., *Leicester and the Netherlands 1586–1587* (Utrecht, 1988)

Oosterhuis, Ton, *Lumey, de vossestaart: Admiraal van de Geuzen* (Amsterdam, 1996)

Opstand en onafhankelijkheid: Eerste Vrije Statenvergadering Dordrecht 1572 (Dordrecht, 1972)

Opstand en Pacificatie in de Lage Landen: Bijdrage tot de studie van de Pacificatie van Gent (Ghent, 1976)

Orange, William of, *The Apologie of William of Orange against the Proclamation of the King of Spaine*, edited after the English edition of 1581 by H. Wansink (Leiden, 1969)

Oudendijk, Johanna K., 'Den coninck van hispaengien heb ick altijt gheeert', in *Dancwerc: Opstellen aangeboden aan Prof. Dr. D. Th. Enklaar ter gelegenheid van zijn 65ste verjaardag* (Groningen, 1959)', pp. 264–78

Parker, Geoffrey, *The Dutch Revolt* (London, 1977) (multiple reprints)

——, *Philip II* (London, 1979)

——, *The Military Revolution: Military Innovation and the Rise of the West, 1500–1800* (Cambridge, 1988)

——, 'Was Parma Ready? The Army of Flanders and the Spanish Armada in 1588', in *Beleid en bestuur in de oude Nederlanden: Liber amicorum prof. dr. M. Baelde*, ed. Hugo Soly and René Vermeir (Ghent, 1993), pp. 279–97

——, *The Grand Strategy of Philip II* (New Haven, CT, 1998)

——, *The Army of Flanders and the Spanish Road 1567–1659*, 2nd edn (Cambridge, 2004)

——, *Imprudent King: A New Life of Philip II* (New Haven, CT, 2014)

Pettegree, Andrew, *Emden and the Dutch Revolt: Exile and the Development of Reformed Protestantism* (Oxford, 1992)

——, 'Religion and the Revolt', in *The Origins and Development of the Dutch Revolt*, ed. Graham Darby (London, 2001), pp. 67–83

——, 'France and the Netherlands: The Interlocking of Two Religious Cultures in Print During the Era of the Religious Wars', *Nederlands Archief voor Kerkgeschiedenis*, 84 (2004), pp. 319–37

Piceu, Tim, *Over vrybuters en quaetdoenders: Terreur op het Vlaamse platteland (eind 16de eeuw)* (Leuven, 2008)

Pi Corrales, Magdalena, *España y las potencias nordicas: 'La otra invencible' 1574* (Madrid, 1983)

Pietromarchi, Antonello, *Alessandro Farnese: L'eroe italiano delle Fiandre* (Rome, 1999)

Piot, Charles, ed., *Correspondance du cardinal de Granvelle, 1565–1583*, 12 vols (Brussels, 1877–96)

Pirenne, Henri, *Histoire de Belgique*, 7 vols (Brussels, 1922–32)

Pluijm, J. E. van der, *De vestingstad Grol: Geschiedenis van de vestingwerken van Groenlo* (Groenlo, 1999)

Po-Chia Hsia, R., and H.F.K. van Nierop, *Calvinism and Religious Toleration in the Dutch Golden Age* (Cambridge, 2002, repr. 2012)

Poelhekke, J. J., *De vrede van Munster* (The Hague, 1948)

——, *Frederik Hendrik: Een biografisch drieluik* (Zutphen, 1978)

——, 'De Infanta Isabel 1566–1633', in *Vrouwen in het landsbestuur: Van Adela van Hamaland tot en met Koningin Juliana: Vijftien biografische opstellen*, ed. C. A. Tamse (The Hague, 1982), pp. 97–111

Pollmann, Judith, *Religious Choice in the Dutch Republic: The Reformation of Arnoldus Buchelius (1565–1641)* (Manchester, 1999)

——, *Een andere weg naar God: De reformatie van Arnoldus Buchelius (1565–1641)* (Amsterdam, 2000)

——, 'Countering the Reformation in France and the Netherlands: Clerical Leadership and Catholic Violence, 1560–1585', *Past and Present: A Journal of Scientific History*, 190 (2006), pp. 83–120

——, '"Brabanters do Fairly Resemble Spaniards After All": Memory, Propaganda and Identity in the Twelve Years' Truce', in *Public Opinion and Changing Identities in the Early Modern Netherlands*, ed. Judith Pollmann and Andrew Spicer (Leiden and Boston, 2007), pp. 211–27

——, 'No Mans' Land: Reinventing Netherlandish Identities, 1585–1621', in *Networks, Regions and Nations: Shaping Identities in the Low Countries, 1300–1650*, ed. Robert Stein and Judith Pollmann (Leiden, 2009), pp. 241–62

——, *Catholic Identity and the Revolt of the Netherlands 1520–1635* (Oxford, 2011)

Postma, Folkert, *Viglius van Aytta als humanist en diplomaat 1507–1549* (Zutphen, 1983)

——, 'Nieuw licht op een oude zaak: De oprichting van de nieuwe bisdommen in 1559', *Tijdschrift voor Geschiedenis*, 103 (1990), pp. 10–27

——, *Viglius van Aytta: De jaren met Granvelle, 1549–1564* (Zutphen, 2000)

——, 'Van bescheiden humanist tot vechtjas: Viglius van Aytta en de crisis van 1566–1567', *Bijdragen en Mededelingen betreffende de Geschiedenis der Nederlanden*, 123 (2008), pp. 323–40

Prak, Maarten, *The Dutch Republic in the Seventeenth Century: The Golden Age* (Cambridge, 2005)

——, *Gouden Eeuw: Het raadsel van de Republiek* (Amsterdam, 2012)

Presser, J., et al., *De Tachtigjarige Oorlog* (Amsterdam, 1941) (multiple reprints)

Puype, J. P., and Marco van der Hoeven, eds, *Het arsenaal van de wereld: Nederlandse wapenhandel in de Gouden Eeuw* (Amsterdam, 1993)

Quatrefages, René, 'Alba Cunctator', in *Alba*, ed. Ebben et al., pp. 50–72
Quilliet, Bernard, *Guillaume le Taciturne* (Paris, 1994)
Rachfahl, Felix, 'Die Trennung der Niederlande vom deutschen Reiche', *Westdeutsche Zeitschrift für Geschichte und Kunst*, 19 (1900), pp. 79–119
——, *Wilhelm von Oranien und der niederländische Aufstand*, 3 vols (The Hague, 1906–24)
Raeymaekers, Dries, *One Foot in the Palace: The Habsburg Court of Brussels and the Politics of Access in the Reign of Albert and Isabella, 1598–1621* (Leuven, 2013)
Reformatorica: Teksten uit de geschiedenis van het Nederlandse protestantisme, ed. C. Augustijn et al. (Zoetermeer, 1996)
Riaño Lozano, Fernando, *Los medios navales de Alejandro Farnese (1587–1588)* (Madrid, 1999)
Rodríguez Pérez, Yolanda, *De Tachtigjarige Oorlog in Spaanse ogen: De Nederlanden in Spaanse historische en literaire teksten (circa 1548–1673)* (Nijmegen, 2003)
——, *The Dutch Revolt Through Spanish Eyes: Self and Other in Historical and Literary Texts of Golden Age Spain (c. 1548–1673)* (Oxford, 2008)
Rodríguez-Salgado, M. J., *The Changing Face of Empire: Charles V, Philip II and Habsburg Authority, 1551–1559* (Cambridge, 1988, repr. 2008)
——, and the staff of the National Maritime Museum, *Armada, 1588–1988: An International Exhibition to Commemorate the Spanish Armada* (London, 1988)
Roey, J. van, *De val van Antwerpen 17 augustus 1585 – voor en na* (Antwerp, 1985)
Roosbroeck, R. van (ed.), *De kroniek van Godevaert van Haecht over de troebelen van 1565 tot 1574 te Antwerpen en elders*, 2 vols (Antwerp, 1929)
——, *Willem de Zwijger: Graaf van Nassau, Prins van Oranje* (The Hague and Antwerp, 1974)
Rooze-Stouthamer, C., *Hervorming in Zeeland (ca. 1520–1572)* (Goes, 1996)
——, *De opmaat tot de Opstand: Zeeland en het centraal gezag (1566–1572)* (Hilversum, 2009)
Sandoval, Prudencio de, *Historia de la vida y hechos del emperador Carlos V*, 2 vols (Pamplona, 1618–19)
Scheerder, J., *De beeldenstorm* (Bussum, 1974)
——, *Het Wonderjaar te Ghent 1566–1567*, ed. Johan Decavele and Gustaaf Janssens (Ghent, 2016)
Schelven, A.A. van, *Willem van Oranje: Een boek ter gedachtenis van idealen en teleurstellingen*, 4th edn (Amsterdam, 1948)
Schepper, Hugo de, 'De mentale rekonversie van de Zuidnederlandse hoge adel na de Pacificatie van Gent', *Tijdschrift voor Geschiedenis*, 89 (1976), pp. 420–28
——, *'Belgium Nostrum' 1500–1650: Over integratie en desintegratie van het Nederland* (Antwerp, 1987)
——, *'Belgium dat is Nederlandt': Identiteiten en identiteitenbesef in de Lage Landen, 1200–1800: epiloog: Koninkrijk der Nederlanden, 1815–1830* (Breda, 2014)
Schiller, Friedrich, *Geschichte des Abfalls der vereinigten Niederlande von der Spanischen Regierung* (Leipzig, 1788), quoted from the edition in

Schillers Werke Nationalausgabe, vol. XVII, part 1 (Weimar, 1970), pp. 7–289

Scholten, Paul, 'Christelijke vrijheid en Nederlanderschap', in H. B. Wiardi Beckman, B. M. Telders and Paul Scholten, *Den Vaderlant ghetrouwe* (Haarlem, 1940), pp. 35–52

Sigmond, Peter, *Zeemacht in Holland en Zeeland in de zestiende eeuw* (Hilversum, 2013)

—, and Wouter Kloek, *Zeeslagen en zeehelden in de Gouden Eeuw* (Amsterdam, 2007)

Soen, Violet, *Geen pardon zonder Paus!: Studie over de complementariteit van het koninklijk en pauselijk generaal pardon (1570–1574) en over inquisiteur-generaal Michael Baius (1560–1576)* (Brussels, 2007)

—, *Vredehandel: Adellijke en Habsburgse verzoeningspogingen tijdens de Nederlandse Opstand (1564–1581)* (Amsterdam, 2012)

Spaans, Joke, *De levens der maechden: Het verhaal van een religieuze vrouwengemeenschap in de eerste helft van de zeventiende eeuw* (Hilversum, 2012)

Spijker, W. van 't, et al., *De Synode van Dordrecht in 1618 en 1619*, 2nd edn (Houten, 1994)

Steen, Charlie R., *A Chronicle of Conflict: Tournai, 1559–1567* (Utrecht, 1985)

—, *Margaret of Parma: A Life* (Leiden, 2013)

Steen, Jasper van der, *Memory Wars in the Low Countries, 1566–1700* (Leiden, 2014)

Stein, Robert, 'Seventeen: The Multiplicity of a Unity in the Low Countries', in *The Ideology of Burgundy: The Promotion of National Consciousness 1364–1565*, ed. D'Arcy Jonathan Dacre Boulton and Jan R. Veenstra (Leiden, 2006), pp. 223–85

—, *De hertog en zijn staten: De eenwording van de Bourgondische Nederlanden ca. 1380–ca. 1480* (Hilversum, 2014)

—, *Magnanimous Dukes and Rising States: The Unification of the Burgundian Netherlands, 1380–1480* (Oxford, 2017)

Stensland, Monica, *Habsburg Communication in the Dutch Revolt* (Amsterdam, 2012)

Stoppelenburg, Nettie, *De Oudewaterse moord* (Oudewater, 2005)

Storms, Martijn, 'Cartografie in camouflage: Sluis (1604) wordt Salvador de Bahía (1625)', *De Boekenwereld*, XXIX/5 (2013), pp. 24–7

Stradling, R. A., *Philip IV and the Government of Spain, 1621–1665* (Cambridge, 1988)

—, *The Armada of Flanders: Spanish Maritime Policy and European War, 1568–1668* (Cambridge, 1992)

Sutherland, N. M., 'William of Orange and the Revolt of the Netherlands: A Missing Dimension', *Archiv für Reformationsgeschichte*, 74 (1983), pp. 201–30; reprinted in Sutherland, *Princes, Politics and Religion, 1547–1589* (London, 1984), pp. 207–36

—, 'The Foreign Policy of Queen Elizabeth, the Sea Beggars and the Capture of Brill, 1572', in Sutherland, *Princes, Politics and Religion, 1547–1589* (London, 1984), pp. 183–206

Swart, Erik, *Krijgsvolk: Militaire professionalisering en het ontstaan van het Staatse leger, 1568–1590* (Amsterdam, 2006)

——, 'The Field of Finance: War and Taxation in Holland, Flanders and Brabant, ca. 1572–85', *Sixteenth Century Journal*, 42 (2011), pp. 1051–71

Swart, K. W., 'The Black Legend During the Eighty Years' War', in *Britain and the Netherlands*, v, ed. J. S. Bromley and E. H. Kossmann (The Hague, 1975), pp. 36–57

——, *William of Orange and the Revolt of the Netherlands, 1572–84*, with introductory chapters by Alastair Duke and Jonathan I. Israel; ed. R. P. Fagel, M.E.H.N. Mout and H.F.K. van Nierop (Aldershot, 2003)

Tepe, Roy, *Oog in oog met de Martelaren van Gorcum. Catalogus bij de tentoonstelling in het Gorcums Museum – 2012* (Gorinchem, 2012)

Thijs, Alfons K. L., *Van Geuzenstad tot katholiek bolwerk: Maatschappelijke betekenis van de Kerk in contrareformatorisch Antwerpen* ([Turnhout], 1990)

Thøfner, Margit, *A Common Art: Urban Ceremonial in Antwerp and Brussels During and After the Dutch Revolt* (Zwolle, 2007)

Thomas, Werner, *La represión del protestantismo en España 1517–1648*, and *Los protestantes y la Inquisición en España en tiempos de Reforma y Contrarreforma*, 2 vols (Leuven, 2001)

——, *De val van het nieuwe Troje: Het beleg van Oostende, 1601–1604* (Leuven, 2001)

——, 'Alba and Religion', in *Alba*, ed. Ebben et al., pp. 116–35

——, and Luc Duerloo, *Albert & Isabella, 1598–1621: Essays* ([Turnhout], 1998)

Tienen 1635: Geschiedenis van een Brabantse stad in de zeventiende eeuw (Tienen, 1985)

Tracy, James B., *Holland under Habsburg Rule, 1506–1566: The Formation of a Body Politic* (Berkeley, CA, 1990)

——, *The Founding of the Dutch Republic: War, Finance, and Politics in Holland 1572–1588* (Oxford, 2008)

Trim, D.B.J., 'Sir Francis Vere (1560/1–1621), Army Officer and Diplomat', *Oxford Dictionary of National Biography*, online edition

Ubachs, P.J.H., 'De Nederlandse religievrede van 1578', *Nederlands Archief voor Kerkgeschiedenis*, 77 (1997), pp. 41–61

Úbeda de los Cobos, Andrés, *Paintings for the Planet King: Philip IV and the Buen Retiro Palace* (Madrid, 2005)

Uijterschout, I. L., *Beknopt overzicht van de belangrijkste gebeurtenissen uit de Nederlandsche krijgsgeschiedenis van 1568 tot heden* (Kampen, [1935])

Valerius, Adriaen, *Nederlandtsche Gedenck-clanck* (Haarlem, 1626)

Valvekens, Emiel, *De Zuid-Nederlandsche norbertijner abdijen en de Opstand tegen Spanje maart 1576–1585* (Antwerp, 1929)

Velius, Theodorus, *Kroniek van Hoorn*, 2 vols (Hoorn, 2007)

Verdugo, Francisco, *Voor God en mijn koning: Het verslag van kolonel Francisco Verdugo over zijn jaren als legerleider en gouverneur namens Filips II in Stad en Lande van Groningen, Drenthe, Friesland, Overijssel en Lingen (1581–1595)*, introduction, translation and explanatory notes by Jan van den Broek (Assen, 2009)

Verheyden, Alphonse, *Le Martyrologe protestant des Pays-Bas du Sud au XVIe siècle* (Brussels, 1960)

——, *Le Conseil des Troubles* (Flavion-Florennes, 1981)

Verhoef, C.E.H.J., *Nieuwpoort 1600: De bekendste slag uit de Tachtigjarige Oorlog* (Soesterberg, 2001)
Vermeir, René, *In staat van oorlog: Filips IV en de Zuidelijke Nederlanden, 1629–1648* (Maastricht, 2001)
Verschure, Han, *Overleven buiten de Hollandse tuin: Raamsdonk, Waspik, 's Gravenmoer, Capelle, Sprang en Besoijen tijdens de Tachtigjarige Oorlog* (n.p., 2004)
Versele, Julie, *Louis del Río (1537–1578): Reflets d'une période troublée* (Brussels, 2004)
Verwer, Willem Janszoon, *Memoriaelbouck: Dagboek van gebeurtenissen te Haarlem van 1572–1581* ed., J. J. Temminck (Haarlem, 1973)
Vetter, Klaus, *Wilhelm von Oranien. Eine Biographie* (Berlin, 1987)
Vis, Jurjen, 'Centrum van de Hollandse reformatie: Opkomst en vestiging van de "ware" religie', in *Geschiedenis van Alkmaar*, ed. Diederik Aten et al. (Zwolle, 2007), pp. 134–45
——, 'Tot meerdere eer en glorie van God. Kunst en muziek in en om de kerk', in *Geschiedenis van Alkmaar*, ed. Diederik Aten et al. (Zwolle, 2007), pp. 169–83
Vliet, A. P. van, *Vissers in oorlogstijd: De Zeeuwse zeevisserij in de jaren 1568–1648* (Middelburg, 2003)
Vondel, Joost van den, *Werken*, ed. J.F.M. Sterck et al., 10 vols (Amsterdam, 1927–37)
Vosters, S. A., *Het beleg en de overgave van Breda*, 3 vols (Breda, 1993)
——, *De Nederlanden in de Spaanse literatuur (van 1200 tot 1700)* (Breda, 2014)
Vrankrijker, A.C.J. de, *De historie van de vesting Naarden*, 3rd edn (Haarlem and Naarden, 1978)
Vrugt, Marijke van der, *De Criminele ordonnantieën van 1570: Enkele beschouwingen over de eerste strafrechtcodificatie in de Nederlanden* (Zutphen, 1978)
Wassink, Jos, and Wil Nouwen, *Boerenschansen: verscholen voor Staatsen en Spanjaarden* (Weert, 2008)
Weis, Monique, *Les Pays-Bas espagnols et les états du Saint Empire (1559–1579): Priorités et enjeux de la diplomatie en temps de troubles* (Brussels, 2003)
Wijsenbeek-Olthuis, Th.F., *Honger* (Leiden, 2006)
Williams, Patrick, *Philip II* (Basingstoke, 2001)
Winter, P. J. van, *Oorlogsduur in oorlogsnamen: Over het gebruik van getallen tot steun van historische voorstellingen* (Amsterdam and London, 1972)
Wittman, Tibor, *Les gueux dans les 'Bonnes villes' de Flandre (1577–1584)* (Budapest, 1969)
Woltjer, J. J., *Friesland in Hervormingstijd* (Leiden, 1962)
——, *Tussen vrijheidsstrijd en burgeroorlog* (Amsterdam, 1994)
——, 'De middengroepen in de Opstand', *Spiegel Historiael*, XXIX (1994), pp. 468–73
——, *Op weg naar tachtig jaar oorlog: Het verhaal van de eeuw waarin ons land ontstond: Over de voorgeschiedenis en de eerste fasen van de Nederlandse opstand* (Amsterdam, 2011)
Zijlstra, S., *Om de ware gemeente en de oude gronden: Geschiedenis van de dopersen in de Nederlanden 1531–1675* (Hilversum and Leeuwarden, 2000)

Bibliography

Zijp, R. P., ed., *Ketters en papen onder Filips II: Het godsdienstig leven in de tweede helft van de 16de eeuw* (Utrecht, 1986)

Zwitzer, H. L., *'De militie van den staat': Het leger van de Republiek der Verenigde Nederlanden* (Amsterdam, 1991)

List of Illustrations

1 Frontispiece: Daniel van den Queecborn (attributed), *Portrait of William, Prince of Orange*, c. 1598. Leiden, University, Academy Building, Icones, nr. 22.
2 *Karel v, heer over de zeventien Nederlandsche gewesten* (Groningen, 1955). Leiden, University Library, 22598:4 (4).
3 From Jan van der Noot, *Lofsang van Brabant* (Antwerp, 1580). Leiden, University Library, 1367 C 28, p. 25.
4 Statue of Charles v. Utrecht, Centraal Museum, inv. no. 1735. Image and copyright Centraal Museum, Utrecht/Ernst Moritz.
5 Tapestry showing the arms of Charles v. Wilhelm de Pannemaker, Brussels, c. 1540–c. 1555. Amsterdam, Rijksmuseum, BK 17260-b.
6 Leiden, University Library, coll. Bibliotheca Thysiana, 737.
7 From Lambertus Hortensius, *Van den oproer der weder-dooperen. Eerst int Latijn beschreven ... ende nu in Nederlandts overgheset* (Enkhuizen, 1624). Coloured by hand and embossed in gold by Dirck Jansz. van Santen, Amsterdam, University Library, OTM 2 C 18.
8 From *Germania Inferior id est, XVII provinciarum ejus novæ et exactæ tabulæ geographicæ* (Amsterdam, 1617). Leiden, University Library, COLLBN, Atlas 93.
9 *Margaret of Parma*, 17th-century engraving. Leiden, University Library, Print Room.
10 From Gerard van Loon, *Beschryving der Nederlandsche historipenningen*, 4 vols (The Hague, 1723–31), vol. 1 (1723), p. 1. Leiden, University Library, 1226 A 2.
11 *The Abdication of Charles v*, 1630. Tapestry from a series of seven depicting the life of Granvelle. Besançon, Musée du Temps.
12 Leeuwarden, Provincial Hall. With thanks to the RKD (Rijksbureau voor Kunsthistorische Documentatie).
13 Jan Vermeyen, *Portrait of Philip II*, 1555. Amsterdam, Rijksmuseum, Print Room, RP-P-1892-A-17329.
14 Bartel Jacobsz. Bart. Zaandam, Zaans Museum, collection ZOV. Inv. no. ZOV-01265.

15 Anonymous, *Portrait of Granvelle*. Leiden, University Library (portrait collection).
16 Anonymous, *Portrait of Lamoraal of Egmont*. Nuremberg, Germanisches Nationalmuseum, Gm 632.
17 Anonymous, *The Mast of the Inquisition*. Leiden, University Library (historical prints).
18 Rotterdam, *Atlas van Stolk*, anonymous drawing in Willem L. van Kittensteyn, *Spieghel ofte afbeeldinghe der Nederlantsche Geschiedenissen*, unpublished manuscript, inv. no. 50442 – 104.
19 Marianum, *c.* 1533. St Leonard's church, Zoutleeuw. © KIK-IRPA, Brussels.
10 Hans Liefrinck I, *Henry of Brederode*. Leiden, University Library, P-124.386.
21 Manuscript by Godevaert van Haecht, not published until four centuries later by Robert van Roosbroeck, *De kroniek van Godevaert van Haecht over de troebelen van 1565 tot 1574 te Antwerpen en elders*, 2 vols (Antwerp, 1929–30). Antwerp, city archives, inv. no. PK 106.
22 Manuscript by Willem De Gortter. Brussels, Royal Library, manuscript 15662, fol. 2r.
23 Anonymous, *Portrait of the Duke of Alba*. Gaasbeek, Gaasbeek Castle. © Lukas, *Art in Flanders*, photograph Dominique Provost.
24 *Het Nievwe Testament, dat is het Nieuwe Verbond onzes Heeren Jesu Christi*. Translated by J. Utenhoven et al. (Emden, 1556). Leiden, University Library, 1498 G 4.
25 St Paul's church, Antwerp. With thanks to Raymond Sirjacobs.
26 Print of the statue of Alba. Leiden, University Library, PK-P-123.280.
27 Propaganda print of the Prince of Orange. Leiden, University Library, PK, PT-104.
28 From Abraham van den Burgh, *Hoe en wanneer Hollant tot een graefschap is afgesondert* (Arnhem, 1647). Leiden, University Library, 1369 D 9.
29 *Atlas van Kittensteyn*. Rotterdam, Atlas van Stolk.
30 *Kenau*. Haarlem, Frans Hals Museum. Photograph Tom Haartsen.
31 Balthasar Jenichen, *Ware Contrafactur bayder leger zu wasser und landt vor Haerlem des Hertzog vonn Alba unnd Prinntzen von Orannien wieso zu dieser zeit belegert ist adi 10 Junnij Anno 1573*. Nuremberg [1575]. Leiden, University Library, COLLBN 009-13-054m.
32 House with the cannonball, waterside. Alkmaar, Appelsteeg 2. With thanks to Louis Sicking.
33 Hoorn, Grote Oost, Bossuhuizen. Photograph: Azarja Harmanny/ Netherlands Institute of Military History, The Hague.
34 Lambert Melisz., Hoorn, Westfries Museum.
35 From *Album amicorum van Janus Dousa*. Leiden, University Library, WHS, BPL 1406, f. 102.
36 View of Dordrecht, from Georg Braun and Frans Hogenberg, *Civitates orbis terrarum* (Antwerp, 1575–1618). Leiden, University Library, COLLBN Atlas 45 I.
37 *Requesens*. Amsterdam, Rijksmuseum, Print Room, RP-P-1948-330.
38 Anonymous, *Portrait of Louis of Nassau*. Leiden, University Library (portrait collection).

List of Illustrations

39 *The Leiden Lion*. Leiden, Regional Archives, inv. no. LB 2006, fol. dl. 2, no. 15.
40 Amsterdam, Rijksmuseum, Print Room, RP-P-OB-79617.
41 *Crossing the Zijpe*. Simancas, Archivo General del Estado.
42 *Queen Elizabeth I*. Leiden, University Library (portrait collection).
43 From Jan Baptist Houwaert, *Milenus clachte* (Leiden, 1578). Leiden, University Library, 1497 C 29: 1, p. 133.
44 *Destruction of the Citadel of Antwerp*. Leiden, University Library (historical prints).
45 From Jan Baptist Houwaert, *Declaratie van die triumphante Incompst vanden ... Prince van Oraignien binnen die princelijcke stadt van Brussele* (Antwerp, 1579). Leiden, University Library, 1367 E 9, p. 18.
46 Johannes Wierix, *Portrait of Matthias of Austria and William, Prince of Orange*. Amsterdam, Rijksmuseum, Print Room, RP-P-1909-1920.
47 Abraham de Bruyn (attributed), *Portrait of William, Prince of Orange*. Amsterdam, Rijksmuseum, Print Room, RP-P-OB-86.370.
48 The Reformation Wall in Geneva. With thanks to Dr Alexandre Vanautgaerden, Bibliothèque de Genève.
49 From Jean-François Le Petit, *La Chronique ancienne de la Hollande*, vol. II (Dordrecht, 1601). Leiden, University Library, 1499 A 13, p. 427.
50 *Orange with his Last Words*. Rijswijk, Rijksdienst voor het Cultureel Erfgoed.
51 From Hendrik Goltzius, *De begrafenisstoet van prins Willem van Oranje* (Haarlem, 1584). Leiden, University Library, PK-P-100.829.
52 Otto Vaenius, *Portrait of Alexander Farnese*. Deinze, near Ghent, Ooijdonk Castle. © KIK-IRPA, Brussels.
53 Beveren, Our Lady in Gaverland Chapel in Melsele. © KIK-IRPA, Brussels.
54 From *Afconterfeytinge der stadt Graue alzo die vanden prins van Parma belegert is* (n.p., 1586). Leiden, University Library, THYSPF 664.
55 Geertruidenberg. The Hague, Royal Library, 128 A 27.
56 *Copia van een brieve geschreven van seker gueden Burger van Groninghen aen een ander sijne medeburger vertrocken in Duytslant* (Antwerp, 1600). Leiden, University Library, COLLBN 054-16-008.
57 *De Lierse furie*. Lier, Stedelijk Museum Wuyts-Van Campen en Baron Caroly. © KIK-IRPA, Brussels.
58 *Maurice and Frederick Henry*, coloured engraving. Leiden, University Library, PK PT-311.
59 *Of-conterfeytinge der stad Hulst, met zyne polders en schansen, waerop den Coronel la Borlotte den 10 July des nachts met synen aenslach heeft gemaket en veel volcks opgebracht, welck hem en vele vanden synen t'leven heeft gecost, anno 1596* (n.p.), coloured copper engraving. Leiden, University Library, COLLBN, port 39, n. 17.
60 Hessel Gerrits, *Albert and Isabella*. Also published in Emanuel van Meteren, *Historiën* (1647). Leiden, University Library, PK, P-122.717.
61 From Francis Vere, *The Commentaries, being Diverse Pieces of Service, Wherein He Had Command Written By Himself in Way of Commentary* (Cambridge, 1657). Leiden, University Library, 1367 C 23, between pp. 178 and 179.

62 From Henrick van Haestens, *De bloedige ende strenge belegeringhe der stadt Oostende in Vlaenderen* (Leiden, 1613). Leiden, University Library, 1123 A 2, title page.
63 From Pompeo Giustiniano, *Delle gverre di Fiandra libri VI* (Antwerp, 1609). Leiden, University Library, 1011 C 4, fig. XXV.
64 Adriaen van de Venne, *Fishing for Souls*. Amsterdam, Rijksmuseum, SK-A-447.
65 Leiden, University Library, PK (portrait collection).
66 *Novissima, et accuratissima Leonis Belgicis, seu septemdecim regionum descriptio* (Amsterdam, 1622). Leiden, University Library, COLLBN port 2 N 61.
67 *Oldenbarnevelt*. Leiden, University Library, Icones, no. 38.
68 *Maurice*. Leiden, University Library, Icones, no. 50.
69 Daniel van Breen, *Privateer on the Shore*, drawing, 1641. Amsterdam, city archives, Heshuysen archive, 523.
70 Anonymous, *Portrait of Ambrogio Spinola*. Leiden, University Library, PK, sign. PT-310.
71 Peter Paul Rubens, *The Vision of St Teresa of Ávila*, c. 1630–35. Lier, Stedelijk Museum Wuyts-Van Campen en Baron Caroly. © KIK-IRPA, Brussels.
72 Diego Velázquez, *The Surrender of Breda*, 1634–5. Madrid, Prado.
73 Anonymous, *La rivée de l'arme navalle de Spaigne devant la Baye au Bresil* (n.p., 1625). Leiden, University Library, COLLBN 054-16-001.
74 Simon van de Passe, *Liberum Belgium* (Free Netherlands). Allegory of the prosperity of the Republic, Amsterdam, 1628. Leiden, University Library, PK P-123.611.
75 From Anonymous, *Nieuws. t'Geusen-rov-mael, en Fransche-covrante* (Delft, 1635). Leiden, University Library, THYSPF 1399. It can be seen as typical of the relative freedom of the printed media in the Republic that a print such as this could be published without restriction.
76 Gerrit van Santen, *Het beleg van Schenkenschans door Frederik Hendrik*. Amsterdam, Rijksmuseum, SK-A-3893.
77 Peter Paul Rubens, *The Triumphal Car of Kallo*. Antwerp, Royal Museum of Fine Arts. © Lukas – Art in Flanders, photograph Hugo Maertens.
78 Cornelis van Dalen, *Maerten Harpertszoon Tromp and the Battle of Downs*, c. 1640. Leiden, University Library, PK 102.74.
79 Monstrans, c. 1640. Hulst, St Willibrord Basilica. Photograph: with thanks to Trude Gielen and Emiel Saman.
80 *The Seventeen Virgins of the Netherlands*. St Petersburg, Hermitage.
81 No. 2.14b. Adriaen Valerius, *Neder-landtsche gedenck-clanck: kortelick openbarende de voornaemste geschiedenissen van de seventhien Neder-Landsche Provintien, 't sedert den aenvang der inlandsche beroerten ende troublen, tot den iare 1625* (Haarlem, 1626), Leiden, University Library, 1497 D 22, p. 13.

Maps pp. 215–17 by Jonathan Bos.

Acknowledgements

There are fortunately a number of excellent general works on the Eighty Years War. They are usually produced by teams of specialists, and that they end up as hefty volumes is clearly not a major concern. This book is an attempt to present a very complex period in the history of the Netherlands in a concise account that is accessible to everyone.

I would never have dared to set out on this venture without the support of a number of people whose varying expertise proved invaluable. My heartfelt thanks to Karel Bostoen[†], Maurits Ebben, Raymond Fagel, Gustaaf Janssens, Erik Swart, Arnoud Visser and Boudien de Vries for reading the manuscript, and for their critical corrections and additions. I would also like to thank my colleagues in the Special Collections department of Leiden University Library for their always helpful assistance in searching for rare illustrations and making high-quality digital reproductions. Lastly, I would like to thank Jan Jouke Tjalsma of our unsurpassed IT department for his unremitting care for the University website on the Revolt: http://dutchrevolt.leiden.edu.

Index

Illustration numbers are indicated by *italics*

Aalst 110
Aarschot 193
Aarschot, Charles de Chimay, duke of 119, 150
Aarschot, Philip de Croÿ, duke of 119–21, 149
abdication 35–6, *10*, *11*
Abjuration, Act of 129, *48*, *49*
Achterhoek 87, 148, 157
Achterraad 45
Admiral of the Sea 157
admiralties 99, 122, 158
Affligem, abbey of 50
aid 18, 41
Aire 123
Alba, Fernando Alvarez de Toledo, duke of 15, 26, 31, 42, 44–5, 69–94, 100, 104, 108, 119, 123–4, 127–8, 138, 140, 146, 178, *23*, *26*, *27*
Albanists 69
Albert of Austria 150–52, 155, 161, 164, 166–7, 171, 179–80, *59*, *60*, *64*, *80*
Alcalá, University of 75
Alkmaar 63, 92–3, 100, 103, *32*
Alps 71
Amboyna 164
America 24, 189
Amersfoort 88, 189
Amsterdam 27–8, 83, 86, 93, 99, 122, 132, 139, 159, 196, *7*
Anabaptists 26–7, *7*

Andalusia 198
Anjou, François, duke of Anjou 109–10, 129–32, 162
Antwerp, bishop(ric) 48, 50, *25*
Antwerp, town 26, 28, 33, 40, 50, 59, 61, 64, 67, 80–81, 111–12, 118, 120–22, 130, 137–8, 147, 158, 166, 169–70, 194, 196, 205, *44*, *53*
French Fury 131
Spanish Fury 112, *43*
Apology see William of Orange
Aragon 22–3
Aranjuez 56
Archangel (Arkhangelsk) 186
archdukes *see* Albert and Isabella Clara Eugenia of Austria
Archivo General de Simancas 10, *17*
Arenberg, Jean de Ligne, count of 53, 78
Armada, Spanish (1588) 139–42, 178
Armada, Spanish (1639) 196–7
Armenteros, Thomas 45
Arminians 174
Arminius, Jacobus 173
Arras, bishop(ric) 48
Arras, town 41, 46, 123–4
Arras, Peace of 124, 128, 149
Arras, Union of 117, 124–6, 128,
Artois 17, 31–2, 58, 60, 123–4, 198, 203, *45*
Asia 179, 186

Assendelft 93
Atrecht *see* Arras
Augsburg, Peace of 26
Augustine, saint 56
Austria 21, 23, 24, 32, *5*
Austria House of *see* Habsburg, House of
Austruweel *see* Oosterweel
Ávila, Teresa of, saint 182, *71*
Axel 122
Aytona, Francisco de Montada, marquis of 190–92, 194

Bahía *see* Salvador de Bahía
Bailleul 60, 61
Bakhuizen van den Brink, Reinier C. 8
Baltic 60, 169–70, 186
bankruptcy of the state 39–40, 110–11, 150
Barnevelt *see* Oldenbarnevelt
Bart, Bartel Jacobsz. *14*
Bartholomew's Day Massacre, St 87, 131
Beeldenstorm, 61–5, 69, *18*
  see also iconoclastic fury
Beemster 170
Belgium 10, 20, 29–30, 80, 206, *3*
Belgium nostrum 113, 203
Benelux 10, 108
Bergen (Hainaut) *see* Mons
Bergen [op Zoom], Jean de Glymes, marquis of 59–60, 95
Bergen, Willem van 144
Bergen op Zoom 128, 138, 146, 166, 181–2, 184, 191
Bergh, Hendrik, count van den 189, 191
Bergh, William IV, count van den 87
Berlaymont, Charles, count of 45, 53, 57–8
Besançon 37
Béthune 123
Beveren 137
Beverwijk
Bicker, Cornelis 199
Bijen-corf der H. Roomscher Kercke 80
Binnenhof 163–4
bishoprics 48–50

Black Legend 51
Blijde Inkomst 20
Blois of Treslong, Willem 67, 84
Blood Council 74
Blood placards 28
Boonen, Jacob 190, 199
Boschuysen, François van 83
bosgeuzen 73
Bossu *see* Boussu
Boulogne 161
Bourbon, Charlotte de 131
Bourtange 98
Boussu, Maximilien de Henin, count of 85, 88, 93
Boussu Houses 93, *33*
Brabant 16–18, 20, 23–4, 29, 38, 41, 45–6, 48–9, 60–61, 77, 79, 86–8, 99, 120, 125, 146–7, 153, 168, 180, 193, 203–4, *3, 5*
Bracamonte, Gonzalo de 78
Bragança, House of 198
Brandenburg 161–2
Braudel, Fernand 43
Brazil 186, 194, 197
Breda 50, 72, 104, 119, 143–4, 146–7, 153, 177, 181, 183–6, 195–6, *72*
  peace talks 40
Brederode, Henry, count of 57, 60, 62, 65, 67, 72, 95, *20*
Bredevoort 149
Brès, Guy de 59
Brill 83–5, 97, 138, 162, 171
Bronckhorst, Dirck 102
Bruges 18, 52, 61, 122, 135, 190, 205
Brunswick, Christian of 183
Brussels 22, 28, 35–6, 38, 42–3, 45–6, 52–3, 57, 61, 71, 73–4, 76, 78–9, 81, 83, 94, 99, 104, 110, 115, 118, 120, 151, 171, 179, *45, 80*
  first Union of 113–14, 117, 124
  second Union of 117
Bruyn, Abraham de *47*
Buen Retiro Palace 186
Burgundian Circle 31–2
Burgundy, duchy 17, 21–4, *5*
Burgundy, House of 17–18, 28
Burmania, Gemme van *12*

Index

Cádiz 158
Calais 141, 151
Calvin, Jean 60, 80, 173
Calvinists 11, 54, 60, 65, 95, 97, 108, 120–25, 204–5
Cambrai 46, 48, 144
camisade 87
Canary Islands 159
Cape St Vincent, Battle of 198
Carlos of Austria, Don 32
Carolus Borromeus, saint 170
Cartagena 71
Castel Rodrigo, Emanuel de Moura Cortereal, marquis of 199
Castile 22–4, 70, 198
Castricum 69
Catalonia 178, 198
Cateau-Cambrésis, Peace of 44, 59
Catholic Church *see* Roman Catholic Church
Catholics 11, 14, 47–8, 52, 54, 64–5, 76, 87, 92, 97, 108, 111, 117, 120–23, 125, 135, 146, 161, 164–5, 167, 170–74, 179, 182, 184, 197, 204–5, *17, 79*
Channel, English 113, 141, 196
Charles V, emperor 12, 14, 19, 23–6, 28–32, 35–40, 44, 48, 79, 119, 121, 134, *2, 4, 5, 10, 11*
Charles I, king of England 187
Charles IX, king of France 59, 87
Charles the Bold, duke of Burgundy 20–22
China 182, *63*
Christian IV, king of Denmark 168
Clerck, Hendrick de *80*
Cleves 72, 73
Cockayne, Land of 33
Coevorden 127, 146, 157
Coligny, Gaspar de 80–81, 83, 87, 131
Coligny, House of 59
Coligny, Louise de 131, 175
Cologne 48, 126
collateral councils 30
Columbus, Christopher 24
Committees of Eighteen Men 115, 121–3
composite monarchy 24

Compromise of Nobles 57, 64, 78, 124, *20, 21, 81*
Condé, Henri I de Bourbon, prince of 80, 83
Condé, House of 59
Confessio Belgica 59
conseillers de robe longue 30
consistories, reformed
Consulta 45
conversos 51
convooien 122, 139, 158
Cortes 32
Coudenberg hill, Palace of 35
Council of Finance 30, 45
Council of State (Brussels) 11, 13–14, 15, 30, 36, 43, 45, 52, 54, 56, 110–11, 113, 134–5, 190
Council of State (The Hague) 139, 166
Council of State (Madrid) 69–70
Council of Troubles 74–6, 104
Counter-Reformation 47–8, 170
Counter-Remonstrants 174–5
Criminal Ordnances 76
Cuba 189
cuius regio, eius religio 26
Culemborg, Floris of Pallandt, count of 62, 64, 78
Culemborg 62, 64

David, king of Israel 142
Dávila, Sancho 101–2, 128
De Gortter, Willem *22*
Deinze 122
Delfshaven 85, *29*
Delft 89, 99, 103, 134, 170, *51*
Delfzijl 144
Dendermonde 65, 87, 122, 135
Denmark 20, 67, 162
Deventer 87, 126, 139, 144
Diest 135, 193
Dijon 17
Dillenburg 72
Does, Jan van der, lord of Noordwijck 102, 104, *35*
Does, Pieter van der 159
Dokkum 99
Dordrecht 86, 99, *36*

Douai 49, 123
Downs, Battle of the 196–7, *78*
Drake, Francis 140–41
Drenthe 28, 126–7
Duke, Alastair 8, 46
Dunkirk 43, 122, 141, 152–4, 158, 169, 178, 186, 194, 197, 199, *69*

East-Friesland 30, 168
East Indies 164, 177
East India Company, Dutch *see* VOC
Eboli, Ruy Gómez da Silva, prince of 69–70
Ebolists 69
Eems river 79, 83
Egmond, abbey of 50
Egmont, Anna of, countess of Buren 26, 44
Egmont, Lamoraal, count of 43–4, 50, 52–3, 55–7, 59, 64, 72, 74, 78–9, 95, 142, 202, 205, *16*
Egmont, Maximiliaan of, count of Buren 26
Eighteen Men *see* Committees of Eighteen Men
eletto 91, 110
Elizabeth I, queen of England 84, 107–10, 137–40, 155, 159, 161–2, *42*
Emden 73, 83, 168, *24*
Emmanuel Philibert, duke of Savoy 42–3
Empire, German *see* Holy Roman Empire
England 36, 42–4, 46–7, 60, 73, 149, 162, 164–5, 180, 196–7
Enkhuizen 83, 86, 88, 99, 159
Enno III, count of East-Friesland 168
Enschede 149
Eraso, Francisco de 69–71
Erasmus of Rotterdam 25, 49
Ernest of Austria 149–50
Escorial, El 152
Essen, Jan van 28

factor 39–40
Fadrique, Don *see* Toledo, Fadrique de

Farnese, Alexander *see* Parma
Ferdinand I, emperor 31
Ferdinand II, king of Aragon 22–3
Ferdinand of Austria 192–6, 198
Fidèles au roy, jusqu'à la besace 58
Fistula dulce canit 102
flag 83, 85, 123, 180, *29*, *35*
Flanders 10, 18, 23–4, 31–2, 38, 41, 45–6, 51, 60–61, 64, 83, 99, 120, 122, 125–6, 168, 180, 197, 199, 203–4, *5*
  French-speaking 46, 51, 60
Florianus, Johannes 137
Flushing 44, 84–5, 108, 111, 129, 138–9, 154, 162, 169, *28*
France 24, 30–31, 35, 42–4, 46, 53, 55–6, 59–60, 63–5, 79, 80, 87, 108–9, 131, 149, 162, 164–5, 187, 192–5, 200–201
Franche-Comté 17, 22, 30, 54, 71
Franciscus Xaverius, saint 182
Frankfurt 73
Frederick III, emperor 21
Frederick Henry, prince of Orange, count of Nassau 131, 148, 168, 175, 177, 184, 187–91, 193–4, 198–200, 205, *58*, *72*, *74*, *75*, *79*
freedom of conscience 11, 13, 77, 97, 111, 134
freedom of religion 11, 13, 67, 77, 97, 134
Friesland 17, 31–2, 46, 87, 99, 125–7, 146, 203, *12*
Fruin, Robert 143
Fuentarebbía 196
Fuentes, Pedro Enríquez de Toledo, count of 149
Fugger, family 23

Gaasbeek 50
Gachard, Louis-Prosper 10
Geertruidenberg 146, 185, *55*
Gelder, H. A. Enno van 58
Gelderland 31, 87–8, 125–6, 148–9, 157, 183, 187, 189
Geldern 194
Gelre 17, 29, *49*
Gembloux, Battle of 121–2

General Pardon 81
Generality Lands 146
Geneva 60, 70, 80, *48*
Gennep 198
Genoa 155
Gérard, Balthasar 132
Germany 26, 32, 73
Ghent 23, 60–61, 63–4, 111, 113, 120–24, 131–2, 135, 205, *79*
Ghent, Pacification of 76, 111–14, 117, 119
Gibraltar 180
Gibraltar, Battle of 159
Gijsels, Artus 198
Giustiniano, Pompeo, *Delle guerre di Fiandra*, *63*
Goes 86, 122
Golden Fleece, Order of the 18, 42, 53, *13*
Gomarists 173–4
Gomarus, Franciscus 173
Gómez da Silva *see* Eboli
Gorinchem, martyrs of 85, 171
Gouda 99, 132, 134
Granvelle, Antoine Perrenot, cardinal 36–8, 41, 45, 49–50, 53–4, 58, 79, 120, 127, 171, 192, *11, 15, 17*
Grave 138, 155, *54*
Gravelines 98, 142, 199
  Battle of 43, *79*
Great Privileges 21
Grevelingen *see* Gravelines
Grol *see* Groenlo
Groenlo 149, 157, 187–8
Groningen, town 62, 78, 126, 146, *56*
Groningen, province 31–2, 46, 48, 77, 126–7, 146, 203
Groot-Privileges 21
Grotius, Hugo 46
guerra de Flandes, la 10
Guise, Henri, duke of 108, 142
Guise, Louis de, cardinal of Lorraine 142
Guise, House of 59

Haarlem, bishop(ric) 50, *25*
Haarlem, town 60, 89–92, 99–100, 107, 122, 170, *30, 31*

Haarlemmermeer 89
Habsburg, House of 21–2, 31, 119, 179
haec libertatis causa 103
Haecht, Godevaert van, *Chronicles 21*
Haga, Cornelis 167
Hague, The 29, 52, 163–5, 175, 179, 194
Hainaut 17, 46, 58, 60, 79, 123–4, 203, *45*
Hanseatic League 20, 168, 180
Haring, Jan 93
Harlingen 99
Hasselaer *see* Kenau Simonsdr.
Havré, Charles Philippe de Croÿ, marquis of 149–50
Heemskerck, Jacob van 159
Heemskerck, Maerten van 63
Heidelberg 73
Heiligerlee, Battle of 8, 11, 77–8
Hein, Piet 189
Hembyze, Jan van 121
Hemiksem, abbey of 50
Henri II, king of France 44, 59
Henri III, king of France 129, 132, 142, 162
Henri IV, king of France 87, 140, 142, 162, 165, 168
Henry VIII, king of England 36, 107
Héraugières, Charles de 144, 147, 153
Hertogenbosch, 's-, bishop(ric) 48
Hertogenbosch, 's-, town 155, 177, 186–7, 189–90, 198
Hertogenbosch, Meijerij van 's- 168
Heusden 98
Heyn, Piet *see* Hein, Piet
Hoe en wanneer Holland tot een graafschap is afgezonderd 28
Hogenberg, Frans, *Beeldenstorm 18*
Hollaer, Marinus 191
Holland 10, 17–18, 29, 31, 45–46, 60, 83, 86, 93, 95, 98, 100, 102, 107–9, 111, 124–5, 130, 157, 180, 186, 194, 199, 201, 203–5
Holland, Garden of 149, 157, *39*
Holland Mission 172
Holy Roman Empire 20–21, 26, 31–2, 35, 54–5, 75, 79, 149, 156, 171, 182–3, 189, *16*

265

Holy See 28, 42
Hoorn 93–4, 99, 159, *33*
Hopperus, Joachim 56
Horn, Philip de Montmorency, count of 52–3, 59, 65, 72, 74, 78, 95, 202
Hortensius, Lambertus 89
Hout, Jan van 102–4, *35*
Houwaert, Jan Baptist, *Declaratie van die triumphante incompst 45*
Hove, Anneke van den 151
Hovius, Matthias 171
Howard, Charles 141
Huguenots 59, 80, 83, 86–8, 182, 201
Huizinga, Johan 9
Hulst 122, 144, 151, 199, *59, 79*
Hungary 31
Huy 153

iconoclastic fury 61–5, *18*
IJ river 93, 107
IJssel line 157, *63*
IJssel river 157, 189
Indies 164, 166, 182, 186
Inquisition, episcopal 51
Inquisition, papal 51–2
Inquisition, Spanish 46, 51, 58
Mast of the Inquisition, The 17
Isabella, queen of Castile 22
Isabella Clara Eugenia of Austria 150–52, 154, 164, 167, 171, 180, 185, 187, 190–2, *60, 64, 80*
Isabella of Portugal 32
Isidore, saint 182
Israel, Jonathan 8
Istanbul 167
Italy 14, 21, 23–4, 31–2, 42, 45, 70, 79, 186

Jansz, Dirck, farmer in Friesland 77
Jauregui, Juan 131
Je maintiendrai 128, *47, 48*
Jean II, king of France 17
Jeannin, Pierre 164–6, *65*
Jemmingen, Battle of 79–80, 101, *26*
Jews 51, 182, 191, 197
Joanna, queen of Castile and Aragon ('the Mad') 22, 35

Joyous Entry 20–22, 86, 114, 120, 152, *80*
John of Austria, Don 88, 113–14, 117, 119, 121–3, 126, 137
Juana of Austria 32
Jülich 181
Jülich-Cleves crisis 167–8

Kallo, Battle of (1638) 196, *77*
Kampen 88, 125–6
Kenau Simonsdr. (Hasselaer) *30*
Kortrijk 122
Kossmann, Ernst H. 9
Kouwenstein dyke 137

Land of Waas (Waasland) 137
Land's Advocate of Holland 176
Lawrence, saint 61
Leest, Antoni van *45*
Leeuwarden 39, 62, *12*
Leicester, Robert Dudley, earl of 138–40
Leiden 63, 99–104, 140, 170, *39*
Leiden University 104, 173, *1*
Leo Belgicus 168, *8, 66*
Lepanto, Battle of 88
Lerma, Francisco Gómez de Sandoval y Rojas, duke of 152, 182
Leuven, town 61, 64, 87, 122, 193
Leuven University 49, 75, 87
Leyden, Lucas van 63
leyenda negra see Black Legend
licenten 122, 139, 158
Liefrinck, Hans, *Henry of Brederode 20*
Liège, bishop(ric) 46, 60, 79
Liège, town 60, 79
Lier 98, 146–7, *57*
Ligne, Jean de *see* Arenberg
Lille 61, 64
Limburg-Overmaas 17, 46, 120, 125, 168
Lingen 29–30, 149
Linköping 63
Lochem 157
Loon, Gerard van, *Beschryving der Nederlandsche historipenningen 10*
Lorraine 71

Louis XI, king of France 21–2
Louis XIII, king of France 168
Louis XIV, king of France 201
Louvain *see* Leuven
Loyola, Ignatius of 182
Lumey, Willem van der Marck, lord of 84–5, 97
Luteranos 51
Luther, Martin 24–5
Lutherans 11, 54, 65, 165
Luxembourg 10, 29, 46, 120, 122, 125, 127

Maas river 31, 79, 84, 138, 191, 198–9
Maastricht 46, 126, 135, 177, 191, 198
Madrid 54, 120, 163, 182
Malcontents 124
Mansfeld, Peter Ernst, count of 127, 149
Mantua 178, 186, 190
Margaret of Austria, governor-general of the Netherlands 24
Margaret of Parma, governor-general of the Netherlands 44–5, 52–4, 56–8, 60, 64–7, 71, 121, *9*
Margaret of Valois 87
Maria of Austria 32
Marianum 19
Markiezenhof 166
Marnix of St Aldegonde, Philip of 79–80, 86
Marnix of Toulouse, John of 57, 67, 80
Mary, duchess of Burgundy 21–2
Mary, princess of Orange, countess of Nassau 119, 150
Mary I, queen of England 36, 42
Mary, queen of Hungary, governor-general of the Netherlands 24, 30
Mary, Queen of Scots 108
Mary Henrietta Stuart, princess of Orange 187
Mary of Portugal, wife of Philip II 32
Matanzas, Bay of 189

Matte, Sebastiaan 61
Matthias, archduke of Austria, later emperor Matthias II 119–20, 206, *46*
Maurice, prince of Orange, count of Nassau 99, 138–9, 143–9, 153–7, 161–4, 167–8, 174–6, 179–80, 184, 187, 191, *1, 55, 58, 64, 68*
Maximilian I, emperor 21–2
Maximilian II, emperor 104, 149
Mechelen, (arch)bishop(ric) 49, 50, 171
Mechelen, town 17, 46, 87–9, 147
Medina Sidonia, Alonso Pérez de Guzmán, duke of 141
Mediterranean 88, 186
Megen, Charles de Brimeu, count of 78
Melisz., Lambert 94, *34*
Melo, Francisco de 198–9
Melsele *53*
Mendoza, Bernardino de 183
Mennonites 11, 28, 52, 54, 56, 80, 100, 125, 151, 165
Metz, siege of 35
Meurs 149
Mexico 24
Middelburg 86, 99–100, 107, 159, 169, 201
Mierevelt, Michiel van *67, 68*
Mierlo, Godfried van *25*
Moluccas 164
Mondragón, Cristóbal de 100, 106–7, 110
Monnickendam 83
Monnickendam, Cornelis van 93
Mons (Hainaut) 85, 87, 123
Montaigne, Michel de 78
Montecuccoli, Raimondo 189
Montferrat 187
Montigny, Floris de Montmorency, marquis de 53, 58, 69, 72, 75, 95
Mook 101
Mookerheyde, Battle of 100–101, 128
moriscos 51
Morocco 167
Motley, John Lothrop 8, 10
Mühlberg, Battle of 31

Muiden 88
Münster 26–8, 30, 48, 200–201
   Peace of 77, 199–202
Musius, Cornelis 97
Muslims 14, 24, 51
mutinies of Spanish soldiers 91–2, 102, 110, 113, 149, 158

Naarden 88–9, 98
Namur 17, 46, 58, 79, 114, 120, 122, 125
Naples 24
Nassau, Adolf of 76–7
Nassau, Catherine of 133
Nassau, Ernst Casimir of 187
Nassau, Henry of 102
Nassau, John of 100, 125–6, 132
Nassau, Justin of 141–42, 184, *72*
Nassau, Louis of 57, 65, 76–80, 84–5, 100–103, *38*
Nassau, William Louis of 99, 143, 146, 149, 153, 168, 176, *55, 64*
Nassau-Siegen, Johan of 191
Nassau-Siegen, John Maurice of 197
Nassau-Siegen, William of 196
National Synod 176
Navarre, Henri of *see* Henri IV, king of France
Netherlands, Kingdom of the 20, 29–30, 128, 177, 203, 206
Neyen, Jan 163, 165
Nierop, Henk van 58
Nieuwpoort 154–5, 195
Nieuwpoort, Battle of 154
Nijmegen 101, 144, 157
Noircarmes, Philippe de 65
Noot, Jan van der, *Lofsang van Brabant 3*
Nördlingen, Battle of 192
Norwich 73
Noue, François de La 85

Oldenbarnevelt, John of 138–9, 146, 149, 153–5, 159, 161–5, 167–8, 170, 174–6, *67*
Oldenzaal 127, 149, 156, 187
Olivares, Gaspar de Guzmán, count-duke of 182, 191–2, 194–6, 198

Oosterweel, Battle of 67, 77, 80
Oostzaan *14*
Ootmarsum 149
Oran 182
Orange, House of 175, 187
Orange, principality 83
Orange, William of *see* William of Orange
Øresund 60, 168
Osnabrück 200
Ostend 153–6, 169, 178, 186, *62*
Ottoman Empire 24, 31, 54
Oudenaarde 61, 122, 132
Oudewater 106
Overijssel 28, 31, 46, 125–7, 146, 149, 156–7, 183, 187
Overveen 60

Palatinate 161–2
Paris 43, 87, 143, 194, 196
Parker, Geoffrey 8–9, 71, 125
Parma, Alexander Farnese, prince, later duke of, 57, 73, 80, 121–4, 126–8, 131–2, 135–43, 146–7, 149, 168, 182, 204, *52, 53, 54*
pater patriae 134
patrimonial domains 31
Paul IV, pope 42
Pax Hispanica 152
pays de par deçà, les 17
Peñaranda, Gaspar de Bracamonte y Guzmán, count of 200–201
Perpetual Edict 113
Peru 24
Philip II, king of Spain 9, 11–14, 20, 28, 30–32, 36–43, 48, 51–2, 54–7, 60, 67, 69, 71, 75, 77–8, 81, 88, 90, 94, 100, 104, 110, 114–15, 119, 127–9, 134, 140–41, 150–52, 171, 182, 204, *2, 11, 12, 13, 17, 45, 48, 49*
Philip III, king of Spain 152, 155–6, 161–2, 164–167, 179, 182
Philip IV, king of Spain 182, 185–7, 190–92, 194, 198–9
Philip the Bold, duke of Burgundy 17
Philip the Fair, lord of the Netherlands 22

Philip the Good, duke of Burgundy 17, 18, 20, 22, 203
Philip William of Orange, count of Nassau 75–6
Philippine 154, 293
Piacenza, citadel of 53
Pirenne, Henri 119, 135
placards 28, 57
Plantin-Moretus Museum *45*
Poperinge 61
Portugal 127–8, 150, 169, 178, 186, 198
Pragmatic Sanction 32
privateers 140, 152, 178, 197, *69*
privileges 74, 76, 152
Privy Council 30, 45
Pro rege, lege et grege 77
Protestants 14, 26, 28, 31, 46–8, 64, 87, 111, 117, 168, 170, 191, 204–5

Queecborn, Daniel van den, *William of Orange 1*
Quinze, les [Arras] 124

Rammekens, fort 138, 162, 194
Reformation 24–8, 35
Reimerswaal, Battle of 100
Religious Peace 117
Remonstrants 174
Rennenberg, Georges de Lalaing, count of 126–7
reputación 14, 161
Requesens, Luis de 94, 99–100, 104, 106, 108, 110, 119, 158, 178, *37*
Request of the Nobles 57–8
Rheims 48
Rheinberg 148
Rhine river 31, 148, 194
right to self-determination 11, 13
right of participation 11, 13
Rijhove, François de la Kethulle, lord of 121
Rijmenam, Battle of 121, 147
Rijnberk 148
Río, Luis del 74
Rochelle, La 83, 187
Rocroi, Battle of 198

Roermond 87–8, 97, 191, 195
Roman Catholic Church 14, 24–6, 36, 42, 43, 47, 49–51, 76, 80, 85, 171, *6, 17, 103*
Roman Catholics *see* Catholics
Rome 48–9
Romero, Julián 87, 89–90
Ronse 122
Roose, Pieter 190, 192
Rotterdam 84–5, 89, 99, 159
Rubens, Peter Paul 170, 196, *71, 77*
Rudolf II, emperor 119, 126
ruwaard (protector) of Brabant 120

Saint-Omer 123, 196
Saint-Quentin, Battle of 43, 79, 127
Salvador de Bahía 186, 189, 197, *73*
Santander 141
Santen, Gerrit van, *The Siege of Schenkenschans by Prince Frederik Hendrik 76*
São Tomé 159
Sas van Gent 199
satisfactions 122
Savoy 42, 71
Saxony, Anna of, princess of Orange 97
Scheldt river 31, 100, 137, 139, 158, 167, 170, 179, 196
Schenkenschans 194, *76*
Scherpenheuvel 170
Schetz, Gaspar 39–40
Schoonhoven 106
Schouwen-Duiveland 107
Schwarzburg, Günther von 104
sea beggars 73, 76, 83–6, 89, 93, 103, 107, *29*
Segovia letters 57
Seventeen Netherlands 16, 203, *3, 46, 80*
Sevilla 189
Sharp Resolution 175
silver fleet 189
Simancas 58, 72
Simons, Menno 28
Sint-Niklaas 122
Sint Philipsland (island) 107
Sint-Truiden 60
Sint-Winoksbergen 122

Slaak, Battle of the 191
Slochteren 78
Sluis 139, 141, 156, *73*
Smeekschrift *see* Request of the Nobles
Solms, Amalia of 187
Solomon, king 142
Sonnius, Franciscus 48, *25*
Sonoy, Diederik 93
Spain 14, 32, 35, 38, 41–42, 44, 50–51, 138, 149, 161, 169, 179, 182
Spanish Road 71
Spinola, Ambrogio 155–7, 163–4, 168, 181–7, *70, 72*
stadtholder 18
Stadtlohn, Battle of 183
States, the 13, 18
States General (Brussels) 13, 14, 15, 18, 21–23, 40–41, 58, 73, 81, 86, 98, 104, 113, 115, 117–18, 120–23, 126–7, 129, 132, 134, 152, 154–5, 166, 191–2, 199
States General (The Hague) 140, 143, 146, 166–7, 176, 187, 189, 201, *75*
States of Artois 123
States of Brabant 50, 110–11, 120, 190
States of Flanders 190
States of Friesland 37, 39, *12*
States of Hainaut 123–4
States of Holland 40, 86–7, 98–9, 103, 106, 117–8, 122, 127–8, 132, 166, 173–6, *48*
States of Zeeland, 98–9, 117–18, 124–5, 146
Steenvoorde 61
Steenwijk 146
Stokkum 79
Straelen, Antoon van 74–5
Stuart, Mary Henriette *see* Mary Henrietta
Supreme Authority 99
Sweden 60, 168, 201
Switzerland 31, 71, 108, 125

Tenth Penny 15, 40, 81–3, 90, 104, *27*
Terborch, Gerard 202

Terschelling 83
Texel 52
Thirty Years War 178–80, 189, 192
Tholen 191
Tiel 157
Tiende Penning see Tenth Penny
Tienen 155, 193–4, *75*
Tilly, Johan Tserclaes, count of 183
Titelmans, Pieter 51–2, 72
Toledo 150, 192
Toledo, Fadrique de (admiral) 180, 186, *73*
Toledo, Fadrique Álvarez de (son of Alba) 88–9, 92, *30, 37*
Tournai, bishop(ric) 48
Tournai, town 46, 59, 60, 65, 124, 128
Tournaisis 46, 124
trade with the enemy 139, 158
transubstantiation 47–8
Trent, Council of 47
Treslong *see* Blois of Treslong
Triest, Antoon 190, 199
Triple Alliance 149
Tromp, Maarten Harpertszoon 196–7, *78*
Turks 88
Turnhout, Battle of 147, *61*
Twelve Years Truce 161–72, 177–80, 200, *65, 66*

une foi, une loi, un roi 64
Utrecht, (arch)bishop(ric) 48–9
Utrecht, province 28–9, 31, 46, 106, 125, 174–6
Utrecht, town 29, 113, 139, 170, 176, *4*
Utrecht, Union of 13, 117, 125, 138, 175–6, 201
Uyttenbogaert, Johannes 175

Vaernewijck, Marcus van 62
Valencia 152
Valenciennes 59–61, 65, 67, 85
Valerius, Adriaen, *Nederlandtsche Gedenck-clanck* 81
Valladolid 32
Valois, House of 17
Van Eyck, Hubert and Jan 63

Vargas, Juan de 74
Veen, Otto van 52
Veere 84, *28*
Velázquez, Diego de 186, 196, *72*
Veluwe 189
Venice 164
Venlo 191, 195, 199–200
Venne, Adriaen van de, *Fishing for Souls* 64
Verdugo, Francisco de 127
Vere, Francis, *The Commentaries* 61
Vermeir, René 198
Vermeyen, Jan Cornelisz., *Portrait of Philip II*, *13*
Veurne 122
Vianen 62, 65
Vienna 120, 190
Viglius van Aytta 45, 48–9, 52, 54, 56, 61, 65
Villavicencio, Lorenzo de 52, 56–7
Vilvoorde 135
Vlissingen *see* Flushing
VOC (Dutch East India Company) 159, 167, 186
Voes, Hendrik 28
Vondel, Joost van den 192
Voorne 84
Vranck, François 140
Vredenburg 113

Waal river 157, 194
waardgelders 175
Walcheren 84, 107, 138
Walsingham, Francis 206
Washington, George 8
watergeuzen see sea beggars
Werff, Pieter van der 102
Wesel 148, 189–90
West India Company, Dutch 167, 189, 197–8
Westzaan 94
WIC *see* West India Company, Dutch
Wierix, Johannes *46*
Wijk aan Zee *69*
Wilhelmus 79, 118, *22*
Willebroek canal 118
William I, prince of Orange, 8, 11, 13, 26, 36–37, 44–5, 49–50, 52–4, 56–57, 59, 64–7, 72, 75–7, 79–80, 83, 85–9, 93, 95–100, 102–7, 110, 113, 115, 117–23, 125–35, 137–8, 142–4, 149, 157, 206, *1, 10, 27, 38, 39, 45, 46, 47, 48, 50, 51, 81*
  Apology 44, 127–8, 134
  Justification 46, 77
  nickname 'the Silent' 72
William II, prince of Orange 187
William Louis *see* Nassau, William Louis of
Willoughby, Peregrine Berty de Eresby, Lord 139
Wittenberg 25
Woerden 106
Woltjer, J. J. 47

Y river *see* IJ river
Ypres 122, 132, 135

Zaandam
Zeeland 17–18, 29, 46, 49, 84, 86, 95, 98–100, 102, 106–9, 111, 122, 125, 130, 137–8, 157–8, 169–70, 180–81, 186, 189, 191, 200–202
Zeelandic Flanders 154
Zeeuws-Vlaanderen *see* Zeelandic Flanders
Zierikzee 106–7, 110
Zichem 135
Zijpe 107, *41*
Zoutleeuw *19*
Zuiderzee 29, 157, 158
Zuiderzee, Battle of the 93, 100, 158
Zutphen 87–9, 132, 139, 144, *49*